China and the
Challenge of the Future

China and the Challenge of the Future

CHANGING POLITICAL PATTERNS

Carol Lee Hamrin

Westview Press
BOULDER, SAN FRANCISCO, & LONDON

Copyright © 1990 by Westview Press, Inc.

Published in 1990 in the United States of America by Westview Press, Inc., 5500 Central Avenue, Boulder, Colorado 80301, and in the United Kingdom by Westview Press, Inc., 13 Brunswick Centre, London WC1N 1AF, England

Library of Congress Cataloging-in-Publication Data
Hamrin, Carol Lee.
   China and the challenge of the future :
changing political patterns
   Includes index.
   1. China—Economic policy—1976–   . 2. China—
Politics and government—1976–   . I. Title.
HC427.92.H34 1990   338.951   86-28960
ISBN 0-8133-7364-6
ISBN 0-8133-0982-4 (if published as a paperback)

Printed and bound in the United States of America

   The paper used in this publication meets the requirements of the American National
   Standard for Permanence of Paper for Printed Library Materials Z39.48-1984.

10   9   8   7   6   5   4   3   2   1

Dedicated with gratitude to Robert,
who first suggested I write a book
about China's future,
and to the Chinese reformers
of the 1980s

Contents

Preface and Acknowledgments

This book highlights information obtained from formal interviews and informal conversations with knowledgeable Chinese in 1985–1987, although it is informed by years of background reading in the Chinese press. During that time, I was a visiting scholar at the Edwin O. Reischauer Center for East Asian Studies at the Johns Hopkins University School of Advanced International Studies (SAIS), while on sabbatical from my work as a research specialist at the Department of State and from my part-time teaching duties at SAIS. Through an introduction by Doak Barnett of SAIS, I proposed to Vice President Zhao Fusan of the Chinese Academy of Social Sciences that I interview officials and scholars involved in the planning process both in Beijing and in some of the special economic zones, the open coastal cities, and the key cities experimenting with reform. The academy invited me for this purpose, and Lin Di of the academy's foreign affairs bureau helped arrange meetings in November 1985 (Shenzhen, Guangzhou, Xiamen, Fuzhou, Shanghai, and Beijing), in May 1986 (Beijing, Tianjin, Shenyang, Anshan, and Dalian), and again in May 1987 (Beijing).

Because of the macroscopic nature of my topic and the speed of change in China, as well as the limitations of my time and abilities and the nature of the interview process, my conclusions can only be suggestive, not definitive. They are a sketch of how some strategic policy decisions were made in China in 1983–1987, not a detailed portrait of how they always have been or will be made. I was able to learn more about economic decisionmaking than about political, ideological, or military policy decisions. Many interviewees were quite ready to discuss the evolution of policy, but not disagreements over policy or the names of disputants. Some found concepts and questions about the structure and process of policymaking too unfamiliar to address clearly. My interviews were wide rather than deep—that is, I interviewed many people from different policy arenas and institutions, but few people from each. My sources included more policy researchers and advisers than policymakers. The most important limitation to my study is its focus on the formation of policy at the higher levels of the system, not on its implementation at lower levels, which many would argue is more than half the story. Along the way, however, I did learn something of how the frustrations, failures, or successes in policy fed back into the next round of decision.

This book focuses on changes in China up through the 13th Party Congress of 1987, concluding with some judgments on trends through 1988. Copyediting of my final draft was completed in early June 1989, arriving in the mail for my review just after the Democracy Movement was crushed by the Beijing massacre of 4 June. In response to these events, I added a subsection to my concluding chapter and deleted more names of interviewees to protect people at a time of great uncertainty.

I gained much personal satisfaction and knowledge from this research opportunity. I express my deep appreciation to Doak Barnett and to SAIS for their support and to my hosts at the Chinese Academy of Social Sciences for their invaluable assistance, which was marked by warmth, efficiency, and great persistence. I am grateful to the individual Chinese scholars and officials who took valuable time to meet with me and who provided me with further introductions and written materials to help me understand the planning process and the broader intellectual and political changes underway in China.

Special thanks are due the U.S. government, which provided me with a paid sabbatical as well as research and travel funds through the Exceptional Analyst Program. I thank my colleagues, particularly Tom Fingar and Chris Clarke, for their help and support. My choice of topic and research efforts were entirely independent, however, and my study is not being used for any official purpose. The conclusions of this study represent my personal views, not the official views of the U.S. government.

I also thank a number of other U.S. scholars who provided timely suggestions, either individually or by arranging seminars to discuss sections of my written work: Gerald Barney, Ralph Clough, Nina Halpern, Harry Harding, Kenneth Lieberthal, and James Reardon-Anderson. Detailed comments on the penultimate draft by Timothy Cheek, Barry Naughton, Suzanne Ogden, Michel Oksenberg, and Robert Suettinger were invaluable in shaping the final product, and I am deeply grateful to them. My friend Louisa Brown offered help with editing at a crucial time, and Susan McEachern, senior acquisitions editor at Westview Press, was very patient, encouraging, and helpful throughout the process of producing this book. Libby Barstow, senior production editor at Westview, efficiently arranged for final editing, indexing, and publication, and Jan Kristiansson provided excellent copyediting.

Carol Lee Hamrin
Washington, D.C.

1
Introduction

Since the early 1980s, the leadership of the People's Republic of China (PRC) has been discussing and revising modernization goals and strategies for the year 2000 and beyond. This study originated as an attempt to understand the policy content and institutional process of such strategic decisionmaking in the Deng Xiaoping era. Thus, one aim of this book is to explain how Chinese leaders and their advisers consciously sort out national priorities and direction by coordinating diverse demands and opportunities and to demonstrate where, when, and how this occurs in the political system.

In China, determining national strategy or direction involves deciding fundamental—moral and ideological—principles, not merely adopting a practical policy framework for problem solving. Therefore, acquiring the power to influence overall guidelines is central to political competition. As a result, this book illuminates the evolution in the 1980s of high-level politics—the use by individual leaders of policy institutions and processes to pursue power and to implement programs. This study also reveals the growing participation in politics of other social groups, especially intellectuals, and related changes underway in the patterns of contemporary Chinese political thought and culture.

I began my investigation with the changes in economic decision-making that took place in the course of drafting official programmatic documents on economic reform, especially the 7th Five-Year Plan (FYP) (1986–1990). I focused on strategic decisions that affected other bureaucratic subsystems in order to look more closely at the problems of policy trade-offs and coordination. I then explored the relationship of economic decisions to decisions in other arenas, including foreign policy, ideology and culture, and political reform. From this emerged a picture of how economic reforms are driving reforms in other arenas of the Chinese system—foreign affairs, ideology and culture, and politics.

I purposefully sought to design my research project to build upon other recent studies that used interviews and other new sources of data to explore the post-Mao decisionmaking structure and process.[1] These works, all by political scientists, tended to focus on the formal, prescribed institutional relations in the policy bureaucracies, although they also traced the evolution of some specific policies. I adopted a complementary historical approach to capture more of the ad hoc, informal, and changing nature of policymaking institutions and processes. I took as my starting point important official policy decisions and then investigated the individuals, institutions, and processes, both formal and informal, that shaped them. One important factor that emerged more clearly from this historical approach was the conceptual revolution in the minds of many policy researchers and officials, as well as some leaders, that spurred more radical reforms by the late 1980s.

Analytical Assumptions

Specialists in contemporary Chinese affairs have long debated the best models for analysis of Chinese politics. I agree largely with one recent discussion of the problem, which recommended incorporating the best elements of three models: (1) a rationality model that assumes a smooth procedural evaluation of policy alternatives, and the choice of a coherent set of policies, by a cohesive group of decisionmakers whose main criterion is the advancement of the national interest; (2) a power model that assumes a more conflictual evaluation of policies, and a less coherent result, achieved by compromise among leaders of competing personal factions whose main criterion is advancement of their own political beliefs and interests; and (3) a bureaucratic model that assumes the emergence of often inconsistent policies through an ongoing process of policy formation and implementation in which semiautonomous bureaucracies pursue different goals and decisionmakers seek to broker the differences using the criterion of widespread acceptability rather than rationality.[2]

The predominance of one or another model in the China field has reflected trends in Western social science as well as the changing degree of access to China and types of information available about China. The suitability of these models also depends to some extent on the time frame; the bureaucratic model is less suited to study of the Cultural Revolution because of the unstable institutional structures and procedures of the time.

These models also reflect different levels of analysis. The rationality model is most appropriate at the level of international politics. It is more concerned with the content of Chinese policy than with the policy process and tends to dominate studies of Chinese foreign policy, which are primarily concerned with how Chinese leaders pursue the interests of the nation in competition with other nations. The power model is appropriate at the level of leadership politics, for understanding the personalities, interests, and strategies of senior leaders who alone have the authority to set programmatic guidelines and make the key decisions on personnel and resource distribution. The bureaucratic model applies at the level of elite politics, where leaders interact with officials in charge of China's main bureaucratic and provincial organizations. The latter are preoccupied with shaping and implementing practical, concrete policy while preserving and enhancing their personal and unit resources. There is yet another level of politics not adequately covered by any of these models, and that is social politics—the interaction of leaders and the bureaucratic establishment with other social groups, primarily intellectuals. This level of interaction was central to the dynamics of the Cultural Revolution and is again of growing importance in post-Mao China; yet analysis of this is the weakest subfield of China studies.

As the emergence of competing analytical models suggests, different dynamics and values characterize each level of politics, and these different political "worlds," or subsystems, generate different, often conflicting, policy imperatives. The long-standing personal relations among elders and their commitment to the values of the revolution produce a dynamic quite different from that which prevails among bureaucrats focused on more pragmatic and material problems. The norms of both of these subsets differ in turn from those that dominate international relations; yet these levels must interact. The historical record indicates that in China, the systemic tensions that result from this interaction produce unstable institutions, sharp shifts in policy, and chronic, unresolved problems.[3]

In my view, the chief weakness in the 1980s reform program was the failure to reform the unitary Leninist political system, which was dominated by the personal authoritarian politics at the top leadership level, to create more autonomous institutions and more flexible procedures capable of brokering competing interests at the levels of international, bureaucratic, and social politics. The Beijing massacre of June 1989 is the most recent example of the disaster this political weakness inflicts on China. Decisions during the crisis were made in the context of personal factional competition at the top, in relative isolation from information and advice regarding the interests of the various bureaucracies, alternative ways of dealing with the social tensions that fueled the Democracy Movement, and the likely effect on China's international economic and political relations.

This book focuses on the level of interaction between leaders and bureaucracies and thus adopts the approaches of both power and bureaucratic models. Whenever I speak of policy programs, I assume that they are less than fully coherent results of bureaucratic compromises and political deals. My study reveals that these amalgams of bureaucratic interests, rather than some hypothetical national interest, shape Chinese foreign policy, yet at the same time foreign actors indirectly have become an integral part of China's bureaucratic politics in the 1980s. This study also indicates that while the interests of most non-bureaucratic social groups are still indirectly and inadequately factored in by China's political system, intellectuals have gained access to decisionmaking at a critical point—as policy coordinators, researchers, and advisers who channel information between leaders and bureaucracies and shape the perceptions of decisionmakers regarding the problems and options facing them.

Together, the interaction of institutions, processes, ideas, actors, and events forms the main patterns of politics in China. Due to the dynamic, nonlinear interactions among many forces and events in a complex system, it is impossible to predict China's future; only the general characteristics of the future can be described. Human history has a fundamentally uncertain, or open, quality.[4] So this study outlines, but does not predict, the constraints, regularities, and potentialities that will shape China's future. For example, the basic political patterns include annual cycles of reform and counterreform; the five-year planning cycle contributes to medium-term fluctuations in economic and political behavior. The outside parameters of longer-term change also emerge in this study. Under Deng Xiaoping's leadership, China has begun to break out of the economic and cultural stagnation created under the post-1949 Leninist party command system. Leaps in learning have occurred; change is irreversible in the ideological and economic subsystems and in the southeastern localities. But the break is not complete; a new equilibrium and a new order have yet to be established and, in my view, are not predetermined. In a sense, then, while this study is not a forecast, it may be an almanac to have at hand as the Chinese people struggle to shape their future.

Waves of Reform

Reform of the Chinese system in the 1980s proceeded in cycles or waves, rather than in a straight linear fashion. Each cycle began with a new policy initiative by reform leaders; was followed by experimental implementation, evaluation, and relevant research by reformist intellectuals and officials; and concluded with the emergence of problems and criticism from opponents of reform requiring a period of readjustment before pressures built or opportunities arose for another reform initiative. The tidal nature of these cycles has been remarked by Chinese participants and outside observers.[5] In fact, such "fluid" terminology seems apt for capturing the important qualities common to social change. There are elements of uncertainty in timing, scale, and unanticipated effects, yet there is a recognizable and predictable overall pattern, order within the disequilibrium.

One reason for the cycles of reform was the tension between the more conservative elders represented by Chen Yun and Peng Zhen, who aimed to balance the economy and reinstitutionalize the Leninist central bureaucratic command system, and the bold younger reformers led by Hu Yaobang and Zhao Ziyang, who became increasingly committed to removing bureaucratic constraints on economic and cultural activity and creating a market-driven economy. Deng Xiaoping maintained his position as paramount leader by arbitrating between these competing wings of his political coalition.[6]

During periods when reformers were ascendant, the central apparatus retreated from much daily administration, which resulted in a partial dispersal of authority from center to localities and from political generalists to administrators, technicians, factory managers, professionals, and entrepreneurs. The greatest gains in decisionmaking power were made by the local bureaucratic elites, intellectuals inside and outside the party, and the rural populace. During episodes of readjustment under the conservatives, general supervision by the central bureaucracy was strengthened. Norms of collective leadership were emphasized, and Leninist institutions and regulations from the 1960s, abandoned by Mao, were resurrected.

Another reason for the policy cycles was the pioneering nature of reform. There was little time and a dearth of the knowledge and abilities required to thoroughly research and construct a comprehensive plan for reform. The program began and remained in a reactive mode: Urgent problems arose, some solutions emerged in practice, policymakers found ways to encourage the spread of those solutions and to coopt or assuage critics and opponents. Although reformers gradually increased their ability to recognize problems and launch policy initiatives quickly and to foresee problems and preempt critics, they always felt themselves to be lagging behind the curve. For example, the rural reforms were actually launched in 1978 by starving peasants and desperate local cadre in Feixi county, Anhui.[7] In the face of a drought worse than any in a century, cadre allowed peasant households to cultivate land on contract and keep the produce after paying a tax in kind. (Similar events led to similar policies after the Great Leap Forward, so the locals were following known but outlawed precedent.)

Staffers of a newly formed party rural development research group came to investigate and obtained support from provincial leaders Wan Li in Anhui and Zhao Ziyang in Sichuan to begin provincial experiments with the contracting system in 1979. It was spread nationwide from there, partly by volunteer, partly by central directive. In the process, a very conscious effort was made to explore new methods of research that would prevent error, address the interests of those involved, and thereby minimize opposition.

Some of the reformers would have preferred to avoid this ad hoc and cyclical approach to urban reform. As early as 1978, policy advisers wanted to thoroughly research a coordinated package of reforms and introduce it quickly in order to minimize and control systemic dislocations.[8] But they were unable to do so, for both political and practical reasons. First, skeptics and critics were more easily cajoled into allowing experiments. Second, reform theorists and officials were at first too ignorant and later too divided among themselves about the proper reform strategy to agree on a package. As a result, urban reform was also introduced in a piecemeal, experimental fashion. Beginning in 1983, former staffers of the rural development research group did much of the urban fieldwork for the State Council's economic reform commission and consciously followed the general principle that had worked so well in rural reform—relaxing controls and sharing benefits widely.[9]

The lessons of the Great Leap Forward and the Cultural Revolution must also be factored into any explanation of the gradual experimentalism of reform. People in China had become allergic to Maoist political campaigns and empty slogans that introduced socioeconomic models to be instantly and rigidly implanted everywhere regardless of applicability. The veteran officials, scholars, and young researchers back in power under Deng had experienced the depth of rural poverty and cadre oppression and knew the fine line between survival and starvation. They also knew the huge information gap that lay between Zhongnanhai (China's White House) and the grain fields. When the reforms began, perhaps the biggest problems facing policymakers and advisers were the lack of policy-relevant information as well as research and intellectual tools. The statistical system was nearly useless, being still in the process of restoration. Researchers suffered from the blinders of dogma, fear, and self-censorship; lost records and years of disuse of intellect; and ignorance of advances in social science outside China.

Thus, experimentalism reflected a search for realistic policy and institutional flexibility. A remark by Zhao Ziyang in early 1980 became the slogan for the decade: "In China, we have a saying—'When you cross the river, you grope for the stones.' But you must cross the river. You can't just jump over it. Sometimes things don't work and you have to start again."[10]

Overview

Chapter 2 provides historical background for the 1980s reform program. The four main chapters that follow explain how the reformers seized or created opportunities and overcame opposition to push their program ahead in successive waves. They began with a change of paradigm, moved on to reforms in policy and personnel, and then began to change the basic economic management institutional structure.[11] In the first wave, they were in the political minority; in the second, they greatly expanded their bureaucratic constituency and institutional base; in attempting to press forward a third wave, they undermined their position of strength.

Chapter 3 covers the first wave (1979–1980) and ebb tide (1981–1982) of reform, during which leaders and advisers under Deng Xiaoping and Chen Yun critiqued the Stalinist development strategy and began an assault on the Maoist personnel and institutions that fostered local party-dominated self-reliance and defense industries in the interior. Followers of Deng and Chen began to diverge in this period, however, when it came to deciding what new institutions should replace the old. More conservative elders under Chen wanted to rebuild the central planning mechanisms, whereas reformers under Deng wanted to create alternative central policy planning bodies and allow some localities (the special economic zones, or SEZs) to experiment with market mechanisms. In a compromise approach, both proceeded in tandem. During the retrenchment that culminated in the triumph of the conservatives at the 12th Party Congress in 1982, reformer advisers nevertheless worked to create a new nonbureaucratic paradigm for the economy. Intellectuals and science administrators proved valuable allies for the reformers against the economic bureaucracy.

Chapter 4 covers the beginning of the second wave (1983–1984) of reform, during which the reformers won a major political skirmish with the conservatives and thereby achieved a breakthrough in policy initiatives. Three major programmatic documents were drafted and adopted as guidelines for urban reform, and the scope for market experiments, including in the SEZs, was expanded. Reformers used promises of an economic miracle and expanded autonomy for municipal and regional officials to expand their constituency to include the local bureaucracies, especially along the coast.

Chapter 5 examines how the reformers were able to maintain the initiative in the face of pressures for another period of retrenchment (1985–1986). Despite criticism and difficulties in controlling the economy, they nevertheless implemented important institutional reforms in the economic administrative system, including in planning, trade, finance, and enterprise management. Much of the central planning and management apparatus was dismantled. Policy reforms and personnel turnover expanded from the economic subsystem to the foreign affairs, science/technology, and propaganda/personnel subsystems. During this flood tide, however, enemies were made among the noneconomic bureaucrats and the elites in the interior as it became evident that there would be losers in the reform process.

Chapter 6 discusses the problems of system transition and political succession that dominated Chinese politics from 1987 into the beginning of 1989. The necessary direction of future reform as well as the obstacles to such reform became clear in this period. The need for reform of the political system and fundamental cultural changes became urgent. Transformation of the old regulation mechanisms of ideological exhortation and mandatory planning into new legal and fiscal-monetary mechanisms had been given a good start under Deng Xiaoping, but the follow-through would take decades, and it would not be smooth. Chapter 7 sums up themes from the book and comments on the systemic crisis of May and June 1989.

Notes

1. These studies include A. Doak Barnett, *The Making of Foreign Policy in China: Structure and Process* (Boulder, Colo.: Westview Press, 1985); Nina Halpern, "Making Economic Policy: The Influence of Economists," in John P. Hardt, ed., *China's Economy Looks Toward the Year 2000, Volume 1. The Four Modernizations: Selected Papers Submitted to the Joint Economic Committee, Congress of the United States* (Washington, D.C.: GPO, 21 May 1986), pp. 132–146; Nina Halpern, "Scientific Decision Making: The Organization of Expert Advice in Post-Mao China," in Denis Fred Simon and Merle Goldman, eds., *Science and Technology in Post-Mao China* (Cambridge, Mass.: Harvard University Council on East Asian Studies, 1989), pp. 157–174; David M. Lampton, ed., *Policy Implementation in Post-Mao China* (Berkeley: University of California Press, 1987); David M. Lampton and Kenneth Lieberthal, eds., *The Structure of Authority and Bureaucratic Behavior in China* (forthcoming); and Kenneth Lieberthal and Michel Oksenberg, *Policy Making in China: Leaders, Structures and Processes* (Princeton, N.J.: Princeton University Press, 1988).

2. Lieberthal and Oksenberg, ibid., pp. 3–18, discussed these models, and the evolution of the China field, in greater detail.

3. Suzanne Ogden, *China's Unresolved Issues: Politics, Development, and Culture* (Englewood Cliffs, N.J.: Prentice-Hall, 1989), pp. 1–12, presented a framework for analysis that focused on conflicting values—socialist, traditional, and developmental—that make it difficult for the Chinese system to resolve key issues. My analysis focuses more on different institutions and processes operating at different levels of the system, but our approaches are quite complementary.

4. The concepts and methodology of nonlinear science presented in James Gleick, *Chaos: Making a New Science* (New York: Viking Penguin, 1987), and in Ilya Prigogine and Isabelle Stengers, *Order out of Chaos: Man's New Dialogue with Nature* (New York: Bantam Books, 1984), echo my experience in analyzing Chinese politics. Neither the reductionist methods of current political science nor traditional historical approaches do full justice to the topics at hand here, but no new methodology exists that could apply to the social sciences some of the insights just now being developed in the natural sciences.

5. A number of articles in the Chinese press have used this metaphor, and Michel Oksenberg, when commenting on an early draft of my work, suggested that the metaphor seemed appropriate here. Harry Harding, *China's Second Revolution: Reform After Mao* (Washington, D.C.: Brookings Institution, 1987), p. 70, stated, "A wavelike pattern has characterized the process, as periods of consolidation or retreat have followed periods of advance, and periods of rapid momentum have given way to a more measured or tentative pace."

Alvin Toffler, *The Third Wave* (New York: Morrow, 1980), p. 21, cited the use of the wave metaphor in several studies of the nineteenth-century United States and then used it for his own analysis of the agrarian, industrial, and postindustrial societies of the West. He emphasized the violent clashing of waves of social change. Gilbert Rozman, ed., *The Modernization of China* (New York: Free Press, 1981), p. 489, cited the waves of reform in Russia (1861), Japan (1868), and China (1905).

6. In this study of the mid- to late-1980s, for the sake of simplicity, I have called Hu and Zhao and their followers of the younger generation *reformers* and all moderate reformers and antireform groups at the other end of the political spectrum (whose spokesman was Chen Yun) *conservatives;* Deng was the arbiter between these groups.

It is difficult to find terms that adequately take into account both policy preferences and personal loyalties, but a number of studies have shown that the dynamics of the system seem to produce "three lines" in the leadership. See Dorothy J. Solinger, *Three Visions of Chinese Socialism* (Boulder, Colo.: Westview Press, 1984); Kenneth B. Lieberthal, "Domestic Politics and Foreign Policy," in Harry Harding, ed., *China's Foreign Relations in the 1980s* (New Haven, Conn.: Yale University Press, 1984), pp. 43–70; and Carol Lee Hamrin, "Competing Political-Economic Strategies," in John P. Hardt, ed., *China's Economy Looks Toward the Year 2000,* in which I focused on the late 1970s and early 1980s and used the terms *moderate reformers* for the Chen Yun group, *radical reformers* for Deng, Hu, and Zhao, and *conservatives* for Stalinists and Maoists. Dorothy J. Solinger, "The Fifth National People's Congress and the Process of Policy Making: Reform, Readjustment, and the Opposition," *Asian Survey* 22:12 (December 1982), pp. 1238–1275, used the terms *readjusters, reformers* and *conservers* for the same three groups.

The dynamics of the system do seem to produce three competing coalitions, but the political spectrum shifts. Although Stalinists (central industrial planners) and moderate reformers (central fiscal-monetary balancers) persisted through the post-1949 period (and have cooperated against radical reformers), Maoists have been replaced by radical reformers as the third main group representing the interests of localities.

7. The following account comes from a conversation with a former member of the rural development center, Washington, D.C., 1985.

In the experimental rural areas, crop yields increased 15–65 percent compared with 5 percent in other areas. By the end of 1980, 20 percent of rural China had adopted similar management reforms; 50 percent had done so by the fall of 1981. Because of continued opposition by the vast majority of provincial leaders, however, the household responsibility system was then spread by fiat, with the first of five annual central directives issued in January 1982. By summer, 80 percent of China's rural areas had adopted the system.

The staff of the rural development center was formed from a personal network of children of mid- and high-level cadre who were at Beijing University when the Cultural Revolution broke out and were sent down to the countryside together. Their real education began then, as they worked with the peasants and read and discussed classic texts of Marxism-Leninism and other Western social theory bought by the pound as scrap paper after Red Guards had ransacked personal and public libraries. The head of the rural development center, Du Runsheng, was one of the architects of rural reform and a personal friend of Wan Li and Zhao Ziyang.

8. Xue Muqiao, "Sum Up Experience, Deepen Reform," *Renmin ribao* [People's Daily], 30 October 1987, p. 5, in Foreign Broadcast Information Service China Daily Report 87–212, 3 November 1987, pp. 35–38; and Halpern, "Making Economic Policy," p. 141.

9. He Weiling, "China's Reform: Background, Present Situation, and Prospects" (1987, unpublished ms.).

10. Zhao Ziyang in an interview given to Fox Butterfield, *China: Alive in the Bitter Sea* (New York: Times Books, 1982), p. 300.

11. My periodization of the reforms of the past decade are echoed by many Chinese commentators, although they tend to play down the discontinuities and emphasize the inevitability of continued progress. See, for example, Gao Shangquan (a vice minister of the reform commission), "A New Phase in Reforming China's Economic System," *Zhongguo jingji tizhi gaige* [China Economic System Reform] 12 (23 December 1987), pp. 7–8, in Joint Publications Research Service China Report 88-014, 17 March 1988, p. 2.

2

The Legacy of the Past

The basic Stalinist political system and economic development model adopted by China in the 1950s was a highly centralized version of the Leninist system similar to Lenin's own war communism of 1918 vintage. All key economic, cultural, and social entitities were nationalized, and along with the national party and state organs, they were run as a single party-state political-economic-social bureaucracy. Divided into functionally defined subsystems, such as those for finance and trade, for industry and communication, and for ideology and culture, this rapidly expanding bureaucracy monopolized decisionmaking in all spheres. The prevailing military mentality was reflected in references to these subsystems as fronts. They were highly compartmentalized; officials tended to remain within one arena throughout their careers and developed appropriate sets of professional values and processes.

Individual units in this system tended to become multifunctional; for example, ministries, factories, or hospitals provided not only their main products or services but were also responsible for housing, medical care, education, counseling, and recreation for their employees. In a pyramid-style hierarchical structure, lower-level entities were absolutely dependent upon higher levels and were subordinate to their command.

Pursuit of a Stalinist development strategy gave resource priority to the rapid growth of heavy industry, especially military industry. Central planners and industrial ministries gained tremendous power over resources as they supervised the nationalization and collectivization of the urban economy, and the industrial centers of China's northeastern provinces gained disproportionately from this wholesale importation of the Soviet system. The geopolitical Sino-Soviet alliance was the basis for China's resulting economic, political, and cultural dependence on the USSR.

But the Stalinist mode of development was difficult to adapt to the Chinese situation. Given China's poverty, the extraction of resources from agriculture for growth in industry did not take China very far. Central planning was hindered by a lack of skilled personnel, poor communication and transportation links, and huge differences among geographic regions in the stage of development. Under central command, those responsible for planning and implementation had little flexibility in adapting to specific functional or geographic conditions and problems. The top-down system was information poor; feedback was weak and distorted. There were complaints from within the elite as well as from the populace about the inefficiencies and inequities of commandism even before the formal adoption of the Soviet-style 1st Five Year Plan (1953–1957) in 1955.

Efforts to reform this basic model began early and continued throughout the next thirty years. Two competing modifications of the Stalinist model emerged: a radical, decentralized Stalinism associated with Mao Zedong and a moderate Leninism identified with Zhou Enlai and Chen Yun. These were pursued alternately throughout the 1960s and 1970s. Often, formal programs during these years reflected an uneasy compromise between the two sets of priorities and strategies. Mao and his colleagues continued to share the goal of rapid industrialization and the Stalinist assumption that this could be achieved through the transformation of society into state or collectively owned and operated units. But they came to disagree profoundly over the pace and method of change.

In 1955, before the ink on the 1st FYP was dry and against the desires of others, Mao began to accelerate the timetable for collectivizing the urban and rural economy in hopes of simultaneously increasing industrial and agricultural growth rates. The communes created in 1958 at the start of the Great Leap Forward extended the hand of the bureaucracy to rural affairs. Eventually, Mao went even farther than Stalin had in promoting ideological uniformity as an adjunct to the collectivization process.

Decisionmaking power was decentralized during the Great Leap Forward to the provincial-level bureaucracies in order to encourage more rapid, localized development of China's internal resources. In the process, party committees at each level gained control over factories and other units in their locality that were formerly controlled by higher levels in the separate functional subsystems. Mao's program aligned the interests of central and provincial party and military leaders responsible for mass mobilization through mandatory production drives and ideological exhortation but at the expense of economic and social administrators with professional credentials and concerns. This approach reflected suspicion of the Soviet Union as well as the West and was characterized by regional autarky and national isolationism in the name of self-reliance. Despite this devolution of power, there was no substantial change in the monolithic mode of management by administrative command.[1]

The Moderate Leninist Approach to Development

The alternative, more moderate effort to reform China's Stalinist system, modeled after Lenin's New Economic Policy (NEP) and various post-Stalin Eastern European reform experiments, was identified with Zhou Enlai and Chen Yun. First formulated in 1956, the moderate program was set aside in favor of the Great Leap Forward and was later adopted in times of crisis, including the early 1960s, the mid-1970s, and the early 1980s. Central economic administrators sought gradual organizational change through regular bureaucratic means and asserted the importance of financial realism and overall coordination and balance among economic sectors and geographic regions. Moderates placed priority on maintaining social stability through economic redistribution, police order, and moral education in Marxist-Leninist orthodoxy. They were willing to accept slower economic growth for the sake of steady growth; military and heavy industries were slighted in order to increase investment in agriculture. This approach favored agricultural and light industrial production and export regions along the coast. General détente was encouraged, especially in the Asian region (ranging all along China's borders: central, northeast, southeast, and south Asia), to reduce the military threat and expand available foreign resources and markets.

In 1956, when Chinese leaders first carried out a comprehensive review of the Soviet model in the wake of Joseph Stalin's death, they were motivated not only by the revelations regarding Stalin but also by indigenous problems stemming from the 1955 crash socialization program. Ironically, just as the Chinese completed the installation of a Soviet-style system, its merits were called into serious question. The review was fueled by elite and popular sentiment opposing overdependence on the Soviet Union and repression at home.

Vice Premier Chen Yun was in charge of the economic section of the policy review as head of the party's finance and economics leading group; Premier Zhou Enlai oversaw the larger effort. Chen's role as primary author of the Soviet-style 1st FYP gave his recommendations for change added authority. In April 1956, Mao presented to a gathering of officials the conclusions of the policy review in a speech titled, "On the Ten Great Relationships"; he described the

review as an effort to find a "Chinese road to socialism." He called
on his audience to learn from Soviet errors so as to avoid following
the same detours.[2] Zhou and Chen used the review to begin drafting
the 2nd FYP (1958–1962), which Chen presented for approval in a
speech to the 8th Party Congress in September.[3]

This new approach could be characterized as balanced development; it was intended primarily to redress the heavy industry bias in
the Soviet model. At the heart of this moderate critique of the Soviet
model was a realization of its human costs and a desire to improve
living standards along with industrialization; China needed grain as
well as steel and guns and housing as well as factories. But Chen Yun's
8th Party Congress speech reflected a different understanding of development, not just a different set of priorities.[4] He saw economic
growth as the outcome of the interaction among various sectors of the
economy. His approach contrasted with the prevailing, predatory Stalinist view that growth in one sector could be achieved only at the
expense of the others. Chen argued that the pace of industrialization
must be slowed to match the necessarily slow pace of agricultural
development because agriculture supplied most of the state's financial
revenue, raw materials for light industry, and exports to pay for technology imports.

Chen's approach also called into question the Soviet-style extensive
development strategy that measured growth as the quantity of material
output achieved by high rates of investment in capital construction.
Chen's speech proposed an intensive development strategy that sought
to improve the efficiency of the economy and quality of products by
using material incentives and market indicators as well as plans to
guide production. This strategy required increased enterprise competition, multiple forms of ownership, and reduced bureaucratic interference
in the economy.

There were important procedural and organizational implications
in this shift of assumptions and priorities (which were also spelled out
by Chen at the congress). In order to balance the budget and control
the supplies of credit and foreign exchange, planning was recentralized
and followed financial indicators. As a result, local party officials again
lost control over resources to officials in charge of the vertical functional
systems. Financial and trade officials became more involved in decisionmaking, thus breaking the monopoly of the planning commissions,
which followed the Soviet style of material supply planning.

Chen Yun's approach required that the state distribute resources
more widely. There was a new emphasis on improved living conditions,
increased wages, and more autonomy and economic benefits for the
localities, factories, peasants, national minorities, and nonparty social

groups. The social views espoused in Mao's April 1956 speech formed the basis for liberalization policies designed to ensure less coercion, more tolerance of alternative views, and a more open attitude toward learning from capitalist as well as socialist countries. Mao indicated that this new socioeconomic approach was premised on an assumption that China now faced a period of relative internal unity and international peace that was expected to last a decade or more.

Implementation of Chen's new development approach was delayed for several years. Its basic assumptions of stability at home and abroad were undermined in late 1956–1958 by the outbreak of popular dissent during the 100 Flowers Movement, the state's harsh reaction during the Antirightist Campaign, and tensions with both Washington and Moscow. Mao shifted to the Great Leap Forward program as a shortcut to development and independence. This approach sought low-cost improvement in agricultural output through mass labor mobilization campaigns and local small-scale, low-technology industries in order to continue the Stalinist industrial policy. Mao aimed to set up complete industrial systems in each large region and province in the name of self-reliance. Chen Yun, however, remained convinced that agricultural output would not expand without modern technological input, which required investments in imports. He also opposed regional self-reliance and remained committed to a truly national economy based on regional specialization.

In the wake of the famine, economic depression, and loss of Soviet assistance that were the fruits of the attempted leap into communism, the moderate program resurfaced. Both the readjustment policies of 1960–1965 and the original draft of the 3rd FYP (1966–1970) reflected the views of Chen Yun, who was again put in charge of the economy with the backing of Zhou Enlai and Deng Xiaoping.[5] Grain was imported; peasants were resettled from the cities to the countryside to save demand on state grain; thousands of inefficient rural enterprises were closed; private plots and rural markets were restored; and the commune was set aside in practice, as output quotas were assigned to families.

But even in the face of rural catastrophe and looming budget deficits, Chen Yun barely won the argument to postpone the inauguration of the FYP from 1963 to 1966 and to reduce its outrageous steel targets. Chen's draft plan focused on restoring and increasing consumption levels (as reflected in the targets for grain and textiles), setting realistic growth rates, and moderating investment levels, with a shift of investment priorities away from steel and machinery to the chemical industry (fertilizer and synthetic fibres) and to imports of foreign technology. Three-fourths of new investment were to go to coastal industry.[6]

This plan was never put into effect; tension between China and the United States over the escalating war in Vietnam led Mao to question the plan's advisability. Mao and his close associates convinced the leadership to pursue a very different industrialization program, which again resembled war communism, during the next decade. In the summer of 1964, Mao was highly critical of the draft plan presented to him and insisted that the plan give more resources to heavy industry and new construction of inland industry and armaments and gear imports less to grain and more to advanced technology. In the wake of the Tonkin Gulf crisis, Mao argued successfully for a drastic acceleration of the pace of inland construction because of the imminent danger of war and the vulnerability of China's coastal industrial regions.[7]

Mao's War Communism:
The Third-Front Strategy

With the U.S. bombing of North Vietnam in early 1965, Mao argued that China should be divided into "three great fronts." The first front was the developed coast and border areas subject to seizure by an invasion force; the second was the central plains and other concentrations of population and industry subject to bombing attacks; and the third was the secure base area in the undeveloped, mountainous interior.[8] The rationale was to minimize the loss of industrial assets located in the first and second fronts in the event of war. The third-front industrial policy thus was highly redistributive; it shifted investment from the north and northeast, where it was concentrated in the 1st FYP, and once again ignored the coast. Not a single large nonpetroleum industrial project was begun in the coastal regions between 1965 and 1971. Eventually, nearly four hundred large-scale factories and their workers, and even some existing rail lines, were dismantled and moved inland.

Complex, large-scale, interprovincial projects were constructed at a frenzied pace by massed government construction teams and the army engineering corps, for the most part under military command posts. But while the state poured the bulk of its resources into third-front projects, financial control of most large civilian enterprises was gradually turned over to the localities, and small-scale local enterprises grew. Austerity and regional self-reliance became the watchwords for Mao's war communism. Planning became increasingly complex and ineffective in matching resources and investment.

The imperatives of military preparation and accelerated heavy industrial development dominated economic planning until the fall of Lin Biao and the beginning of Sino-U.S. détente in 1971. Economic decisions in this period must be viewed at least in part as military strategy, not development strategy. Even though Sino-U.S. tensions were already moderating by 1966, tensions with the Soviet Union were growing and led to border clashes in 1969, a renewed war scare, and a second phase of war construction. The nuclear and aerospace industries, built in the far northwest, received high priority. Probably two-thirds of budgeted industrial investment went to the third front at its peak, and one-fifth of this went to military industry. The signs of war preparations probably had effective deterrent benefits. Yet the third-front strategy was much more than defense strategy, given the long-term investments such as the Panzhihua steel plant, the Yangzi River dam, and petroleum complexes clearly designed to create an entire industrial base that could survive a prolonged war.

The third-front strategy was useful politically for Mao and Lin Biao. Mao sent critics such as Li Fuchun, longtime head of the planning commission, and Peng Dehuai, former defense minister, out of Beijing to work in the third-front area. Yu Qiuli, a Mao protégé, became head of a new planning leading group, and Lin established personal control over military industries (civilian control was not restored until 1974). It would appear that Mao and Lin took advantage of the international threats, perhaps exaggerating them, so as to force their preferred policies, personnel, and organizations with added urgency.

Mao's war communism became increasingly radical and utopian in its methods, but ironically and tragically it looked to the past for its model. Mao praised the Yan'an era of the 1940s, when a militarized supply economy and tight social and ideological discipline characterized the anti-Japanese wartime base areas. He turned to the army as the model for social discipline and unquestioning obedience to his personal command. Mao's personality cult elevated him to the position of emperor, even to that of a savior-god, beyond reach of statute or moral appeal. His program was radical in its methods but essentially reactionary in nature, with its antimodern, antiurban, anti-intellectual, anticommercial, and antiforeign biases.

The growing hidden dangers in the economy were suddenly exacerbated when the 4th FYP (1971–1975), known as the "flying leap," called for extremely high investment rates and output targets. Large numbers of huge projects were begun by every construction ministry, most of them starting early in the plan cycle in 1970–1971. State investments increased 49 percent in 1970 and another 13 percent in

1971. The economy was totally out of control, which sparked a leadership crisis.

The End of the Third-Front Strategy

In 1972, following Lin's death, the third-front strategy was brought to a sudden halt with an urgent readjustment program. Work on major projects was suspended and left unfinished; construction teams were transferred out of the region. The strain on resources and the appalling waste made continuation of the strategy impossible. Huge inefficiencies resulted from inadequate transportation links between the inland plants and their sources of supplies and markets. Because of difficulties of terrain, poor planning and design, and construction flaws, many of these major projects failed to come on line until the 1980s. (Some still lie rusting, never to be completed. In the 1980s, one of China's senior economists claimed that up to $100 billion may have been wasted in infrastructure development since 1949; the bulk of it would have to have been in the third front.[9] The additional cost of neglecting the coast is incalculable; the price in energy scarcity and transportation bottlenecks is still being paid today.) From an economic point of view, the third-front strategy was a disaster even surpassing the Great Leap Forward.

During the 1970s, both before and after Mao's death, there was a constant struggle between proponents of Mao's radical Stalinization and those who backed a return to the Chen-Zhou moderate Leninism. Central and local planners also waged a battle over revenues, with the latter holding the majority of new revenues for the first time. Economic administrators struggled to shut down the worst third-front construction projects and limit local projects, but these administrators met little success in the face of the powerful interests now vested in the status quo.

Because of this political-economic struggle, officials were stymied in their efforts to direct a development program and were reduced to using what portion of investment they did control simply to balance current accounts in the economy. In 1975, Deng Xiaoping attempted to recentralize the economy and improve industrial management as part of a ten-year plan. He was opposed by the radicals, and with the deaths of Zhou and Mao in 1976, economic activity ground to a halt. All efforts to create a version of the Soviet political-economic system suited to China came to a dead end.

Waves of Reform After Mao

The decade following Mao's death was shaped by the political interests and personal relationships among China's remaining revolutionaries. These elders, among whom Deng Xiaoping and Chen Yun were the most senior, together dismantled the Maoist system and repudiated Maoist priorities. They did so in the name of a more moderate, regularized Chinese Leninist system and a more realistic orthodoxy that placed priority on material development as a prerequisite for egalitarian and collectivist goals.

Continued political and economic instability following the deaths of Zhou and Mao provided the opportunity for a thorough challenge to Maoism by the old guard. Deng Xiaoping, Chen Yun, and other elder revolutionaries purged by Mao reasserted their prior claim to leadership against younger leaders such as Hua Guofeng who had gained influence during the Cultural Revolution. An alliance between Deng and Chen and their protégés gradually succeeded in reasserting the priorities of the moderates and gaining control over key levers of power, beginning with the famous 3rd Plenum of late 1978. The plenum challenged Mao's legacy with its ideological shift from class struggle to modernization as the party's legitimizing purpose, its call for a major shift of investment to agriculture and consumer goods and the legitimation and expansion of markets, and its decision to normalize Sino-U.S. relations (symbol of the intent to break out of isolationism).[10] The 3rd Plenum thus ushered in a major resorting of priorities that would characterize the decade to follow.

Political instability was moderated for much of the following decade, in part because the spectrum of political opinion was narrowed by the thorough discrediting of the Maoist program and in part because other leaders acknowledged Deng's status as chief political arbiter. The leadership as a whole agreed on several essential aims: eliminating terror and restoring a sense of normality, steadily raising standards of living to rebuild confidence in the party, and expanding foreign economic ties to supplement scarce domestic resources. Nevertheless, political-economic cycles of reform and retrenchment emerged, with hesitation in reform during 1981–1982, 1985, and 1987–1989.

The Roots of Reform

The post-Mao reform program was the latest in a series of efforts begun before 1949 to adapt the basic Leninist party command structure to the task of fulfilling the twentieth-century dream of restoring China's historical greatness. The program drew its context from the mandate the Chinese Communist party inherited from its earlier years and from the institutional legacy imparted by previous attempts to reform the political system.

The Modernization Mandate

Once the party had won the anti-Japanese and civil wars and had established a nationwide monopoly on political power and economic resources, it turned to the tasks of economic development. In the mid-1950s, the party promised that under its centralized command, China would industrialize and socialize the economy within fifteen years (by 1965) and then during several more decades would become a world power. (The party is still striving to fulfill this promise.) Mao Zedong, in the opening address to a special national party conference held to ratify the 1st FYP, set forth the program: "We may be able to build a socialist society over three five year plans, but to build a strong, highly industrialized socialist country will require several decades of hard work, say, fifty years, or the entire second half of the present century."[11] Mao's speech also revealed the nationalistic sentiment that fueled these goals—the urgent desire to catch up with or surpass the most powerful capitalist countries in the world.

The fifteen-year timetable and the model for the first stage (1950–1965) were inspired by the Soviet Union's experience from 1920 to 1935. The party leadership assumed that setting up a Soviet-style centralized and collectivized socioeconomic system would automatically produce steady economic development. Thus, China did not have a development strategy, but a set of political and economic goals and a model. After 1956, Mao attempted to speed up the timetable through forced collectivization and crash industrialization programs. Moderate leaders sought to retain a more realistic time frame, however; Premier Zhou Enlai set forth a two-stage development agenda in 1964 (reiterated in 1975) that essentially postponed the goal of industrialization to 1980 but still called for full modernization by the year 2000.[12]

Before Mao and Zhou died in 1976, China succeeded in establishing a nationwide administrative and industrial infrastructure. But Chinese leaders met with continual failure in their efforts to sustain steady economic growth, expand political participation, build stable and harmonious sociocultural institutions and shared public values, and address long-term population and ecological concerns. The historical record shows that although the overall growth of the Chinese economy after 1949 was quite respectable, the growth pattern was most notable for its fluctuations.

The downturns in China's economic growth had origins in fluctuations in agricultural output, but they were exacerbated by serious flaws in the political system. Decisionmakers often responded to economic trends too late and too sharply; investment decisions amplified the effect of resource scarcities. Differences among Chinese leaders over policy and power too often escalated into pitched battles between high-level factions. These battles paralyzed the policy process or resulted in wild swings from one policy extreme to another. Social tensions became entwined with political conflict in explosive ways. The most notable examples of resulting instability were, of course, the Great Leap Forward (1958–1960) and the Great Proletarian Cultural Revolution (1966–1971). One Chinese source in early 1987 cited secret figures attributing a $32 billion financial loss to the Great Leap Forward period and a $135 billion loss to the Cultural Revolution. Other losses, in human and ecological terms, can never be fully measured but were enormous. In the early 1960s alone, 20–30 million lives were lost due to policy-induced conditions of starvation or illness.[13] Chinese leaders as well as critical intellectuals came to recognize that their failures stemmed in part from serious inadequacies in the political system and sought to remedy them through reforms.

The Leninist System

The object of reform both under Mao and in the 1980s was the highly centralized and monolithic political-socioeconomic system imported from the Soviet Union in the early 1950s, which concentrated control over important material and human resources, information, and decision power in the hands of the political bureaucracy and increased the compartmentalized, or cellular, nature of Chinese society. This system built upon and fortified key elements of the traditional authoritarian Chinese political culture, which accepted unbounded state prerogatives and patronage relations based on personal loyalty (this is typical of a patrimonial dependency culture). Power in traditional and Leninist Chinese society did not trickle down to the citizenry but rather migrated into the hands of a few powerful patrons at the top and produced dictators at the apex. As a result, the bureaucratic system was managed primarily so as to maintain and expand the power and privileges of the bureaucratic elite and to distribute the perquisites of power within the bureaucracy. Efficient socioeconomic development and wider distribution of its benefits were secondary goals. As in similar societies, the Chinese system was inflexible and lacked adaptive power to combine social and material resources in novel ways.[14]

Chinese dissidents who criticized the political culture and system as a kind of feudal socialism in which the people were exploited by a new class were jailed as leaders denied that the Communist party was a ruling class with special interests of its own. Yet the average Chinese spoke naturally and often of the party's rule as one that enforced maintenance of special rights for a privileged stratum.

In 1980, Deng Xiaoping himself described the contemporary Chinese bureaucratic system as differing from both the traditional and Western types by virtue of its bureaucratism, overconcentration of power, patriarchal methods, life tenure in office, and privileges. His proposed solution was administrative reform, starting at the top, not just changes in thinking and behavior.[15] Dissidents seemed to differ from reformers more in prescription than in diagnosis. While dissidents demanded new channels for popular participation in decisionmaking, Deng made it clear that change must be initiated and controlled by the leadership. During his tenure, sporadic and tentative attempts were made to change the following chief characteristics of the Leninist system.

The Structure of the Bureaucracy. In theory, the system of Chinese leadership was separated into party, government, and military bureaucracies, but in fact these were a single political bureaucracy divided into functional systems (vertical "branches") and geographic localities (horizontal "areas"). These two cleavages typically provided the framework of competing bureaucratic interests on which competing personal factions were constructed. Members of the Politburo's standing committee plus a few semiretired elders held senior responsibilities in one or more of several broad policy arenas—government (economic) affairs, party (personnel and propaganda) work, foreign affairs, and security (internal and military) affairs. These leaders of the oligarchy accrued and exercised power through formally assigned bureaucratic responsibilities and through informal patronage networks; the formal and informal links among and within the bureaucratic units were of equal significance.[16]

Membership on informal groups, such as leading groups, coordinating or document-drafting groups, and advisory groups, tended to be personally assigned by top leaders. These groups could be used by leaders to strengthen the communication and coordination among the normally self-contained units of the bureaucracy, or the groups could be used to build up power factions by monopolizing important information and bypassing the regular bureaucracy.

The tight integration, or fusion, of politics and economics in China's monolithic system reflected the state ownership of the major means of production, which made all important economic decisions political in nature. In addition, the absence of an institutionalized approach to leadership competition and change meant that political struggles for power took place within the bureaucratic policy and personnel processes. The stakes in debates over policy priorities were high, given the potential impact on patronage resources. With the absence of limits on terms of tenure in office and the illegality of challenging incumbent leaders, political competitors stood to lose all or gain all.

As a result, there were powerful incentives for established insiders to monopolize the policy process by retaining tight control over information and decisionmaking and by placing only loyal supporters in key policy posts. Aspiring outsiders were motivated to subvert or bypass established policy procedures and to disrupt implementation of the program in process. When a leader lost power the victors tended to repudiate all his policy preferences, remove his supporters, and weaken the institutions that were the base of his power as guarantees against his comeback.

Incentive for cooperation to ensure policy stability and continuity was weak. For many actors both inside and outside the bureaucracy, the main avenue for influencing policies made without their consultation was to obstruct or distort implementation to their advantage. Add to this the absence of formal local autonomy in China, and the complexity and sensitivity of national policy debates grew exponentially. Intra- and interprovincial as well as central-local conflicts of bureaucratic interest all entered into the national policymaking process. Truly national interests or the special interests of those social groups outside the bureaucracy did not find an adequate institutional voice in such a system.

Competing Policy Programs. Political programs in China tended to be presented in the form of programmatic policy documents that articulated long-term goals and overall direction and justified these by a set of ideological principles. These documents, when officially adopted by top party and state congresses, were intended to function as the official party line that set the parameters for more concrete policies, legislation, and personnel decisions. The party line became the criterion for legitimizing political-economic behavior at all levels. These programs had powerful implications for the balance of power and distribution of resources within the bureaucracy. Thus, the political strategies of both institutions and individuals at the center revolved around shaping programs or party lines in their favor and subverting implementation of those that were not.

The Leninist concept of the correct party line gave policy a moral component that made compromise agreement and flexible approaches to policy problems exceedingly difficult. When one leader's approach prevailed, the general line would be made or revised accordingly. Alternatives could not be broached openly without challenging the official line of the top leader. Such challenges were considered illegitimate because they questioned the myth of the infallibility of the party (and its leader). Challengers thus had to wait for problems to arise, or create them, to spur a policy review. Therein lay the incentive for outsiders quietly to sabotage the prevailing economic program or exaggerate its faults. Even small problems could bring on a serious political attack that led to policy stagnation, fluctuation, or reverse.[17]

Debates over national strategy took place in great secrecy and with tremendous conflict at the very top among a few dozen party politicians, rather than at lower levels, in other institutions, or in public arenas. The programs that emerged rarely resembled well-researched development strategies but were closer to U.S. campaign platforms in level of simplicity, remoteness from reality, and subservience to particular political interests. Program implementation, moreover, became closely tied to the legitimacy of individual leaders, who viewed the questioning of an official program as disloyalty.

Under the personal dictatorship of Mao, of course, the party line degenerated into simplistic slogans or personal directives from Mao that the citizen saluted in word and deed to prove loyalty to the great helmsman as the personification of the party and the revolution. Only the great leader had the privilege of contemplating a vision or strategy for the future of the nation. For anyone to question his program or offer an alternative was an act of lèse-majesté. Under Deng Xiaoping's more enlightened and collegial leadership throughout most of the 1980s, broader discussion of the national program was encouraged within the elite, although Deng retained his informal title (and power) as chief architect of the blueprint, as the Chinese press frequently pointed out. The elements of political and economic rationality in the party line grew to the point where Zhao Ziyang's work report to the 13th Party Congress in 1987 sounded like a report from the chair of the board to the stockholders.

Political-Economic Cycles. In a regularized Leninist system, two five-year cycles—the five-year economic plan and the five-year party congress term—had an important impact on the shaping of alternative programs and on the nature of competition among their proponents. Although these cycles were neither formally integrated nor exactly coincidental, the two were always intimately related. The plan set the budgetary priorities, and the party congress report set the ideological and political priorities of the program.

A loose analogy would be the U.S. presidential campaign cycle, which imposes an arbitrary timing on policy debate and the production of campaign platforms. In China, the need to formulate a five-year plan tends to elicit high-level, all-inclusive policy reviews in which estimates for the near future are made regarding domestic problems and resources and international challenges and opportunities. These then shape the more concrete deliberations that must go into the formal plan, such as the defense share of the budget, the priorities given to heavy or light industry, and so on. The FYP then becomes a major component of the more overtly political programs set forth at party congresses.[18]

In the post-Mao period, both the 6th and 7th FYPs (1981–1985 and 1986–1990 respectively) were drafted in close conjunction with the programs for the 12th and 13th Party Congresses: The former plan was finalized shortly following the 12th congress in late 1982; a special party conference held in late 1985 endorsed a party proposal to the National People's Congress that set directions for the latter plan. In both cases, the focus of the plan served to legitimize complementary changes in the structure and membership of the Central Committee organs.

Although more specialized policy reviews occur when unexpected events call for them, the record indicates that China's most serious and far-reaching strategic debates and political struggles have occurred in finalizing FYPs, even when the outcome has been a (not infrequent) decision to scrap or totally revise the plan. This suggests that major international and domestic developments have greater political impact at the end stage of a five-year cycle because they will be used as evidence to prove or disprove the rationale for one program or another.

There is reason to conclude that the integrated political-economic five-year cycle itself has contributed to the record of debilitating political and economic fluctuations. Economically, local officials have a strong incentive to increase investments and wages near the end of a plan cycle because their share of the next budget is based on the last. Similarly, officials are wise to use a high proportion of their new allotments in the first year of the plan in case the plan is later revised. Thus, the leadership is confronted by two years of imbalance in income and expenditures that fuel budget deficits and inflation. Moreover, this tends to occur in the midst of leadership competition for power so that those responsible for the plan are objects of criticism and demands for new directions.

The reform program of the 1980s had roots in previous efforts to adapt the Soviet model to Chinese realities. It did not spring full-blown from the mind of Deng Xiaoping or the pages of a development textbook. Rather, it was the product of previous Chinese and Eastern European modifications of the Soviet model combined with insights and institutions borrowed from nonsocialist development experiences.

Notes

1. This point was made by Chen Yizi, the main drafter of the political reform section of the 13th Party Congress work report, in a July 1986 speech published as "Reform of the Political Structure Is a Guarantee of Reform of the Economic Structure," *Shijie jingji daobao* [World Economic Herald], 10 August 1987, pp. 3–4, in Foreign Broadcast Information Service China Daily Report [FBIS-CHI] 87–174, 9 September 1987, pp. 20–26.

2. Mao Zedong, *Selected Works,* vol. 5 (Beijing: Foreign Languages Press, 1977), pp. 284–302. For a detailed study of the domestic and international events affecting policymaking from 1956 to 1960, see Roderick MacFarquhar, *The Origins of the Cultural Revolution, Volume 1. Contradictions Among the People, 1956–1957* (New York: Columbia University Press, 1974), and *Volume 2. The Great Leap Forward, 1958–1960* (New York: Columbia University Press, 1983).

3. David M. Bachman, *Chen Yun and the Chinese Political System* (Berkeley: University of California Center for Chinese Studies, 1985), pp. 57, 63ff.

4. For the following description of Chen's views, I have relied heavily on Bachman, ibid., and the introduction to Nicholas R. Lardy and Kenneth Lieberthal, eds., *Chen Yun's Strategy for China's Development: A Non-Maoist Alternative,* trans. Mao Tong and Du Anxia (Armonk, N.Y.: M. E. Sharpe, 1983), pp. xi–xliii.

5. Bachman, ibid., pp. 70, 73–76.

6. Barry Naughton, "The Third Front: Defence Industrialization in the Chinese Interior," *China Quarterly* 115 (September 1988), p. 352. The following discussion of the third-front investment program is based on pp. 352–386.

7. Kenneth G. Lieberthal and Bruce J. Dickson, *A Research Guide to Central Party and Government Meetings in China: 1949–1986* (Armonk, N.Y.: M. E. Sharpe, 1989), pp. 147–148, mentioned Mao's relevant comments at a September 1963 work conference, in June 1964, and at an August 1964 meeting of the Secretariat.

8. Naughton, "The Third Front," p. 353, explained the geographical logic of developing the "big third front" (*da san xian*) as a secure rear base area; it included all of Guizhou, Yunnan, Sichuan, Gansu, Ningxia, and Qinghai; a part of Shaanxi; and the western, mountainous parts of Henan, Hubei, and Hunan.

9. Qian Jiazhu, quoted in the *Hong Kong Standard,* 2 April 1987, p. 8, in FBIS, April 2, 1987, p. K26. These figures are very general. Qian said 200 to 300 billion yuan, which in the mid-1980s equaled $70 to 100 billion. A report in *China Daily,* 1 April 1989, p. 1, in FBIS-CHI–89-062, 3 April 1989, p. 53, said that construction costs for the third-front industries were well over 300 billion yuan.

10. For a detailed account of the politics of the 1978–1982 period, see Carol Lee Hamrin, "Competing Political-Economic Strategies," in John P. Hardt, ed., *China's Economy Looks Toward the Year 2000, Volume 1. The Four*

Modernizations: Selected Papers Submitted to the Joint Economic Committee, Congress of the United States (Washington, D.C.: GPO, 21 May 1986), pp. 72–89.

Briefly, from the death of Mao and Zhou in 1976 to 1980, the leadership under Chairman and Premier Hua Guofeng tried to restore normalcy, resumed the task of creating an economic plan to guide work to the year 1985, and sketched an overall program for modernizing agriculture, industry, national defense, and science and technology by the year 2000. Although economic development was the stated aim of the modernization program, its underlying imperative was to restore the legitimacy of the Chinese Communist party after the debacle of the late years of Mao Zedong. The leadership made an effort to rebuild central institutions but allowed no fundamental change in the Maoist approach.

An economic development plan was publicized in February 1978; like its predecessors, it avoided tough-minded decisions on conflicting priorities and instead promised something for everyone. The shortcut this time was to be a massive whole plant import program, later dubbed the Great Leap Westward. With the upsurge of contracting late in 1978, a huge gray cloud of budget deficits and foreign debt loomed. At the 1978 3rd Plenum of the 11th Central Committee, Chen Yun reviewed the lessons to be learned from leftist economic mistakes since 1949, and the plenum resolution affirmed that the strategy of the 1956 8th Party Congress was to be used for guidance. Chen thereafter was put in charge of the economy.

11. Mao, *Selected Works,* vol. 5, p. 155.

12. Deng Xiaoping, *Selected Works (1975–1982)* (Beijing: Foreign Languages Press, 1982), p. 14, repeated Zhou Enlai's agenda in a March 1975 speech to economic administrators from throughout the country.

13. *Wenweipo* (Hong Kong) [Literary Gazette], March 1987. The extent of the postleap famine is still undetermined because of government reluctance to publish the facts as well as problems in statistical information from that period and different ways of extrapolating figures from the 1982 census data. It is also difficult to determine how much of the blame should go to bad weather and how much to mismanaged governmental response. For a discussion of the problem, see Thomas P. Bernstein, "Stalinism, Famine, and Chinese Peasants," *Theory and Society* 13:3 (May 1984), pp. 339–377. The highest death figure I have cited was suggested in an unpublished talk by a U.S. government demographer in 1984. An equal number of babies not born because of malnutrition or death of parents adds to the demographical "gap."

By the late 1980s, Chinese specialists were intensively researching and debating the nature and causes of cyclical fluctuations in the economy. See Zheng Kaizhao, "Exploration of the Question of Cyclical Fluctuations of China's Economy," *Renmin ribao* [People's Daily], 3 February 1989, p. 5, in FBIS-CHI–89-028, 13 February 1989, pp. 55–56; and Louise do Rosario, "More Swings Than Roundabouts," *Far Eastern Economic Review,* 2 March 1989, pp. 48–49.

14. According to Kenneth Jowitt, *The Leninist Response to National Dependency* (Berkeley: University of California Institute of International Stud-

ies, 1978), pp. 31–32, in a Leninist-modeled system, which he called neotraditional, the bureaucracy is "an instrument for recognizing or ignoring new claimants on the national patrimony who . . . [request] a protected and privileged place. Control over resources [is] parceled out to discrete cliques, patron-client chains, and ministerial fiefs." The state is only "the most prominent and powerful corporate 'gatekeeper' in a society that rest[s] on a whole series of corporate 'gatekeepers.' Just as the national elite monopolize[s] access to the . . . national economy, so a plethora of sub-elites monopolize[s] access to a variety of 'closed' social domains within the society." The resulting clientelist, bureaucratic, political-economic system is characteristic of all Communist systems modeled after the Soviet Union.

Also see Kenneth Jowitt, "Soviet Neotraditionalism: The Political Corruption of a Leninist Regime," *Soviet Studies* 35:3 (July 1983), pp. 275–297; Kenneth Jowitt, "An Organizational Approach to the Study of Political Culture in Marxist-Leninist Systems," *American Political Science Review* 68 (September 1974), pp. 1171–1191; and Andrew Walder, *Communist Neotraditionalism: Work and Authority in Chinese Industry* (Berkeley: University of California Press, 1986).

15. Deng, *Selected Works,* pp. 302–325, in a speech to an enlarged meeting of the Politburo.

16. This description of lines of authority borrows from Kenneth Lieberthal and Michel Oksenberg, *Policy Making in China: Leaders, Structures, and Processes* (Princeton, N.J.: Princeton University Press, 1988), p. 22.

See Carol Lee Hamrin, "The Party Leadership System," in M. David Lampton and Kenneth Lieberthal, eds., *The Structure of Authority and Bureaucratic Behavior in China* (forthcoming), for a discussion of how the leadership divides responsibilities for functional sectors. See Jonathan Unger, "The Struggle to Dictate China's Administration: The Conflict of Branches vs. Areas vs. Reform," *Australian Journal of Chinese Affairs* 18 (July 1987), pp. 15–46, for a discussion of how functional and geographic divisions of responsibility overlap and conflict. See John Wilson Lewis, *Political Networks and the Chinese Policy Process* (Stanford, Calif.: Stanford University Press, March 1987), on informal personal networks.

There is no direct evidence that the leadership divides responsibilities for different geographic localities, but individual leaders have always been closely identified with and involved in the politics of favored localities, often those where they were born, where they served during the war years, and where they held bureaucratic posts after 1949.

17. This view of the effect of the general line has been echoed by a young Chinese policy adviser involved in the reform program from the beginning. See He Weiling, "China's Reform: Background, Present Situation, and Prospects" (1987, unpublished ms.). To deal with this polarizing effect, the reformers' strategy was to "relax administrative economic controls; push forward; stop and wait; readjust; begin again."

18. In the mid-1950s, debate over the 2nd FYP (1958–1962), a blueprint for which emerged in April 1956, and politicking for the 8th Party Congress

later in the year were closely linked. In the ensuing decades from the Great Leap through the Cultural Revolution, Mao's radical allies successfully sabotaged efforts to regularize either state plans or party programs. But the cycles still shaped politics—the Cultural Revolution was launched to preempt a reformist economic plan and party program then in draft. Lin Biao's campaign to supercede Mao in 1969 and his militarized economic plan of 1970 were part of the same effort.

The final struggle for the succession to Mao between Deng Xiaoping and the radicals took place in the context of drafting documents for a new FYP. Kenneth B. Lieberthal, with James Tong and Sai-cheung Yeung, *Central Documents and Politburo Politics in China* (Ann Arbor: University of Michigan Center for Chinese Studies, 1978), discussed the documents involved, although Lieberthal did not spell out the fact that they were being used to formulate a ten-year plan for 1975–1985. The same documents became the basis for finalizing the ten-year plan after Mao died.

3

The First Wave and Ebb Tide: Search for a New Model (1979–1982)

The first wave of reform in 1979–1980 constituted the abandonment of Stalinism and Maoism through deregulation of the Chinese economy and of Chinese minds. Difficulties in stabilizing the economy and setting priorities for the 6th FYP (1981–1985) fueled continual and eventually far-reaching efforts to open up new policy options.

The leadership's first move involved readjusting investment priorities to give greater resources to agriculture and light industry and to center innovation on agrarian policy. The hallmark of Mao's cellular, self-reliant economy—the commune—was gradually abandoned. The leadership's second move, which was prompted by the urgent and immediate need for new financial resources, was to create special economic zones to attract foreign investment. These policies represented an attempt, like Lenin's New Economic Policy of 1921, to use the local market and the international market as supplements to the state-owned planned economy, that is, to use capitalism to build socialism. The reach of the bureaucracy was limited in order to get whole sectors of society off the dole and back to production.

But very soon afterward, in 1981–1982, economic and social disorder reminiscent of the fluctuations that occurred during the Mao period prompted a slowdown in market reform. As the central authorities relaxed controls, chronic repressed excess demand for investment created a rapid expansion of out-of-plan investment; this in turn caused sectoral imbalances, especially energy shortages, and inflationary pressures as consumer purchasing power expanded rapidly.[1] These problems prompted Chinese leaders to tighten the reins; they began rebuilding central command institutions in all sectors, modeling them after the

8th Party Congress (1956) plans. But this led to economic recession by late 1981, which raised equal alarm concerning the slow growth rate and idled capacity.

The continuing inadequacy of either centralized or localized command approaches to the economy and the elusiveness of steady economic growth fueled a search for new, untried solutions. Top leaders initiated a major political reform that during the years would have immense but largely unanticipated consequences—the leadership opened up the policy process to a handful of trusted intellectuals. As policy advisers, they reviewed alternative development experiences and proposed a new economic development strategy. Their input resulted in a discernible trend toward greater realism and coordination in policy-making. Even though officials might not grasp the intricacies of quantitative modeling, its results were not hard to understand. When economists came up with new figures showing China's per capita weaknesses in natural and human resources relative to other countries, these figures deflated grandiose and magical schemes of leaping into economic development. Modernization goals were stretched out over a longer time frame, and strategic consideration was made of the steps required to achieve them.

At first the policy researchers focused on Eastern European models, but they very quickly began to experiment with the concepts and methods of Western development economics. As researchers and policy-makers became more aware of the growing gap between China's performance and those of capitalist countries, especially in Asia, the pressures of international competition began to force consideration of systemic reforms not envisioned in the late 1970s.

Discarding Old Models

Although the discussions at the work conference leading up to the 3rd Plenum in late 1978 had demonstrated the need for a major review and overhaul of the economy, the bureaucratic and personnel structure, in which the planning commission and industrial ministries monopolized policy, continued to foster old thinking. To remedy this, Chen Yun and Li Xiannian wrote a letter to the central leadership recommending that a new finance and economy commission be set up under the State Council to oversee rewrites of the annual plan for 1979 and the ten year plan through 1985. This proposed commission replicated the policy body used by Chen to salvage the economy from earlier crises.[2]

In March 1979, a party work conference was convened to discuss the economy, and Chen made a forceful argument for a drastic cut in steel investment, caution in borrowing from foreign countries, and the restoration of economic balance. To demonstrate his case for a slow-down, Chen argued that quite a few of the targets for the ten-year plan made more sense for the year 2000, and he called for a three-year period of readjustment. Deng Xiaoping supported him.[3]

For the first time a significant number of third-front projects were cancelled. The readjustment policy included a general strategy for re-focusing development on the neglected coast, the first-front home of agriculture, light industry, and international trade. This intent was evident in the 1979 decisions to simultaneously open the SEZs, allow joint ventures, and begin offshore oil exploration with foreign cooper-ation.[4]

The work conference decided to establish the Shenzhen and Shan-tou SEZs near Hong Kong, the Zhuhai SEZ near Macao, and the Xiamen SEZ opposite Taiwan. The specifics of this decision were typical of the early, experimental phase of reform—ad hoc, unresearched, and heavily influenced by personal ties and preferences. Discussions of the goals for the zones reflected considerable operational vagueness, the result of lack of consensus within the leadership.[5]

The work conference also reviewed and approved the experience of enterprises that had begun experimenting in late 1978—in Sichuan under Zhao Ziyang and in a few other provinces—with new authority over use of investment funds and production decisions. The endorse-ment of the party work conference then resulted in government approval for new regulations for experimental enterprises. These mushroomed to 4,000 by the end of 1979 and 6,600 by the next summer, one factor prompting the retrenchment of 1981.[6]

Worried that reforms were allowing local investment to quickly get out of control, Chen Yun continued arguing on behalf of stabili-zation measures, but with little success. Press articles complained that everyone agreed to readjust the economy but disagreed about how. In September, Chen warned against excessive use of foreign loans, appar-ently worried that factories would use the loans to avoid being reor-ganized or shut down. He repeated pleas for greater realism in planning and balance in investment.

Deng Xiaoping continued to back Chen's insistence on realism and revised his own earlier ambitious growth targets. In late 1975, he had set a goal of $1,000 per capita value of output as the target for 1985; this had remained the target for the overambitious 1978 plan for the year 1985 as well as for new plans in draft in the planning commission. But in late 1979, Deng stated that China aimed to quad-ruple its per capita value of output from approximately $250 in 1980 to $1,000 by the end of the century, thus postponing the 1985 goals fifteen more years. He later revised even this goal downward to $800–1,000, on the advice of experts, to factor in the projected population increase.[7]

Deng and Chen thus poured cold water on a fifteen-year plan (1975–1990) then in the making. The draft was intended to update the 1978 plan, extending the time frame to take into account the late date. But drafting still exhibited the chronic Great Leap Forward, high-output-target approach. The general attitude was typically metaphysical: "If the 'four dragons' [Taiwan, Hong Kong, South Korea, and Singapore] can develop at super speeds, why can't we?" The relatively moderate goal of $1,000 per capita output by the year 2000 sent planners back to the drawing board once again.[8]

Deng's New Year's Day 1980 address even more clearly revealed his intent to inject realism into planning. He explained that China could not easily catch up with Singapore and Hong Kong, whose current per capita value of output was already $3,000, because conditions—limited arable land, huge population, and a weak economic foundation—were much less favorable. Pointedly eschewing decades-old language about catching up with and surpassing the advanced countries of the world, Deng insisted that "in order to narrow and eventually eliminate the gap created over two or three centuries, or at least over one century, we must be determined to work hard with a pioneering spirit for a long period of time. We have no alternative."[9]

Deng's mandate for economic officials was threefold: to create a set of guiding principles, to propose several feasible plans for reforming the economic system, and to draft a long-term economic development program. Deng set a one-year deadline, which reflected his intention to convene the 12th Party Congress earlier than required (before 1982). The planning commission dropped completely the old ten-year plan as well as its fifteen-year draft plan and began to create a five-year plan for 1981–1985 and a twenty-year plan for 1981–2000.[10]

The alliance between Chen and Deng against the Soviet-style planners, to whom bigger and faster were better, payed off politically in 1980, especially for Zhao Ziyang. He became a member of the standing committee of the Politburo and head of a finance and economic leading group.[11] The membership of this party group was essentially the same as that of Chen Yun's State Council commission, and at first Zhao no doubt still bowed to the views of Chen Yun and Li Xiannian, even though Zhao nominally had a higher rank on the Politburo standing committee. The weight of economic decisionmaking gradually shifted toward Zhao, however. In the fall of 1980, he became premier as Chen and Li and other elderly vice premiers gave up their state jobs. The State Council was reorganized, and in the spring of 1981, the commission was formally disbanded.

Leaders Turn to Specialists

During 1979–1980, a major reform occurred in the decisionmaking process that was to prove critical to the success of Deng Xiaoping's reform program through the 1980s. Building on the 1978 campaign to repudiate dogmatism and raise the stature of intellectuals, the party mobilized the intellectual community in an effort to inject realism and professionalism into policy decisions. In 1978, the Academy of Social Sciences had been established as an institution separate from the Academy of Sciences. Now leading intellectuals from the social science academy and from government research organs were assigned to economic policy research groups. It was the beginning of a very gradual harnessing of intellectual forces for development that was made difficult by residual anti-intellectual attitudes among officials and by the preference among many academics—who had come out of the Cultural Revolution era demoralized, out of touch with modern thinking, and intimidated by political forbidden zones—for apolitical, ivory tower work. (Indeed, politicians complained throughout the 1980s about the lack of quality, policy-relevant research.)

Hu Qiaomu and Deng Liqun were put in charge of organizing this effort. Each wore two hats: political hats as the top party propaganda functionaries responsible for overseeing all intellectual activities in China (including the press, the arts, education, and research) and academic hats as president and vice president in charge of economic research at the social science academy. The two men had spent their careers running the party's policy research organs going back to the 1940s and, along with Hu Yaobang, had been in charge of drafting economic plans for Deng Xiaoping and resurrecting science and social science research bodies in the mid-1970s.

Shortly after the March 1979 work conference, Deng Liqun recruited four high-level policy research groups and instructed them to identify the reasons for past economic failure and to devise new economic policies.[12] These four groups were reorganized and placed under the State Council when Zhao Ziyang became premier in late 1980 and again were restructured along with the rest of the State Council in 1982. But essentially, they answered to the party's finance and economic leading group headed by Zhao. The groups were as follows:

- The technical transfer group headed by Wang Daohan, vice minister of economic relations with foreign countries[13]

- The structural readjustment group under Ma Hong, concurrently a vice president of the social science academy and director of its institute of industrial economics[14]
- The economic theory group headed by Yu Guangyuan, a vice minister of the science and technology commission and a vice president of the social science academy, with Dong Fureng, deputy director of the academy's economic research institute, as his deputy[15]
- The economic system reform group, headed by the minister of finance, Zhang Jingfu, who was told to begin work on an overall plan for reform[16]

A number of task forces subordinate to the four groups were set up to address special problems, including price reform, urban collective enterprises, population projections to the year 2000, and alternative economic models.[17]

The prestigious members of these groups were longtime economic officials and researchers well known to each other, each with multiple personal and official ties in the main economic bureaucracies, especially the commissions of the State Council. Not surprisingly, three of the four original research directors were officials who had worked with Chen Yun in the late 1940s and early 1950s in the difficult task of taking over urban China.[18] Further, most of the senior specialists appointed in 1979 had been part of an informal, small-scale economic policy discussion group organized in the immediate post-Stalin period that had met biweekly from 1956 to 1966 at the economic research institute (whose director was famous economist Sun Yefang).[19] A special relationship was forged back then between Chen Yun and these men, as their research supported Chen's views during the 1956 review of the Soviet model and the early 1960s post–Great Leap reconstruction. At the time, Yugoslavia's exploration of an alternative to the Soviet model provided the general inspiration for both Chen and Sun to part ways with Moscow. (Maoist attacks on Yugoslav revisionism in the early 1960s were no doubt aimed at squelching these unorthodox economic theories at home.)

Without a doubt, the professional and personal loyalties of many years duration that joined leader to leader, leader to specialist, and specialist to specialist in large part explain why, in 1979, changes in economic policy could be so actively and quickly pursued. There was no lack of interested or qualified people or of ideas, and Zhao Ziyang proved willing to use them. Zhao's high evaluation of the policy role of specialists was first reflected during his reform effort in Sichuan, when he personally directed the work of the provincial academy of social sciences and even headed the economic research institute. Zhao's encouragement of bold research and experimentation by specialists would become a hallmark of his leadership style.[20]

Exploring New Options

The new policy of readjustment adopted in March 1979 raised difficult theoretical and practical questions. Why had there been such imbalance in favor of heavy industry and such neglect of light, consumer industry? Why had no attention been paid to living standards (and thus the Chinese people were desperately poor despite industrialization)? What was the ultimate purpose of increasing production? How could production be made more efficient? Was China's basic development model, imported from the Soviet Union, the heart of the problem? In short, all the questions economists and officials first began to ask in 1956 had returned in force.

Predictably, Chinese researchers took up the discussion where they had left off before the Cultural Revolution and scrambled to catch up on changes in thinking that had occurred during their fifteen-year absence from the larger socialist community. In April, the economic research institute headed by Xue Muqiao held a conference on the law of (market) value; its stress on the centrality to economic reform of reestablishing the market sector made a big impact. Sun Yefang quickly became a celebrity as the chief Chinese author of the view that commodity production and exchange were as essential to socialist as to capitalist societies. (Since the late 1950s, Sun had led the critique of the anticommercial ideological bias behind the promotion of a unified natural economy in which money and markets would be abolished and goods directly distributed to users.)

Throughout 1979–1980, debate on economic theory raged within the community of specialists, many of whom were absorbing new concepts and facts from voracious reading in foreign economic theory and from visits abroad. In a forward to a collection of his major writings, Yu Guangyuan acknowledged the great impact on his views of visits to Yugoslavia and Romania in March 1978 and to Hungary in 1979, which helped him to rethink the possibilities of non-Soviet styles of socialist development. Liu Guoguang of the economic research institute and Su Shaozhi, who succeeded Yu as head of the institute of Marxism-Leninism, were with him in Hungary. Yu became a proponent of the view that China should move beyond ad hoc reformism and imitate the Hungarian model: introduction of basic overall reform preceded by thorough research and consensus decision on the principles and means of reform.[21] Yu Guangyuan and others again became regular participants in reformist forums such as the annual international conference, Socialism in the World, coordinated by the director of the Yugoslav party's Center for Social Research. Meanwhile, hundreds of foreign theoretical and economic experts on socialist development also visited China.[22]

In 1980, after Deng Xiaoping's call for a reform plan, the intellectual environment became even more open, and research and experimentation became even more far-reaching. The task force on alternative socialist development experiences, headed by Liu Guoguang, tried to summarize and evaluate, but heated disagreement over what lessons could be learned continually postponed any publication of findings. By August, the new economic reform office (former economic reform group) had created a draft reform plan, "On Preliminary Views Concerning Reform of the Economic Structure," that proposed that China develop a commodity (market) economy regulated by central guidance rather than by mandatory plans.[23] The economic theory group opened up the sensitive issue of private and nonstate collective ownership and convened two national conferences in 1980, one in Shenyang on urban collective enterprises and one in Chengdu on diversification of ownership of the means of production. Other controversial ideas were floated, including the suggestion that orthodox Marxist economic theory itself needed reforming.[24]

This openness reflected the fact that researchers had begun looking beyond Eastern European experience in their reading and their travel in an effort to find effective economic development policies. Officials and researchers working on SEZ-related topics, for example, soon became familiar with capitalist experiences. Academy specialists including Xue Muqiao, Ma Hong, and Xu Dixin cooperated with those from Zhongshan University and the import-export commission under Gu Mu in a study of foreign economic development zones (EDZs) (geographic regions allowed to give preferential treatment such as tax breaks to attract foreign investors). In September 1980, Zhu Rongji, then a vice chair of the import-export commission and later mayor of Shanghai, was funded by the U.N. to survey EDZs. He visited Southeast Asia, Ireland, and Sri Lanka. Travel thoroughly convinced specialists that China's earlier approaches had so far succeeded only in widening the gap between China and the rest of the world and therefore had to be discarded.[25]

Theoretical discussion began to shift away from the more orthodox Marxist concepts in use from 1950 to 1979 and centered on discovering economic laws, setting plan goals and targets, and balancing sets of polar contradictions, such as production and consumption. Specialists were attracted to the more complex multifactor approach central to the larger body of Western literature on development strategy. For example, the science and technology commission's institute of scientific and technical information, which purchased, translated, and summarized reference material, in late 1979 sent an analysis of theories on alternative development strategies through internal channels to top leaders. Institute director Lin Zixin, also a deputy director of the science policy research office, was asked to present these theories in a speech to a large assembly of officials and researchers in early 1980. (At this meeting, specialists called into question Deng's stated goal of $1,000 per capita income by the year 2000, pointing out that adjustments for population growth would lower the goal to $800.)[26] In 1980, economist Dong Fureng also became a proponent of such concepts after attending a U.S. conference on alternative development strategies.

According to Tong Dalin, a close colleague of Yu Guangyuan and in 1980 also a vice chair of the science and technology commission, these explorations were very influential in building leadership consensus to discard the Soviet model.[27] Picking up on Deng's expressed desire to find a new road to modernization of a truly Chinese type, Tong, Yu, and others argued—based on wide-ranging reading in foreign economic development theory—that the Soviet model was merely a variant of the conventional development strategy of Western industrial development. This effort to imitate the West but at a faster pace, they argued, led inevitably to Stalinist-Maoist big pushes and great leaps in order to catch up with the West. In early 1981, influenced by their views, Hu Yaobang declared officially that China would follow no single model in its modernization program.

Growing Disagreement

Although the leadership seemed to agree, even on purely nationalistic grounds, to base future decisions on a realistic assessment of Chinese reality, there was more than enough room for heated disagreement over how to proceed and how far to go in modifying the basic Soviet-style system that China had inherited from the past. In the fall of 1980, with soaring inflation, overissuance of currency, and looming budget deficits, signs of disagreement between proponents of stabilization and reform appeared.

In September, leaders convened a national meeting of provincial level party secretaries during which there was major disagreement and a decision was made to withhold judgment on the rural responsibility system and the role of the market while allowing reform experiments to continue. The draft economic reform plan was shelved. Two months later, Deng Xiaoping and Chen Yun reviewed economic policy at a party work conference, and the leadership decided to recentralize control of the economy and put reforms on hold.[28] In his speech, Chen Yun recalled the lessons learned from China's bitter post-1949 experience with leftist errors. He argued for careful planning and control over prices, foreign loans, and technology imports and for a careful review of reforms, including those in the SEZs, before again moving ahead. He held up the post–Great Leap 1960s readjustment as a model of careful reform; he thus implied that reform to date had been another chaotic leap forward. Chen also called for a strict reimposition of ideological and social controls, and he raised the spectre of the recent crisis in Poland as an example of what China could expect if the party did not improve economic and propaganda work.

Deng Xiaoping agreed to Chen's insistence that the readjustment period be extended into the period of the 6th FYP. But he tried to point out that this readjustment was different and more limited and was not a retreat. Deng stressed the complementarity of reform and readjustment and similarly defended the efforts to emancipate thinking as compatible with upholding party rule and Marxist orthodoxy.

Throughout 1981 and 1982, as planners went back to the drawing boards one more time, there were continuing signs of disagreement over the contents of the 6th FYP and the 12th Party Congress political platform. The National People's Congress session in December 1981 was still unable to approve the 1982 annual plan and the FYP, already overdue, nor were the twenty-year goals and the congress program decided.

During the 1981–1982 retrenchment, Chen Yun was able to assert strong authority in economics even though formal responsibility had been passed to Zhao Ziyang. Yao Yilin and Wan Li were placed in charge of a newly created State Council economic readjustment office, and the work of the reform office became secondary.[29] This was evident especially in late 1981, when Zhao Ziyang quoted Chen Yun's insistence that the planned state sector remain dominant. Early in 1982, Chen's speech to the 8th Party Congress in 1956 was given wide publicity as a guide for current policy, and his birdcage analogy for using economic plans (the cage) to constrain the market (the bird) became a household phrase.[30]

But the impact of the retrenchment was felt in other areas as well. Hu Qiaomu and Deng Liqun gained control of the propaganda apparatus with a mandate to reimpose Marxist-Leninist orthodoxy. Dissidents were jailed for challenging the party monopoly, and new controls were imposed on religious and ethnic groups. In foreign policy, there was a shift to neutrality vis-à-vis the superpowers.

A New Paradigm for Chinese-Style Socialism

In the face of this major setback, Hu Yaobang, Zhao Ziyang, and the reform-minded intellectuals became close allies in keeping the reform vision alive. Hu was responsible for the drafting of the 12th Party Congress platform and Zhao for the drafting of economic plans; they used these responsibilities to research and shape a more convincing program of reform. With the central economic apparatus generally in the hands of bureaucrats committed to central planning, the reformers tried to compete by strengthening the policy research groups, reshaping them into think tanks and experiment centers. By launching reform experiments in important urban and coastal localities, they held out promises of gain in exchange for support from local officials.

In February 1981, Hu Yaobang gave a talk on future living standards and lifestyles in China and asked specialists to begin work on analytical sketches depicting what China might be like in twenty to fifty years.[31] He was apparently seeking some inspiring goals to put forth at the party congress scheduled for later that year. Researchers fine-tuned Hu's request into a directive to explore a new target model for a developed China and a new strategy for development. They suggested specific projects that would serve the general purpose. Ma Hong was given special responsibility for coordinating the research effort.[32] Under his aegis, three projects were begun in 1981 at the national level: a development strategy seminar—a series of symposia held to explore what should be China's development strategy; a target model study—an extension of the studies of alternative development models to include Western developed countries and Asian experiences as well as socialist countries and to review China's thirty-year history of development; and a China 2000 study—an experiment in Western forecasting methods modeled after the Global 2000 study done in the United States. Meanwhile, Zhao Ziyang spearheaded a fourth endeavor—research and experiments in regional and urban development.

Hu's statement that there was no fixed model for China's development was meant to encourage a freer exploration, but in fact, there were clearly understood limits. In addition to the obvious requirement that the model be socialist, economists were also committed to researching methods of development that would achieve a quadrupling of the gross value of industrial and agricultural output by the year 2000. In a sense, they were being asked to provide evidence for a decision already made on other grounds, a task quite familiar to Chinese researchers.

The political basis for this target was Deng Xiaoping's per capita output goal of $800–1,000; the professional basis was future projections by the planning commission of China's average growth rate based on the previous thirty-nine years.[33] This crude methodology begged the question of whether there was any basis for assuming the next twenty years of development in China would or should resemble the past. Nor was anyone welcome to question whether this type of target, or this specific target, was appropriate. Similarly crude methodology was used by the population task force in 1979–1980; after projecting growth rates in population, water resources, and domestic grain production to the year 2000, the task force concluded that China should aim for a population of 1.2 billion, which required a one-child policy. Other socioeconomic factors and demographic factors were not taken into account.[34] The quality of such policy research improved dramatically in the early 1980s through the research projects organized in response to Hu Yaobang's request for new thinking about China's future.

The flurry of research activity and local experiments between early 1981 and the spring of 1982 were intended to get a better picture of the economic realities and to reassert reform priorities. This period of policy review, debate, and experimentation reflected the enormous intellectual and political challenge of defining a new development strategy suited to China's capabilities and compatible with the basics of party rule.

The Development Strategy Seminars

The symposia that began in Beijing in late February 1981 were chaired by Yu Guangyuan and Tong Dalin, who represented the theory group and the reform office, respectively, and were hosted alternately by six different governmental research bodies. The meetings convened monthly at first and then bimonthly and continued in various forms through 1986. Other key advisers involved were Xue Muqiao, foreign affairs specialist Huan Xiang, economist Liu Guoguang, and other prominent former students of Sun Yefang. At first, as many as three or four hundred people attended; later, a number of smaller and more specialized meetings were created.[35]

The participants in the original symposia viewed themselves as a policy brain trust whose urgent mandate was to conceive a new political-economic program. The results of their discussions were circulated internally in China, both in summary as memos to top leaders and as compilations of speeches in a special information series. The key advisers in the inner circle were longtime party members and therefore enjoyed such status that they could also send personal memos to senior leaders calling attention to good ideas and recommending policy initiatives.[36] Rawer data or opinion was sent up through internal newsletters, such as the science and technology commission's *Express*, to avoid the tedious internal coordination required of more formal documents. Personal contacts were frequently employed as well by those fortunate enough to have patrons at high levels who could pass ideas along over bridge or at lunch.[37]

Throughout 1981 and 1982, the specialists continued their discussions on conventional and alternative development strategies and interacted with and influenced other projects underway. For example, based on comparisons of the experiences of China and India, the task force on alternative economic models concluded that both countries had been trying different variants of the conventional approach of the West and that although both had experienced partial success, neither had achieved sustained development in all sectors.

According to Tong Dalin, the development strategy seminars paid special attention to problems of distribution of wealth.[38] Advisers concluded that because development in the capitalist West had led to polarities in income, China had to search for an alternative development strategy that considered distribution of wealth and quality of life as well as growth in production. According to the economists, late in 1981 their group coined the phrase "Chinese-style socialism" to symbolize these balanced objectives; the phrase was adopted the following year by Deng Xiaoping in his speech to the 12th Party Congress.

By late 1981, the preliminary findings of the seminar found expression in a dozen new guiding principles for economic work set forth by Zhao Ziyang at the people's congress in December 1981;[39] these were intended to shape both the FYP and the twenty-year plan. Economist Dong Fureng saw in these principles a four-part shift of priorities: from achieving rapid economic growth to improving living standards; from favoring key sectors (such as steel and heavy industry) to balanced sectoral development; from promoting economic self-sufficiency to encouraging opening to the outside world; from emphasizing extensive development (expanded plant capacity) to supporting intensive development (improving efficiency of existing infrastructure).

Dong also specified the many policy areas in which much research and setting of priorities were still needed. He emphasized that this shift in strategy highlighted the problematic relationship between development strategy and economic system and contended that in order to implement the new strategy, "It is imperative to carry out corresponding restructuring in our country's economic system."[40]

The growing influence of this view, which was shared by the other seminar participants, was evident in May 1982 when the State Council created the economic system reform commission. Headed by Zhao Ziyang, this prestigious organ was given a mandate to research and draft a plan for comprehensive reform to go into effect with the 7th FYP in 1985. The commission also began to launch local reform experiments in order to try out its policy ideas. During the next few years, its commissioners and researchers played a central role in efforts to expand the support base for reform.

There was a general upsurge of reformist activity in the spring of 1982 following Zhao Ziyang's expressed judgment that the retrenchment had been successfully completed; in his view, a proper sectoral adjustment and a healthy economic situation were conducive to a resumption of reform efforts. This decision and renewed discussion of reform resulted in a much more favorable attitude toward economic reform in the final version of the 6th FYP adopted in November 1982. In comparison with the December 1981 economic principles, which called for prudence in reform, this plan mandated the creation of a general program for reform of the economic system as well as the steps to carry it out. The plan explicitly allowed for the development of diversified economic forms and modes of operation and encouraged energetic development of foreign economic relations and trade rather than merely adherence to the open policy. A call in the December 1981 statement of principles for strengthening self-reliance was dropped altogether.[41]

But even as reformers sought to end retrenchment and move on to reform, residual pressures for setting higher growth targets, intrinsic to command economies, reemerged. Central and local planners complained that plant capacity was sitting idle with the slowdown in growth. Some researchers defended former command styles of management; one argued, for example, that China had always had development strategies by another name—the main tasks and measures of each FYP. This author explicitly defended the strategies of the 1st FYP and the 1957 draft of the 2nd FYP, including their emphasis on rapid growth of heavy industry. Clearly, this author represented those who thought of development strategy as output targets in a long-term plan and who persisted in the view that the system merely needed fine-tuning.[42]

The revised 6th FYP showed evidence of the still strong influence of these views, especially in its admonition to intensify construction of national defense and defense industry and move to a higher level of modernization of military equipment. The 12th Party Congress goal of quadrupling material output by the year 2000 was probably, in part, an appeal by Hu Yaobang and other reformers for the support of the traditionally minded, who were unhappy with the slow growth imposed by stabilization policies.

An uneasy compromise among the several points of view was evident in the final drafting of the congress program. The program qualified the goal of quadrupling output with the caveat that it be achieved only in concert with increased economic results. This rather unsophisticated approach, which set quantity and quality side by side as equal goals, did not by any means resolve the contradiction between them. In fact, this political solution came back to haunt the leaders once they realized that local leaders with leftist mindsets were trying to quadruple every target in sight without regard to economic rationality. In their eagerness to show their loyalty to the 12th congress leadership, some local leaders even offered to quadruple earlier than required or to quintuple output.

Debate over development strategy continued into 1983, as specialists began work on drafting the next FYP. A report summing up discussion at a national development strategy seminar in early November 1983, for example, revealed the persistent lines and polemical nature of debate.[43] Yu Guangyuan found himself defending the whole enterprise of exploring development strategy against those who saw the concept itself as capitalist. In his usual clever fashion, Yu explained that the West was actually just borrowing belatedly the concept of strategy developed first and best by Marx, Lenin, Stalin, and Mao. Yu went on to argue that China should adopt and develop the science of socioeconomic development strategy, which was an organic combination of general science and Marxist science.[44]

The Target Model Study

Liu Guoguang and other economists from the economic research institute of the social science academy had been conducting studies of development experiences both in China and in other countries as part of a task force on alternative economic models. The first phase of their work fully explored China's economic history and produced a mixed scorecard as of late 1982. The study pointed out the leftist errors from 1958 to 1960, the continuing mistakes and disorganized development strategy from 1966 to 1976, the shortcomings of the 1953–1957 Soviet period, and the imbalances in the economy from 1976 to 1978. Yet in comparing China with other developing countries, analysts concluded that some serious drawbacks had been avoided, such as inequitable distribution of income, chronic unemployment, sustained inflation, and heavy foreign debt.[45]

In this early phase (1981–1982), Liu's task force focused on two issues central to the drafting of the 12th Party Congress program, which was to define authoritatively China's strategic goal and target model for the year 2000. The two issues were how to measure and balance growth in production and improved living standards in setting a strategic goal and how to relate plan and market in the target model for the economy. In exploring these issues, the task force demonstrated the complexities of development revealed through comparative analysis and gradually broke away from simplistic traditional concepts that pitted socialist against capitalist countries. Yet the task force's recommendations were hesitant and vague, of the and/or variety, which reflected political disagreement at the top.

Regarding the first issue, the study pointed out that the goal of development was multifaceted and had to include such concerns as growth in total national income, increase in output of major industrial and agricultural products, modernization of the entire national economy, and raising of the material and cultural living standard to that of middle-income countries. Similarly, regarding the second issue, the study emphasized that no single definitive socialist model existed; rather, the socialist world encompassed several alternatives, each with a different combination of plan and market. The study identified five socialist models: war communism, the conventional centralized planned economy, the improved centralized planned economy, the planned economy containing a market mechanism, and market socialism. Each had strong and weak points; none could be completely affirmed or repudiated. (These "models" actually differed more in degree of central administrative control than in kind. The main point of the exercise was to justify growth of the market sector as fully socialist.)

The preceding study helped introduce flexibility into the 12th Party Congress program; although it retained Chen Yun's insistence on the plan as primary and the market as secondary, the program also argued for a shift away from mandatory planning and toward guidance planning. This was viewed as a temporary compromise; Liu Guoguang's group was given a mandate to further pursue the controversial topic of linking plan and market, which was the group's main focus throughout 1983. Liu later recalled that some were arguing for very marginal reform of the Soviet model through decentralization and local diversity. They judged the Soviet model to be 70 percent good, 30 percent faulty. Others argued that the original model should be thrown out altogether, that China should retain only the basic socialist principles of public ownership and distribution according to work, and that these principles should be applied flexibly. There were different interpretations of the maxim that a planned economy was a corollary of public ownership. Some viewed the central plan as basic, even though they agreed it should follow the law of value; others viewed only public ownership as basic to the socialist system.[46]

The First China 2000 Study

The idea for a third project—to provide alternative economic projections to those generated by the planning bureaucracy—was planted during the winter of 1980–1981, when Russell Phillips, executive vice president of the Rockefeller Brothers Fund, followed up on a visit to China by sending a copy of the *Global 2000 Report to the President* to Lin Zixin, then director of the science and technology commission's institute of scientific and technological information of China (ISTIC). Secretary of Agriculture Robert Berglund also gave a copy of the study to the then vice minister of the agricultural commission, Du Runsheng, when he visited Washington, D.C.[47] Du was a driving force behind the rural reforms; he also had close ties to Yu Guangyuan, Tong Dalin, and their associates at the science and technology commission.

These individuals were part of a loose network of officials who had been involved in efforts since 1950 to upgrade Chinese science and technology; they were China's "scientific reformers."[48] Few others in China had such a realistic understanding of the resource and technological obstacles to China's modernization. Yu Guangyuan had sounded the alarm in 1978 with a series of very sobering seminars that focused on long-term environmental, ecological, and population constraints. The conclusions of Yu's seminars flatly contradicted the complacent assumption of the Maoist era that China's future was assured by its vast natural and human resources.

These same scientific reformers also understood the complex role of science in development. They were trying to temper the optimism of Chinese leaders who assumed that acquisition or creation of advanced technology would automatically spin off into economic and cultural development. They were gaining a new understanding of the complexities of technology transfer and were the first to emphasize the software side of science-related imports—that is, education and management, theory and strategy, and policy. The difficult task of coordinating science policy and economic policy fueled the search for new ideas and methodologies.[49]

Lin Zixin and his associates immediately saw the value of the *Global 2000 Report* for addressing policy concerns. Lin quickly had the study translated; in January 1981 a summary was circulating at higher levels of the Chinese leadership, and in March the report was published in Chinese.[50] In February, when Hu Yaobang called on China's researchers and planners to draw up a target model and output projections for China in the year 2000, Lin and others saw it as an opportunity for an experiment in long-range forecasting using methods new to China.

Gerald O. Barney, who directed the Global 2000 study, was invited to lecture in China in July 1981 on the serious environmental, resource, and population problems shaping humankind's long-term future.[51] His sobering talks found echoes in the thinking of China's top planners and researchers, who were struggling with how to reconcile China's ambitions to quadruple output by the year 2000 with severe resource constraints and leadership demands for realism. Discussions during his visit centered on problems of rural development, including population growth and food needs, so central to the post-Mao conviction that China must first feed its people and then worry about growth.

Barney met with Tong Dalin, Lin Zixin, and others and when asked what China should do recommended that China make better use of human resources; address the problem of soil erosion (the seeping away of China's lifeblood); and do a study of China in the year 2000. These suggestions had big reverberations even before Barney left China. He was told at the end of his visit that the science and technology commission would be proposing that it begin a China 2000 study. Commission officials clearly intended to document and publicize widely the serious problems China faced in its modernization program and the consequent need for major changes in policy. By the fall of 1981, the State Council had approved the study, putting it officially under the umbrella of one of the research groups created in 1979—Ma Hong's technical economic research center—with ISTIC as the main research body.

The official documents launching the study mandated a long-range, strategic, and interdisciplinary study, with an emphasis on policy recommendations and analysis of policy implementation. To fulfill this mandate, the study's coordinators set out to create a pioneering report based on the principles of systems science. Most elements in this approach were completely new to China, including integrating the natural and social sciences, combining quantitative with qualitative analysis, developing a comprehensive view of the whole socioeconomic/ scientific/technological system before investigating its specific components; and exploring both short-term and long-term prospects.[52]

Although such an approach sounded commonplace to Western readers, it was unprecedented in China. Natural scientists and military researchers had long been familiar with system thinking and cybernetics, but social scientists were isolated from trends in these fields. Thus, in October 1981, when work began on *China Toward the Year 2000,* researchers first concentrated on developing forecasting models and experimenting with applied mathematics and computer techniques.[53]

The study team was chosen from among those who had attended the fifty hours of lectures given by Barney in July 1981, in which the methodology and data sources for every sector of the U.S. study were reviewed in depth. Barney discussed utility and limitations of many types of projection models and focused on integrating and analyzing projections developed independently in many different agencies, a technique that was developed in the Global 2000 effort. Barney urged his audience to ask each ministry what projection models were then in use. When he returned in 1983 for more lectures, Barney was told that in 1981 the team had been able to find only one projection model in the entire Chinese government.[54]

The study's pioneering effort at forecasting, in addition to introducing new social science research methodology, also opened a new path for policy research. In the past, academic research had steered clear of policy issues out of fear of political reprisal. By presenting alternative best- and worst-case scenarios based on their projections, China 2000 specialists found a way to point indirectly and safely to preferable policies in order to influence internal debates. They also indirectly suggested the possibility of policy failure without breaking the unwritten requirement for official optimism. The resulting realism cloaked in optimism was reflected in the opening remarks of the study: "The prospects for China in the year 2000 are bright, but the difficulties in advancing toward the year 2000 are arduous."[55]

By the summer of 1982, preliminary drafts of *China Toward the Year 2000,* which drew on information and research from more than one hundred government organizations, had already influenced other planning documents, such as the "Agriculture 2000" and "Technology 2000" plans, that became sections of the twenty-year outline plan. The technical economic research center had organized meetings between the study staff and the drafting group in the planning commission, which in May 1982 was completing both a draft of the twenty-year outline plan and the final version of the 6th FYP.[56]

Although the China 2000 study group and the planning commission used essentially the same data, the methodologies and perspectives were quite different. China 2000 focused on information about resource constraints that planners setting ambitious output targets tended to overlook. Thus, the main impact at this early stage of the study was to impress on planners the need for sober realism. The scarcity of resources in every sector and the daunting population pressures clearly implied that to achieve a quadrupling of output might be very difficult without a tremendous effort to increase conservation and improve efficiency. Chinese planners and officials were forced to take off their rose-tinted glasses.

The study's staffers found it hard to woo the planning commission from its old approach of arbitrarily balancing competing demands with little regard for resources, but *China Toward the Year 2000* was given partial credit by others for the more holistic approach to the FYP and its increased focus on reform compared with the preliminary draft of late 1981.[57] The final plan also rewrote a vague 1981 reference to "tackling key problems in science research" and specified instead the importance of applied science and technology and increased educational and cultural levels. The plan also added two fundamental tasks that had emerged as priorities from the efforts of the science and technology commission: rigid population control and intensified environmental protection efforts.

In August 1983, more complete findings of the China 2000 study were discussed at a seminar sponsored by the China futures research society, of which Lin Zixin was deputy secretary-general. The study was published and circulated internally at that time and later made public in September 1984. It was composed of ten chapters projecting trends to the year 2000 and making tentative policy suggestions.[58]

The study's conclusions, among others, were that achieving the quadrupling goal would be very difficult; that overcoming current difficulties required improved, more realistic planning; that addressing interrelated problems in economic, social, scientific, and technical development must occur in a comprehensive rather than piecemeal fashion; and that promulgating palliative measures for population, energy, and transport problems would prove fruitless.

To back up this rare frankness, the study pulled together page after page of startling figures on waste and inefficiency in every sector of the economy, including unused plant capacity, stockpiles of useless goods, delays in capital construction, obsolete equipment, and lack of export competitiveness. Examples of expensive industrial plants imported without regard for energy requirements underscored the crying need for careful feasibility studies. The study showed the causal linkages among worker illiteracy, low productivity per capita, and industrial injury and accidents. For example, workers at Baotao iron and steel company (where 64.9 percent were illiterate or semi-illiterate) had caused fatal accidents in 1979 and a downgrading of fine quality steel in 1981 because they could not read directions. "In the papermaking factories of Shanghai, some equipment manufactured in 1903 is still in operation. . . . The cultural levels of China's workers are even below those of Japanese peasants. . . . There are now 17 million farm-machine operators throughout China, and two-thirds of them are unqualified for their jobs."[59]

Neither leaders nor specialists were satisfied fully with the first-stage results of the China 2000 report, knowing all too well that the range of topics was narrow; coverage of them was shallow and based on inadequate statistical information; most projection methods were simply trend extrapolations through regression analysis; and the lack of integrated analysis left unexplored the interrelationship of sectors and problems. Yet, the study also caught the imagination of China's reformers by pointing out new directions in research and reform that might create solutions to these problems. In August 1983, as Ma Hong's aides were making a new annual work plan, they decided to propose a more formal, official project of a similar nature after Premier Zhao wrote of the first study: "The study of China in the year 2000 is a great project. Whether or not we can come up with a treatise of good quality is of great significance, and we should strive to make it a success."[60]

On 21 October 1983, Ma Hong addressed a special symposium, convened by the State Council and attended by representatives of all government departments, on the subject of an overall development strategy for the economy, society, science, and technology. Ma summed up the efforts of research specialists to date and suggested new directions. His speech seemed to be premised largely on the results of the China 2000 study, which he praised at length for its attempt to integrate economic with noneconomic factors of development and to turn concentration on development strategies in specific fields into focus on a comprehensive development strategy.[61]

Explorations in Local and Regional Development

While major research projects were under way in Beijing that were to reshape the paradigm China used to think about national development, a complementary effort to rethink local and regional development was taking place. By the early 1980s, there was a growing recognition among reform officials and researchers that China's isolation from the outside world was not its only problem. Internal administrative barriers prevented economic specialization according to comparative advantage, the expansion of commerce, and the spread of technology. Factories were unable to exercise their new autonomy so long as vertical administrative monopolies controlled the economy. China needed to open up on the inside as well as to the outside. Although the newly constructed SEZs could bring in foreign investment, China's scattered cities and industrial and resource bases were the true building blocks for the future.

In late 1980, Zhao Ziyang encouraged specialists to research the natural economic functions of cities. Local officials were told to create research groups similar to those set up in late 1979 under the State Council and to explore development strategies suitable to their own geographic areas. The first to do so were economic research committees set up in mid-1981 in Shanghai, Sichuan, and Liaoning.[62] In November 1981, as part of his explication of China's new development strategy, Premier Zhao stated as one aim the organization of rational economic networks based on large and medium cities. He specifically mentioned seven, all on the coast: Shanghai, Tianjin, Guangzhou, Dalian, Qingdao, Fuzhou, and Xiamen.[63] That same year, experiments in comprehensive urban restructuring began, first in the medium-sized cities of Shashi (July 1981) and Changzhou (March 1982).

Just as the needs of enterprises forced the reform of city management, so the urban reform experiments raised the issue of regional economic zones. During 1982, Zhao initiated discussion about centering development on a number of economic macroregions, beginning with Shanxi and Shanghai. In early 1983, Deng Xiaoping praised Zhao Ziyang for suggesting this approach, saying there should be more regions and not necessarily just on an experimental basis.[64]

From the beginning, a major concern in discussions of local and regional development was the revitalization of China's major metropolis, Shanghai. There is some indirect evidence that evolving plans for Shanghai reflected the strong influence of Japan's postwar development experience. Chen Yun reportedly hoped to emulate Japan's focus on two key regions (Tokyo and Osaka) by developing Shanghai (his home area) and Tianjin, thereby encouraging regional and national spin-off effects. Beginning in 1980, Chen's longtime colleagues, including fellow post-1949 east China officials, became boosters of this approach. Local officials in Shanghai and in neighboring cities and counties were persuaded to cooperate only with great difficulty, however, because they all worried that their wealth would be siphoned off by the others.[65]

The Challenge of International Competition

Exposure to the outside world, along with the new policy research and local experimentation in 1981–1982, transformed the mental landscape of China's policymakers and advisers. The introduction of new social science methods of systems analysis and new concepts of development strategy began to remedy the inadequacies of China's traditionally empiricist epistemology. Most policy research in the past, when it was allowed at all, had continued in the tradition of investigation—that is, unsystematic collection of data to be analyzed on an experiential rather than theoretical basis. Socioeconomic issues, and natural science issues as well, were viewed in moral and political terms as right or wrong, black or white. Policy decisions amounted to the imposition of visionary goals with little consideration of concrete limitations or to a juggling of immediate, conflicting demands. Input from analysts rarely resembled complex, integrated policy options; the integration that did occur took place at the very top of the compartmentalized bureaucracy, where politicians rather than specialists considered the policy trade-offs.

New sources of information and ways of analyzing it also forced a departure from a traditional Chinese historical orientation and the adoption of comparative and futurist perspectives. Previously, the criterion for policy appraisal had been China's own recent past. Compared with the relative chaos of the 1930s and the war years, of course, progress since the founding of the People's Republic in 1949 seemed clear and led to self-congratulatory complacency. Isolated from knowledge about the outside world, the elite and the public were easily persuaded that the country was doing well.

With the opening up to outside information, including travel abroad, however, comparisons of China's current situation with other nations, and of the coastal region with Hong Kong and Taiwan, starkly revealed China's relative backwardness and the severity of its problems. For example, *China Toward the Year 2000* pointed out that China had far less per capita farmland than did the Soviet Union, the United States, and India and demonstrated that although China had built an industrial base, it was still not an industrial country. The target model study judged that although China since 1949 had succeeded in moving from a stage of dire poverty to one in which the populace had adequate food and clothing, other countries had progressed even further.

In particular, new comparative information about the results of postwar progress in Japan and the newly industrialized economies (NIEs) of Asia greatly shook the normal complacency in officialdom. How could these tiny entities—Taiwan, Hong Kong, South Korea, and Singapore—with so few resources and supposedly reactionary socioeconomic and political systems so far outperform China? In the last century, they had all been part of a prosperous maritime China. Just under the surface lurked the momentous historical conundrum of twentieth-century Asia—why did the Chinese mainland fall so far behind Japan in the race to modernization? To varying degrees, the four NIEs had pursued the Japanese model of economic development: government-regulated "Confucian capitalism." Nothing brought these issues home quite so pointedly as a comparison of vibrant Hong Kong and stagnant Shanghai, whose current respective roles as Asia's financial and trade center and a sleepy backwater had been just the reverse at the start of the century.

Even more alarming were predictions about major future trends in China as compared with those likely to occur in industrial countries during the next fifteen years. Straight-line projections of China's current dilemmas into the future contrasted sharply with plans elsewhere for industrial restructuring to smooth the transition into postindustrial information societies. Influential foreign sources of information about trends and plans outside China included the European Economic Community, *Interfuture,* and *Japan in the Year 2000,* a study put together by a group under the famous economist Sabaru Okita, who had acted as an informal personal adviser to China's top leaders.[66]

In the immediate post-Mao period, China turned to socialist experiences in its own past and in Eastern Europe for new development models. But by 1983, these appeared second best in comparison to the dynamism evident in the capitalist economies of Asia. By early 1983, reform research and experimentation had convinced a sizable number of younger reform officials and advisers that China needed a new socioeconomic paradigm, one that encompassed a mixed plan-market economy, a scientific culture, and an ideology based on a democratic and humanistic version of Marxism. Such a program implied the need for a generational change in personnel and a major revamping of the Leninist system. But other officials throughout the bureaucracy remained convinced that more marginal modifications of system and theory would suffice. The gap was growing between more conservative elders and more radical younger reformers in Deng's camp. In 1983–1984, the newly perceived pressures from regional and international competition were brought to bear on Chinese decisionmaking in ways that led first to a political showdown and then to a major programmatic breakthrough.

Notes

1. For an excellent explanation of these systemic fluctuations, see Barry Naughton, "Industrial Planning and Prospects in China," Eugene K. Lawson, ed., *U.S.-China Trade* (New York: Praeger, 1988), pp. 185–186.

2. Chen became chair, Li became vice chair, and the vice premiers and senior ministers formed the membership. Vice Premier Yao Yilin, Chen's close associate, became the chief executive officer. For a history of the commission, see David M. Bachman, *Chen Yun and the Chinese Political System* (Berkeley: University of California Center for Chinese Studies, 1985), pp. 106–108.

3. Nicholas R. Lardy and Kenneth Lieberthal, eds., *Chen Yun's Strategy for Development: A Non-Maoist Alternative,* trans. Mao Tong and Du Anxia (Armonk, N.Y.: M. E. Sharpe, 1983), pp. xxxvi–xxxvii; and *Chen Yun wenxuan, 1956–1985* [The Selected Works of Chen Yun] (Beijing: People's Publishers, 1986), p. 229.

4. Interview with a senior official in the SEZs office of the State Council, November 1985. Formal regulations guiding SEZ development were formulated

in 1980. I am grateful to Ezra Vogel for telling me that the idea for the zones actually originated in the 1970s in Guangdong. Guangdong officials investigated export processing zones elsewhere, including Taiwan, and were particularly impressed with Singapore. In 1978, Guangdong and Fujian were given special foreign trade and investment rights to move in this direction.

In an interview with staff of the Shekou industrial zone, Shekou, November 1985, I was told that Shekou director Yuan Geng pioneered the idea while serving as an official of a PRC-owned but Hong Kong–based shipping corporation in the 1970s. He had been looking in vain at expensive Hong Kong land to find a good place to invest on behalf of the company. Yuan thought of his home area, Bao'an county, in southern Guangdong, and began in 1978 to set up a plant for tearing down old ships and selling them as scrap in Hong Kong. When the bottom fell out of the construction industry in Hong Kong, he shifted his interest to industrial production, and in early 1979, Yuan gave a briefing to Deng and other top leaders on his ideas for attracting foreign investment.

According to Xinhua xinwen she [New China News Agency, hereafter Xinhua], 30 October 1986, in Foreign Broadcast Information Service China Daily Report [FBIS], 31 October 1986, p. K1, the idea for some sort of economic zones was then proposed formally at the March 1979 work conference by two senior veterans of the party and army, Xi Zhongxun and Yang Shangkun, who had been assigned to Guangdong in 1978, through the patronage of marshall Ye Jianying. Yuan Geng may have served under Ye; he helped "liberate" the Shekou area in the late 1940s. Deng approved the zone idea, saying, "During the war, wasn't Yan'an a special zone?," implying the need to recognize and work from the special characteristics of each of China's regions and move away from uniform nationwide policies. To reassure skeptics worried about Chinese sovereignty, Deng Xiaoping insisted that these zones were not zones for political privilege, but only "special economic zones."

5. For an excellent study of the debates throughout the years regarding the orientation of the SEZs, which I have used here, see George T. Crane, "China's Special Economic Zones: The Political Foundations of Economic Performance" (Ph.D. diss., University of Wisconsin, 1987). I am grateful to George Crane for sharing this material with me. Also see George T. Crane, "China's Special Economic Zones," *Chinese Economic Studies* 19:2 (Winter 1985–86), pp. 4–7.

6. Bruce L. Reynolds, "Reform in Chinese Industrial Management: An Empirical Report," in John P. Hardt, ed., *China Under the Four Modernizations, Part 1: Selected Papers Submitted to the Joint Economic Committee, Congress of the United States* (Washington, D.C.: GPO, 13 August 1982), p. 128.

7. Deng Xiaoping, *Selected Works (1975–1982)* (Beijing: Foreign Languages Press, 1982), p. 244. I was told about the revision by an official involved in the discussion, interview, Beijing, November 1985.

8. Interview, ibid.

9. Deng, *Selected Works,* p. 245.

10. Interview with an official at the state economic commission, Beijing, May 1986.

11. *Chen Yun wenxuan,* p. 372. It is possible that Zhao and Yao Yilin co-headed the group or that Yao was chief deputy. See Xinhua, 2 November 1987, in FBIS, 87–211, 2 November 1987, p. 46, which stated that Yao at an unspecified time had headed this group and which credited him with proposing a speedup of reforms in 1980. In September 1980, Yao took over the planning commission.

12. The following information on the four economic policy research groups and their evolution comes from conversations with Nina Halpern and from her articles, "Making Economic Policy: The Influence of Economists," in John P. Hardt, ed., *China's Economy Looks Toward the Year 2000, Volume 1. The Four Modernizations: Selected Papers Submitted to the Joint Economic Committee, Congress of the United States* (Washington, D.C.: GPO, 21 May 1986), pp. 132–146; and "Scientific Decision Making: The Organization of Expert Advice in Post-Mao China," in Denis Fred Simon and Merle Goldman, eds., *Science and Technology in Post-Mao China* (Cambridge, Mass.: Harvard University Council on East Asian Studies, 1989), pp. 157–174.

When these groups were under the finance and economic commission, Yao Yilin, its secretary-general, gave them instructions, whereas Deng Liqun, Zhang Jingfu (a commission member), and Ma Hong (who was appointed a vice president of the social science academy in July) convened meetings. Officially, these groups may have been under the dual leadership of the commission and of the propaganda sector, thus accounting for Deng Liqun's role. By 1982, Deng Liqun was head of the Secretariat's policy research center and the propaganda department.

13. In 1980, this group became part of the import-export control commission and then in 1982, along with the commission, was merged into the foreign economic relations and trade ministry.

14. In 1980, this group became the technical economic (research) center. It concentrated on sectoral and project analysis. A collection of the center's influential studies is available as Ma Hong and Sun Shangqing, eds., *Zhongguo jingji jiegou wenti yanjiu* [Studies on Problems in China's Economic Structure] (Beijing: People's Publishers, 1981).

15. I learned much about the work of this group in interviews with Yu Guangyuan, Beijing, May 1986, and with Dong Fureng, November 1985 and May 1986. Its difficult task was to emancipate minds from outmoded leftist ideology, as Dong later explained in a speech listing the breakthroughs in economic theory most critical to advancing economic reform. See *Guangming ribao* [Enlightenment Daily], 20 June 1987, p. 3, in FBIS, 8 July 1987, p. K20. The group continued to meet informally throughout 1986 (and perhaps longer).

16. This group had chronic difficulty in obtaining opinions and inputs from central ministries reluctant to allow finances and resources to pass out of their hands into those of the enterprises. Reynolds, "Reform in Chinese Industrial Management," p. 133. In 1979, the group drafted a "preliminary opinion on an overall outline of reform," but there was general agreement that a reform plan was premature until more study and more experimentation were performed.

The economic system reform group became a state council office in 1980–1981, under the supervision of Vice Premier Wan Li. The office created four research centers: for technical economic research (under Ma Hong), for price research, for economic legislation research, and for economic research (which focused on macroeconomic issues and was headed by Xue Muqiao, concurrently director of economic research in the planning commission).

17. Information on the task forces can be found in Cyril Chihren Lin, "The Reinstatement of Economics in China Today," *China Quarterly* 85 (March 1981), pp. 40–41. I was told by officials at the science and technology commission, interviews, Beijing, November 1985, that Song Jian pioneered population projections; and by economist Liu Guoguang, director of the economic research institute at the social science academy, interviews, Beijing, November 1985 and May 1987, about his task force on alternative socialist development models, which later expanded to cover other developing countries. This type of study was conducted continually by the task force in the early 1980s and is now the regular responsibility of a comparative group within the institute.

18. Chen's former political secretary, Zhou Taihe, was a key figure in the reform group until 1985. Barry J. Naughton, "Sun Yefang: Toward a Reconstruction of Socialist Economics," in Carol Lee Hamrin and Timothy Cheek, eds., *China's Establishment Intellectuals* (Armonk, N.Y.: M. E. Sharpe, 1986), p. 131, mentioned that Sun and Wang Daohan served in the east China industrial bureau in the early 1950s. Zhang Jingfu then was in the east China branch of the finance and economy commission. Ma Hong worked under Chen Yun in northeast China in the late 1940s and like Chen suffered political eclipse in the early 1960s for his criticism of the Great Leap Forward.

19. Interview with Yu Guangyuan, Beijing, May 1986. The discussion group's organizers—institute director Sun Yefang, Xue Muqiao, and Yu Guangyuan—and its participants, including Liu Guoguang, Dong Fureng, and He Jianzhang, were China's most prominent theoretical economists. Naughton, ibid., pp. 128–131, discussed some of the close personal ties. Sun and Xue were related and had been born in the same Jiangsu locale near Shanghai as had Chen Yun. Along with famous anthropologist Fei Xiaotong and economist Qian Jiazhu, Sun and Xue in the 1930s were part of a famous group of underground Shanghai communists who did research on the rural economy under U.S.-trained economist Chen Hansheng. Lardy and Lieberthal, *Chen Yun's Strategy*,, pp. xvii, xxxiii, discussed the influence of Yugoslavia on Chen.

According to Naughton, ibid., pp. 137, 142, as Sun Yefang explored alternatives to Stalinist economics in 1956, he was greatly influenced by the views of Oskar Lange in Poland on the use of "economic levers." Sun's ties with Hungarian reformers were especially close; they exchanged visits in 1955 and regularly thereafter until the Cultural Revolution and then resumed them in the late 1970s. (The economic discussion group may have been modeled after the party economic advisory committee set up in Hungary in 1955.) In the early 1960s, Sun developed policies for enterprise autonomy based on theories about the "law of value"—that is, the importance of using price and profit indicators to regulate the economy through price setting and taxes. These proposals were quite similar to, but developed independently from, those of Wlodzimierz Brus in Poland. Brus's ideas eventually were to inspire the Hungarian economic reform of 1968.

According to Yu Guangyuan, the economic discussion group was attacked during the Cultural Revolution for relying on the three volumes of Karl Marx, *Capital,* instead of on Mao's works and did not reconvene until after Mao's death, when group members began to discuss past economic errors and current problems in the context of criticizing the Gang of Four. Hu Qiaomu's landmark speech of July 1978, which called for a discovery of economic laws and management of the economy by economic means, greatly encouraged theoretical exploration. Soon afterward, long-range research plans for the social sciences were drafted to reflect these policy priorities.

A talk by Chen Yun in March 1979 further rehabilitated non-Stalinist experiments and theories, including *Capital,* which Chen is said to have read three times during his Cultural Revolution incarceration. He defended Yugoslavia's development of the market sector and blamed both Soviet and Chinese failures on neglect of market regulation based on the law of value. Thus, economists were officially invited to explore Eastern European economics. In the years to follow, they became pioneers in broadening the policy base to include professionals, a trend that gradually spread from economics to other functional arenas.

20. Interview with officials at the Liaoning social science academy, which has special ties with its counterpart organization in Sizhuan, Shenyang, May 1986. Striking examples of Zhao's attitude were his insistence on sitting in the audience rather than on the podium when Sun Yefang lectured in Chengdu in 1978 and his later personal visit to Sun on his deathbed in 1983, as mentioned in Naughton, ibid., p. 151. Chen Yun may have been encouraged to pass on his economic authority to Zhao Ziyang by their common respect for political economists in general and Sun Yefang in particular.

21. Yu Guangyuan, *Lun wo guode jingji tizhi gaige, 1978-85* [On My Country's Economic System Reform] (Changsha: Hunan People's Publishers, 1985), pp. 1-5.

22. Interview with Dong Fureng, Beijing, November 1985. These experts included Brus, now at Oxford University, and Ota Sik from Czechoslovakia.

23. Interview with Liu Guoguang, Beijing, May 1987; and Xue Muqiao, "Sum Up Experience, Deepen Reform," *Renmin ribao* [People's Daily], 30 October 1987, p. 5, in FBIS-CHI-87-212, 3 November 1987, pp. 35-38.

Interviews with Hungarian reformers in Budapest, May 1986, revealed that since 1968, there have been similar advisory committees in Hungary on issues such as culture and youth policy. Each is led by a party member chosen at a party congress; the members are all specialists who need not be party members but must be elected by the central committee. According to them, China has considered adopting such an approach.

24. Interview with Dong Fureng, Beijing, November 1985.

25. I was told about the EDZs studies by Zheng Ge, deputy director of the SEZs office, interview, Beijing, May 1986; he also mentioned that U.S. free-

trade centers were investigated in 1985. A number of interviewees emphasized the impact of travel on their thinking.

26. Interviews with officials from the science and technology commission, Beijing, November 1985.

27. The following is from interview with Tong Dalin, Beijing, November 1985.

28. Xue, "Sum Up Experience," p. 36. Chen Yun's speech of 16 December 1980, is in *Chen Yun wenxuan,* pp. 248–254; Deng Xiaoping's speech of 25 December 1980, is in Deng, *Selected Works,* pp. 335–355.

29. *Wen wei po* (Hong Kong) [Literary Gazette], 31 January 1981, in FBIS, 31 January 1981, p. U1.

30. Chen Yun's speech to the congress is in *Hongqi* [Red Flag] 2 (16 January 1982), p. 58; his birdcage analogy appeared in comments on planning on 25 January 1982, in *Chen Yun wenxuan,* pp. 278–280.

31. Hu Yaobang was cited in Ma Hong, "Toward an Overall Development Strategy for the Economy, Society, Science, and Technology," *Jingji wenti* (Taiwan) [Economic Issues] 1 (25 January 1984), pp. 2–9, in Joint Publications Research Service China Report [JPRS CEA] 84–059, 19 July 1984, pp. 13–26.

32. Interviews with an official of the science and technology commission and with Ma Hong's aides, Beijing, November 1985. According to them, Ma shared this responsibility with the editors of *Renmin ribao* and *Hongqi,* which suggests that the research offices of party media organs continued to play an important policy research role.

33. Interview with officials of the Liaoning economic research center, Shenyang, May 1986.

34. Interview with a demographic researcher, Washington, D.C., 1987.

35. Information on the seminar comes from an interview with Yu Guangyuan, Beijing, May 1986; and from Yu Guangyuan, *Jingji shehui fazhan zhanlue* [Economic and Social Development Strategy] (Beijing: China Social Science Publishers, 1984).

The specialists not only fleshed out the projects in response to Hu Yaobang's directive; they helped shape the thinking that prompted his directive. The basic ideas behind both the economic symposia and the China 2000 study had already been implanted in the minds of top leaders through briefings and recommended readings. Hu's February 1981 comments thus were a green light for projects ready to roll. The first session of the symposium, for example, was held almost immediately on February 26. Yu Guangyuan, when asked about the linkage, described Hu's ideas and his own idea for the symposium as a matter of "mutual influence" through which both came to the "same view without discussion."

According to Ma Hong, "Toward an Overall Development Strategy," the hosts for the seminar were the policy bureau and science and technology information institute of the science and technology commission; the economic research institute of the state planning commission; the economic research institute and the world economics institute of the social science academy; and the technical economic center. As of late May 1986, when the thirty-third session convened, the Beijing-based specialists were still meeting on the last Monday of the month to discuss national development strategy. On Tuesday and Wednesday, specialists from outside Beijing came to the capital to discuss regional development strategies; the ninth of these sessions was held in May 1986. On the last Thursday of each month, Yu Guangyuan addressed the delegates of both sections of the symposia on topics in political economy. On Friday, he convened a symposium (four had been held as of May 1986) to discuss strategy by sector, such as food, building materials, insurance, and textiles. On Saturday, an association for territorial economics organized by Yu had a lecture forum on such topics as how to use the resources of the Yellow and Yangzi Rivers, ocean resources, transportation, energy, and so on.

According to Yu and Dong Fureng, these seminars were organized on Yu's personal authority. Although this seems to conflict with the statements of others regarding Ma Hong's role as sponsor, the public listing of the original host organizations, and the role of Tong Dalin as co-convenor, it is probable that on the basis of his personal stature and connections Yu was the main actor in obtaining the necessary official sponsorship. By 1986, during the other weeks of the month, Yu could be found almost anywhere in China leading research teams and speaking on development topics on behalf of his nonprofit, nongovernmental liaison service unit for regional development strategy (formed in August 1984), which coordinated outside consulting projects done by the staff of various bureaucratic units and professional societies (fourteen as of May 1986), while staff members retained their original jobs and salaries.

36. Yu and Tong represent a generation of intellectuals who joined the party before 1949 and thus proved their loyalty and their usefulness early on. They met in Yan'an in 1939–1940 and in the 1950s and 1960s were both in the propaganda department. Interviews with aides to national security adviser Huan Xiang, Washington, D.C., 1986, confirmed that he had similar status.

37. Interviews with science officials, Washington, D.C., and Beijing, 1985 and 1986.

38. Interview, Beijing, November 1985. Tong said he was especially influenced by Theodore Schultz's writings on poverty.

39. Zhao Ziyang, work report to the National People's Congress in December 1981, in FBIS, 16 December 1981, pp. K1–35.

40. Dong Fureng, "Further Develop the Study of China's Economic Development Strategy," *Renmin ribao,* 11 May 1982, p. 5, in FBIS, 17 May 1982, p. K7.

41. *The Sixth Five-Year Plan of the People's Republic of China for Economic and Social Development (1981–1985)* (Beijing: Foreign Languages Press, 1984).

42. Zhou Shulian, "Seriously Study the Historical Experience of China's Economic Development Strategy," *Renmin ribao,* 24 May 1982, p. 5, in FBIS, 1 June 1982, pp. K3–6. In interviews in Beijing in November 1985 and May 1986, Dong Fureng emphasized the continuing difficulty of changing people's operating conceptions of planning and development.

43. Academic trends report, *Renmin ribao,* 1 June 1982, p. 5, in FBIS, 3 June 1982, pp. K1–2. The reporter referred to some comrades who stressed

rapid development and adherence to the socialist road (read, the Soviet model); some who stressed comprehensive balance and ideological orthodoxy (read, Chen Yun's approach); and some who focused on raising economic efficiency through application of science and technology (read, the reform approach).

44. Yu Guangyuan, speech at a development strategy seminar, *Guangming ribao,* 13 November 1983, p. 3, in FBIS, 23 November 1983, pp. K16–18.

45. The following information is from an interview with Liu Guoguang, Beijing, May 1987; and from Liu Guoguang, *Zhongguo jingji fazhan zhanlue wenti yanjiu* [Studies on Issues in China's Economic Development Strategy] (Shanghai: Shanghai People's Publishers, 1984), which presented the findings of the task force. Even earlier phases of this study may have been used in Chen Yun's December 1980 speech summing up economic lessons from China's previous thirty years, but I have no proof of this.

After 1982, this task force on alternative economic models was able to draw on a large body of research on the Soviet Union and Eastern Europe undertaken by China's functional and geographic specialists, mandated and funded by the 6th FYP for social sciences. For a study of the blossoming of academic research and debate on the Soviet Union in internal publications during the early 1980s, see Gilbert Rozman, "China's Soviet Watchers in the 1980s: A New Era in Scholarship," *World Politics* 36:4 (July 1985), pp. 435–474. Early writings critiqued Stalin and the Soviet model and rehabilitated Bukharin and Lenin's New Economic Policy. I assume, based on knowledge of the usual approach to social science planning, that this surge of research reflected official funding priorities. My interviews with Soviet specialists, Beijing, May 1986, confirmed Rozman's findings that they tended to be more positive about the Soviet Union than did economic specialists and U.S. specialists, in part because they were not equipped to do comparative and socioeconomic analyses that would fully explore the flaws in the system.

46. Interview with Liu Guoguang, Beijing, May 1987, confirmed by my reading of articles in the Chinese press throughout 1982.

47. I am most grateful to Gerald O. Barney, study director for *The Global 2000 Report to the President: Entering the Twenty-First Century,* three vols. (Washington, D.C.: GPO, 1980), and now director of the Global Studies Center in Arlington, Virginia, for sharing with me information regarding the origin and development of the China 2000 study. Through him, I met Lin Zixin and Zheng Guanglin, who worked on the first study, and through them, Wang Huijiong and Li Boxi, aides of Ma Hong who were responsible for the second study.

The Global 2000 report provided the first integrated U.S. governmental study of trends affecting all the key economic resources and recommended domestic and foreign policy actions to sustain the nation's resource strength over the long term.

48. Interviews with science officials, Washington, D.C., and Beijing, 1985 and 1986, revealed to me the importance (and complexity) of personal ties for understanding the political influence of this loose grouping. At the apex, they benefited from the protection and patronage of Politburo member and veteran

military figure Nie Rongzhen. In the 1960s, Nie was responsible for development of civilian and military science and technology, and influenced this arena again in the 1980s. Zhang Jingfu (vice premier and economic commissioner in the early 1980s) served as Nie's secretary and his chief assistant at the science and technology commission before the Cultural Revolution. At that time, his secretary was Wu Mingyu, head of the policy bureau of the science and technology commission in the 1980s. Two other key reform officials were part of this network because of responsibilities before the Cultural Revolution: Du Runsheng who was secretary-general of the academy of sciences, under the direction of the commission, and Yu Guangyuan, who was the propaganda department official responsible for science. Wu Mingyu also had other important political ties; he had been a bridge partner of Deng Xiaoping for years, and Deng's daughter, Deng Nan, served in the policy bureau in the 1980s. Wu's own longtime secretary, Lin Zixin, of the commission's science and technology information institute, was also Ma Hong's close friend, neighbor and aide.

49. Gerald Barney based on conversations with Lin Zixin in Beijing, July 1981.

50. Interview with Zheng Guanglin, Beijing, November 1985.

51. The following information is from Gerald Barney, unpublished trip report, July 1981.

52. Interviews with Wang Huijiong and Li Boxi, Beijing, November 1985.

53. Interviews with Zheng Guanglin, Washington, D.C., 1985, and Lin Zixin, Beijing, 1985 and 1986.

54. Several sources indicated that the one existing model—a demographic model at the Aerospace Agency—was that used by Song Jian, a cyberneticist soon to become science commissioner. An article in *Beijing Review,* 9–15 May 1988, pp. 12–15, discussing think tanks in China cited the deputy director of the Beijing information and cybernetics research institute, who stated that in 1979 Song Jian initiated the first long-term forecasts in the population field.

Barney learned that T. C. Yang of Shanghai Jiaotong University also seemed to have played a role in introducing Western-style system modeling to China. A 1930s Ph.D. from M.I.T., Yang reestablished old school ties and in 1980 translated into Chinese the book *Industrial Dynamics,* by Jay W. Forrester of the M.I.T. Sloan School of Management. In 1982–1983, Wang Qifan, a student of Yang, studied with the group working on Forrester's system dynamics national model, which was billed as an effective tool for policy analysts to balance short-run versus long-run goals, integrate forces of supply and demand, and interrelate human, financial, and natural resources.

Barney also provided the China 2000 team with two extensive reports: Gerald O. Barney and Sheryl Wilkins, eds., *Managing a Nation: The Software Sourcebook* (Arlington, Va.: Institute for 21st Century Studies, 1986); and Gerald O. Barney, "Global Issues and Methodology: An Introduction" (Arlington, Va.: Institute for 21st Century Studies, 1986). In addition, Zheng Guanglin, a member of the first-stage team, spent a year in 1984–1985 in Washington, D.C., training with Barney; Zheng assembled a large notebook devoted largely to information on methodology that could be useful in China.

55. For summaries of the conclusions of the first study, see Zheng Guanglin, "The Future of China: Collected Papers," ed. Gerald O. Barney (Arlington, Va.: Global Studies Center, 10 April 1985); and Year 2000 Research Group, *Gongyuan 2000 nian de zhongguo* [China Toward the Year 2000] (Beijing: Science and Technology Documents Publishers, September 1984), published as a special issue of JPRS CEA–86–023, 6 March 1986.

56. Interviews with study staffers, Beijing, November 1985 and May 1986.

57. Interviews, ibid.; interviews with economists at the social science academy, November 1985 and May 1986.

58. Zheng, "The Future of China"; Year 2000 Research Group, *Gongyuan 2000*. The ten chapters covered population, energy, farmland, water supply and demand, forest resources, mineral resources, food supply and demand, communications and transportation, water consumption and conservation, and a general discussion of development problems.

Beginning in early 1983, Ma Hong's staff was increasingly involved in the China 2000 project, having obtained additional funding for it in March as a key research project for philosophy and social sciences in the 6th FYP budget. According to Tong Dalin, suggestions on overall development issues were fed into the report from the economic development strategy seminar. In May 1983, participants in a report meeting to the state council recommended tasking the China association of science and technology with organizing the nearly one hundred related professional societies to participate in the research. That summer, Barney returned to China for two weeks of lectures and discussions focused on specific questions addressed in the study.

59. Year 2000 Research Group, *Gongyuan 2000*, p. 209.

60. Zhao's written comment was cited by Ma Hong, "Toward an Overall Development Strategy."

61. Ibid.

62. Interview with officials and staff of the Liaoning economic research center, Shenyang, May 1986. Their mandate was to do surveys of the current economic situation, to be followed by twenty-year (1980–2000) development strategy forecasts (*fazhan zhanlue yuce*). Both the development strategy seminar and the China 2000 study originally were to explore issues of local and regional development as well as sectoral development, but neither project made much progress in this area because of lack of time and information.

63. Zhao, work report to the National People's Congress, p. K22. The following information on city experiments is from *Liaowang* [Outlook] 50 (16 December 1985), pp. 19–21; 51 (23 December 1985), p. 24; and Wu Peilun, "The Process of China's Urban Reforms" (parts I–II), in FBIS, 15 January 1986, pp. K14–25.

64. Deng Xiaoping, *Build Socialism with Chinese Characteristics* (Beijing: Foreign Languages Press, 1985), p. 14. Deng claimed that Zhao first put forward the idea of establishing economic zones, to begin with Shanxi and Shanghai, in late 1982. But other evidence suggests that Zhao was responding to local lobbies with powerful representation at the center. He had always appeared hesitant to advance Shanghai interests at the expense of other coastal areas, especially Guangdong (where his own ties were strong).

65. Boosters included Xue Muqiao, Yao Yilin, Bo Yibo (also the leader of the Shanxi boosters), Zhang Jingfu, and the Shanghai leadership, including Mayor Wang Daohan as well as first secretary Chen Guodong and second secretary Hu Lijiao. Bo Yibo, Xinhua, 19 October 1983, in FBIS, 20 October 1983, p. K1, mentioned that he and other members of the advisory commission had helped in the design and preparation for economic regions. Xue Muqiao, "Free Ourselves from Worn Out Ideas and Research Modern Development Strategy," *Shijie jingji daobao* [World Economic Herald], 29 April 1985, p. 3, in FBIS, 14 May 1985, pp. K7–12, mentioned that the Shanghai zone was first proposed as early as 1980 and went on to discuss the reasons for local resistance ever since.

66. Conversations with Barney and Zheng Guanglin. Zheng, "The Future of China," page 147, listed the major works he had translated by 1984.

4

The Second Wave:
Ideological Struggle
and Policy Breakthrough
(1983–1984)

From January 1983 to January 1984, China experienced several sharp twists in policy that reflected the rapid unraveling of the very tenuous 12th Party Congress compromise between proponents of relatively moderate and more radical reform. When Hu Yaobang and Zhao Ziyang tried to speed up the timetable for reform, a conservative coalition of party elders and propaganda and security officials formed against them. In 1983, Deng Xiaoping passively sided first with one and then the other group; finally, in 1984 he actively intervened to open a window for a major reform breakthrough. Deng succeeded in gaining leadership endorsement of policy guidelines on reforming the management of the economy, science and technology, and education. This opened the way for rapid introduction of market reforms in urban China. As these events unfolded, two things became apparent—the close connection among ideology, policy, and power politics and the linkage between domestic and foreign policy.

Reform Offensive

Early in 1983, Hu Yaobang used his position as general secretary (the official chief ideologue) to launch a major publicity campaign on behalf of the reform program. In calling for a year of reform, he attempted to speed up the timetable for introducing reforms into the urban economy. In a speech at a national conference on ideological and political work in January, Hu said the notion of the inseparability of modernization and reform was an extremely important guiding ideology.[1] He stressed the paramount importance and pressing need for reform and advocated a search for new ideas, a breaking away from old conventions, and the promotion of cadre bold enough to carry out reform. In apparent response to criticism that reforming the institutional superstructure was a variant of the Maoist politics-first approach to development, Hu insisted that the program of comprehensive reform differed from Mao's theory of continuing revolution in its criterion for introducing reforms—namely, whether reforms contributed to economic development and the people's prosperity.

Humanistic Socialism: Hu Yaobang's Effort to Reform the Party

By encouraging decollectivization and the use of material incentives, the reform program had challenged the Maoist insistence that individual interests must give way to those of the state. Maoist values of egalitarianism, heroic self-sacrifice, and uniformity of thought and behavior had long been empty shells given the mass cynicism in China by the 1970s. But even the remaining shell of Maoism quickly crumbled in the 1980s as Deng Xiaoping encouraged mental emancipation and people were given more freedom for individual thought and pursuit of material interests. Both religion and commercialism gained adherents at the expense of orthodoxy, despite tighter restrictions after 1981. (By rough unofficial count, practitioners of protestant Christianity, for example, grew exponentially from perhaps 2 million in 1979 to 20 million by the mid-1980s.)

A group of influential theorists in the party responded to these spiritual trends by attempting to construct a new version of Chinese Marxism. As part of the de-Maoization effort of 1978–1980, the group had criticized the feudal nature of Chinese society under Mao. In the early 1980s, these theorists began exploring the importance of humanism. On the one hand, they genuinely wanted to spark a Chinese Renaissance. On the other hand, they wanted to provide an ideological defense of the reform program against its more orthodox party critics, woo the intelligentsia into the party, and also attract support for the post-Mao regime from the disaffected populace.

Hu Yaobang came to be viewed as the patron of these and other like-minded highly educated party officials, mostly those in their sixties or younger, who tended to blame the Soviet system, not just Mao or the Cultural Revolution, for China's problems. Many of them had been sent to jail in the 1957 campaign against rightists and had been returned to positions of prominence by Hu. These party intellectuals believed that only radical systemwide reform, including a shakeup of the cadre system, could regain popular support for the regime and bring about a renewal of public morality. Knowing the tremendous cynicism among youth, Hu and his protégés, including those who ran the party's youth program, sought to woo young people with a new ideology of humanistic socialism and greater freedom from ideological control. Of certain practical relevance, too, was the fact that major ideological reform could be used to justify an overhaul of the propaganda and security apparatus and replacement of Hu's orthodox critics with like-minded reform loyalists.

On 13 March 1983, a meeting of the entire central elite was held in Beijing to showcase a major address by Hu Yaobang on the centenary of Karl Marx's death.[2] His speech was remarkable in its transparent effort to counter Maoist anti-intellectualism and set the stage for a major role in China for intellectuals. Playing down the concept of proletarian rule, Hu praised Karl Marx as an intellectual and a scientist committed to a nondogmatic search for understanding of complex, changing reality. Hu similarly praised V. I. Lenin and the Bolsheviks, along with Mao Zedong and other Chinese Communists, for their realistic linking of Marxism with local conditions to produce the Soviet and Chinese revolutions. But Hu made no mention of Joseph Stalin whatsoever and gave short shrift to Mao's post-1949 contributions.

Hu defended the current leadership against charges that it had abandoned Mao's ideology by redefining that ideology and placing at its center Deng Xiaoping's slogan "Seek truth from facts." In this context, Hu defended the rural reforms against the accusation that socialism was losing its foothold in the Chinese countryside; he defended the party's policy on intellectuals against those who claimed that workers and peasants were being shunted aside in favor of intellectuals. Hu's speech stressed the importance of recruiting and promoting trained intellectuals, especially scientists and engineers. He made it clear that intellectuals were the main force behind China's whole development effort in an era when science was an increasingly important element in production. China had to assimilate all the achievements of modern (read, Western) science and culture if it hoped to modernize.

In a paper given at a subsequent symposium on Marxism, theoretical adviser Zhou Yang repudiated his own 1960s critique of humanism and called for an alliance between bourgeois and Marxist humanism. "In my opinion, only Marxist humanism can supercede bourgeois humanism (which attracts some of our young people exposed to Western thought)." Zhou based his views on the well-known explorations of Marx's early writings by Wang Ruoshui, deputy editor of

Renmin ribao (People's Daily); the newspaper later published Zhou's essay over the objections of more orthodox propaganda officials who did not want to grant these views the appearance of official dogma.[3]

Others in the group of theorists close to Hu, including Yu Guang-yuan, convenor of the development strategy seminar, and Su Shaozhi, director of the social science academy's institute of Marxism-Leninism, openly admitted at the centenary symposium that Marxism worldwide was in crisis, that Marxist-Leninists must address many issues raised by modern Western science and social science, and that Marxist-Leninists must update concepts and methodology in the process. The inspiration for this exploration was Eastern European Marxism as well as non-Marxist European socialism.

Theorists were treading on particularly sensitive ground when they spoke of popular alienation from the party and attacked bureaucratic privilege as the heart of China's problems. Although they called primarily for moral education and democratic procedures within the party as a solution, their writings were reminiscent of the heretical claims by Cultural Revolution activists (1966–1968) and Democracy Wall dissidents (1978–1980) that the Soviet-style system itself was fundamentally flawed and must be replaced with an alternative socialism. Wang Ruoshui later was explicitly accused of suggesting that a new Cultural Revolution was necessary to overturn the privileged caste of party officials and thus of providing a theoretical basis for dissident activities.[4]

These theoretical writings on humanism both responded to and encouraged a wave of anti–Cultural Revolution literature on related themes: the human degradation of the Maoist era; the importance of private feelings and imagination; human love and individual fulfillment; sexual liberation; and the universal validity of religious experience. Some of this literature was quite political and depicted party cadre as less than heroic. These themes tended to undermine the orthodox argument that socialism in China had created a society morally superior to capitalism; these authors made the point that greed and love were universal and that the struggle for survival could be found anywhere, perhaps especially in China.

Hu Yaobang's ideological campaign set the stage for further expansion of reform policies in those arenas under his direction as party chief—rural affairs, the SEZs, intellectual affairs, and culture. Central directive no. 1 for 1983 encouraged peasants to get rich as soon as possible, a slogan that was such a bald statement of the shift to material incentives that it thereafter incited constant contention.[5]

Hu also reinvigorated efforts to improve living and working conditions for intellectuals and called for the introduction of experimental political reforms in the management of grass-roots units, including factories and schools. For example, Minister of Culture Zhu Muzhi announced that cultural troupes would be allowed more autonomy in organizing themselves, arranging their work, and retaining box office receipts; they would be required to contribute to their own financial support. The leadership of Shekou in Shenzhen was encouraged to experiment with elections for factory leaders.[6]

Hu Yaobang's reform campaign was intimately tied to his effort to promote reform loyalists in key posts. During the early part of the year, Hu Yaobang and his staff began drafting a document of guidelines for party rectification to be endorsed at the plenum scheduled for the fall. The reform campaign in part was intended to shape the criteria for promotion and demotion or expulsion of party members. Hu's January speech defined a revolutionary cadre as one who would boldly carry out reforms, thereby weakening the argument that some veterans of the revolution should be retained in leading posts on the basis of past contributions and seniority. The other criteria for personnel decisions—that the cadre corps should become younger, better educated, and more professionally competent—all favored the new generation of party officials recruited and trained while Hu Yaobang headed the Communist Youth League in the 1950s and 1960s.

Expanding the Reform Coalition in the Localities

During 1983, Hu and Zhao appeared to seek support for reform from local SEZ and municipal authorities; both men held out the promise of greater local control over resources formerly disposed of by central or provincial planners. As the lengthy preparation for the 7th FYP (1986–1990) got under way in early 1983 following belated endorsement of the 6th plan, there was strong competition among officials in the localities for access to future resources. They argued and maneuvered for separate and favored treatment in the national plan. Shenyang, for example, was trying to draft its plan early so as to impress central officials that it would manage resources well and should be granted special experimental status such as Chongqing had. Coastal cities and provinces were lobbying for permission to set up more SEZs.[7] This situation provided important political opportunities.

In January 1983, Zhao Ziyang visited Hainan Island, and shortly thereafter the leadership issued instructions that gave Hainan some of the flexibility in foreign trade and investment enjoyed by the SEZs. In February, Hu Yaobang visited Shenzhen SEZ, Shekou, and Hainan and encouraged officials to further expand the open door policy. (Debate had persisted throughout 1982 over the proper orientation of the zones as they were drafting their 6th FYPs.) Hu rejected gradualism and isolation for the zones. He endorsed the view that they should pursue high growth rates based on importation of advanced industrial technology and high levels of foreign investment and that they should become crucibles for testing management reforms for the rest of the country.[8]

In February 1983, Chongqing became the first large city to be added to the earlier list of medium and small cities that could begin planning their economic development under national rather than provincial guidance. Experiments eventually included expanded decision-making power for enterprises; reorganization of science and education work to serve production; assignment of construction projects through contract bidding; expansion of the collective and individual sectors; commercialization of housing; deregulation of prices and interest rates; and expansion of markets and trade centers.

At the same time, a drastic streamlining and reorganization of both provincial and city administrative organs and a turnover of top officials were taking place. Cities expanded their jurisdictions over surrounding counties to create more natural economic networks. Nearly one-fourth of China's counties came under municipal jurisdiction. Many state enterprises were shifted from the control of the central industrial subsystems to control by city officials.[9]

Following an investigation trip to the Shanghai area by Vice Premier Yao Yilin from December 1982 through January 1983, the State Council created a special planning office for the Shanghai economic region (encompassing the municipality and areas from several neighboring provinces with which Shanghai had strong economic ties). Zhao and Yao stressed that the Shanghai region was intended not only to spur Shanghai's economic take-off and thereby to aid national economic revitalization, but it also was to be a pioneer in comprehensive economic reform and a means of reforming the planning system. The first conception of the region included only the city's immediate vicinity, but very soon Japanese advisers recommended a larger macroregion, and Chinese academics spoke of including the whole Yangzi River delta. In August 1983, a planning conference was held in Shanghai to begin work on a regional 7th FYP intended to be "an ambitious and feasible blueprint for the economic development of the delta."[10]

In 1983, the two other major Yangzi cities gained more autonomy from provincial authorities: Wuhan was given independent status in the national plan as Chongqing had been earlier, and both were opened to foreign shipping. Press reports about the new Yangzi macroregion stressed the importance of attracting foreign assistance and investment from overseas Chinese originally from the region. Shanghai trade and investments in Hong Kong increased, no doubt building on the large community of former Shanghai residents there. The stated aim of Shanghai's new plans, which centered on the importation of new equipment and technology to upgrade existing industry, was to reach by the end of the century the level of the world's developed countries in the 1980s.

By June 1983, three new regional planning offices had been set up under the State Council: the Shanghai economic region planning office, the Shanxi energy base planning office, and the northeast energy and communications planning office. The latter two regions were important energy bases for the energy-poor coast. These offices were not under sole control of the planning commission, but along with the SEZ office also answered to the foreign investment leading group. Thus, Zhao and other leading reformers could experiment with new methods of economic planning in these important industrial and energy bases. The new offices were tasked with improving intraregional coordination and creating overall regional development strategies that would then shape local 7th FYPs.[11]

The 1983 reorganization was symptomatic of a broader shift of development priorities that gave precedence to the coastal cities. As the new regions were taking shape in the summer, Tong Dalin, a vice chair of the reform commission and co-convenor of the development strategy symposium, unveiled a new development strategy, which he called "relying on the East and moving to the West." Originated by Tong and several colleagues in Shanghai, this concept was influenced by the history of the economic development of the U.S. western frontier.[12] Tong recommended concentration on developing the Songliao plain in the northeast and China's three main river deltas, beginning with the coast and moving upriver. Under this strategy, the Yangzi River region all the way up to the Chengdu plain would eventually include half of China; the development of the Yellow River would move up toward Shanxi; and the southern gold coast—Fujian and the Pearl River delta in Guangdong—eventually would extend economic sway over Guangxi, Yunnan, and Guizhou.

This new approach, which emerged from the development strategy seminars, was also influenced by thinking about the global technological revolution underway. One influential participant in the symposia, Huan Xiang, a senior adviser to Deng and Zhao on economics and international affairs, was also a Shanghai booster. In 1984, when thinking and writing about the new technological revolution became more public, he advocated creating a Silicon valley in the Shanghai area.[13]

The somewhat utopian tinge to these visions had clear political appeal. Throughout the remainder of the decade, this East to West development strategy was hotly debated, as officials in the localities sought to move their cities or provinces higher up on the list of national investment priorities. The general consensus held, however, that throughout the 1980s the infrastructure and energy needs of agriculture and light industry on the east coast would have priority; in the 1990s, central China's basic industries and resources would be the focus; and after the year 2000, the northwest and southwest would gain the development limelight. Mao's third-front strategy had given way to a first-front strategy; not surprisingly, the coastal regions favored reform, and inland areas feared for their interests.

The Conservative Reaction

Quite a few powerful groups found their interests threatened by the post–12th congress reform campaign led by Hu and Zhao in 1983. Rural party cadre could lose their jobs; the interior provinces and northeastern provinces were being ignored in the budget; central and provincial planning officials were being asked to share decisions with financial officials and economic experts; the propaganda apparatus was told to allow independent writing and publishing; and veteran party and military officials were being pressured into retirement. Reformers were in the minority in the bureaucracy and even in the Politburo, but they had Deng Xiaoping's backing. Their hopes for expanding their support base lay in the party rectification campaign planned for late 1983–late 1986, through which they could promote supporters and retire or dismiss opponents.

During 1983, party elders and establishment bureaucrats, represented by party elder Hu Qiaomu and propaganda department director Deng Liqun, had been pressing an alternative solution to the crisis of faith in the party. Ironically, Hu Qiaomu, Deng Liqun, and others like them in general political and security work had served Deng Xiaoping well in the fight against Maoism in the late 1970s. But now, having gained positions of influence with the reestablishment of the Leninist central bureaucracy, they became conservatives defending the status quo against further reform. No longer cooperating with Hu Yaobang, they became his chief critics and competitors.

These conservatives had been preparing for a nationwide education campaign in Communist ideology. A study outline—a sort of Chinese Communist Manifesto—had been circulated for discussion and revision and was ready for publication and distribution for study during the rectification campaign.[14] Sprinkled throughout the document were implicit criticisms of reform, from the misuse of bonuses and profits to the commercialization of culture. The outline insisted that all reforms must be integrated with education in Communist ideology, a theme conspicuously absent in Hu Yaobang's speeches. Citing Chen Yun frequently, the document encouraged suspicion of foreign capitalists and stressed the priority of an independent foreign policy. It defined true patriotism as belief in communism.

In effect, the conservatives were indirectly questioning the legitimacy of the reform program, regardless of its economic efficacy. They thereby sought to stress the revolutionary criterion for promotion—ideological orthodoxy—over criteria of age and education. They also sought to defend traditional methods of propaganda control and censorship, which legitimated their own positions at the top. The conservatives had a strong official rationale for their approach—the 12th congress resolution's insistence that Communist ideology must remain the core of China's spiritual civilization.[15]

Both reformers and conservatives sought support from Deng Xiaoping in the coming showdown. Judging from his actions in the summer of 1983, he tried to respond to orthodox concerns without allowing a new mass campaign. He approved a limited campaign against heterodoxy within cultural circles that was to focus on spiritual pollution without raising the politically loaded slogans of antirightism or procommunism. The draft documents on communism were set aside in favor of Deng's newly published *Selected Works* as the more pragmatic primary study materials for the rectification campaign.

When the 2nd Plenum was held in October, its results at first seemed quite favorable to reformers, despite the absence of personnel changes. Hu Yaobang and his associates were in charge of the commission responsible for rectification, although the group was heavily salted with party elders. The guidelines for rectification primarily targeted Cultural Revolution leftists, unlawful officials and reform opponents for expulsion from the party, although these guidelines also called for vigilance against bourgeois ideology and spiritual pollution. Other than these latter vague references, controversial ideological issues seemed to have been set aside; the plenum communiqué announced that a conference on ideology was scheduled for late 1983.[16]

Immediately after the plenum closed, however, a major ideological campaign burst forth, launched by Deng Liqun with the backing of party and army veterans who gave speeches at various forums calling for the eradication of spiritual pollution (defined vaguely as promoting lack of faith in socialism and the party).[17] They cited speeches at the plenum by Deng Xiaoping and Chen Yun (not officially published until several years later) attacking rightist laxity among party members who allegedly were soft on bourgeois thought and behavior. Conservatives clearly were attempting to shift priorities in the rectification campaign from attacking antireformers to attacking reformers. Although conservatives reassured nonparty groups that this campaign was for party members only, it quickly disintegrated into a dogfight among competing factions within the party core groups that existed in every organization in China, including those in the government and ostensibly unofficial organizations.

Within a few weeks, the editor and deputy editor of *Renmin ribao*, Hu Jiwei and Wang Ruoshui, were removed from office and Zhou Yang was forced to give a self-criticism at a meeting of the central advisory commission, of which he was a member. Nevertheless, he apologized only for the bad influence his writings might have had, not for the views they expressed. All three men became instant folk heroes, especially among youth, from whom they received thousands of letters of support. In the campaign, humanist themes linked to Wang's theory of alienation were savaged as selfish egoism, base profit-seeking, or nihilism. Fans of Tolstoy, Freud, Sartre and modernist literary styles were attacked, as were unnamed proponents of liberty and democracy.[18]

The official party paper, now in the hands of Deng Liqun, published a series of harsh commentator's articles in October that contained thinly veiled criticism of Hu Yaobang and an editorial in early November that criticized capitalist tendencies in the countryside.[19] The press contained negative comments about the United States. Religious followers suffered harassment or even arrest for holding unorthodox or superstitious views. The general tenor of the campaign, which blamed outside influences for China's moral and spiritual problems, was an implicit critique of the open door policy. SEZ officials, in particular, became defensive about their economic and social policies and tried to prove that they had been vigilant against spiritual pollution. Soon, young students, workers, and military recruits were being taken to task for their hair and clothing styles and their taste in music and literature.

Gradually, however, in response to domestic and foreign alarm, limits were set on the campaign:

- On 17 November, the party's youth paper exempted colorful lifestyles from criticism.
- On 20 November, Hu Yaobang stressed that the campaign must be conducted so as to improve economic work.
- At the end of the month, Deng Liqun set new lines of demarcation in conducting the campaign.
- On 8 December, a central party directive placed the countryside off limits to the campaign without clarifying whether spiritual pollution actually existed there.

- Shortly thereafter, economic theorists were exempted.
- On 16 December, Li Xiannian told the archbishop of Canterbury that the campaign was not aimed at faith in religion, which was protected by law.
- On 18 December, leaders speaking at a national science and technology work conference put science off limits.

Planned visits by Hu Yaobang to Japan in November and Zhao Ziyang to the United States in January probably added to the political weight of foreign reaction.

Intellectuals made a major contribution in limiting the campaign by refusing to go along with ritual criticism and self-criticism. For example, when graduate students at the social science academy were called in to discuss an article written by Politburo member Hu Qiaomu to attack unorthodox views on humanism, they bravely withheld praise, raised impolite questions, and pointed out that key sections were confusing. As a result, the reporters present were unable to publish an article in the youth newspaper, as planned. Many academy researchers and writers and artists refused to criticize their colleagues, thus making for sparse turnouts at conservative forums publicized in the press. Young theorists working on the controversial rural policies in the Secretariat's research group registered unhappiness with their boss, Deng Liqun, by arranging to move as a group to the State Council where they enjoyed Zhao Ziyang's protection.[20]

By the end of the year, the campaign had been limited to its original target—allegedly heterodox writers, artists, and political theorists. Nonetheless, the brief but sharp public display of leadership struggle both revealed and exacerbated a deadly serious competition between Hu Yaobang and Deng Liqun, who represented two wings of Deng Xiaoping's unwieldy political coalition with two different approaches to rebuilding the party's legitimacy.

The political standoff between the newly polarized camps was evident into early 1984. For a time, the conservatives seemed to have the upper hand; they used the nintieth anniversary of Mao's birth, 26 December, to organize an outpouring of praise for Mao that was almost a posthumous rehabilitation. They sponsored forums and symposia on Mao Zedong's ideology, praising the current relevance of his views in all fields, especially his rather philistine opinions on literature and art. On 28 December, a *Renmin ribao* commentator insisted once more that criticism of spiritual pollution must remain an important part of the rectification campaign. Yet a New Year's day editorial in the same paper reflected a sudden turnabout by insisting that work in all spheres—

including the rectification campaign—must be subordinate to economic construction. Spiritual pollution was barely mentioned.

Scientific Socialism: The Politics of "Third-Wave Fever"

In the midst of this struggle between Hu Yaobang and Deng Liqun, Zhao Ziyang provided the key that turned the lock in favor of reform. The key policy theme—the overriding importance of technological development—was one Zhao knew would gain Deng Xiaoping's support. The key policy mechanism was the State Council think tanks, advisory groups, and planning offices under Zhao's control, which were mobilized to counter the party propaganda apparatus under Deng Liqun's control.

During 1983, China's elite had been exposed to futurist writings from the West as well as the results of *China Toward the Year 2000*. On National Day, 1 October 1983, Deng Xiaoping wrote an inscription for a specialized middle school that seemed to signal his support for the new futurist thinking among his chief advisers: "Education [implicitly including political education] should be geared to the needs of modernization, the world and the future."[21]

Premier Zhao on 9 October instructed a small group of specialists to do a concentrated study of the new global technological revolution and to recommend appropriate measures for China. In his instructions, Zhao briefly summed up Western views of the coming "third wave" of global technological change, that is, the revolution in information technology (the agrarian revolution was the first wave, and the industrial revolution was the second wave in writings by Alvin Toffler). Zhao stated that "we should study it conscientiously and, in light of our actual conditions, define the proper economic strategies and technological policies to be adopted for long-term plans, covering ten or twenty years, especially science and technology plans. . . . The new world industrial revolution is an opportunity as well as a challenge."[22] Zhao stressed that China must not only learn about the new trends but must learn from them so as to find ways to narrow the economic and technological gap between China and the developed world.

Intellectuals Defend Themselves and Reform

Zhao's statement also reflected a behind-the-scenes bid to fight off orthodox pressures on the new priorities, methods, and ideas being developed by his economic advisers. His welcome of the technological revolution was taken from an article written in the summer of 1983 by senior foreign affairs adviser Huan Xiang, director of the State Council's international studies center and a leading member of the development strategy seminar. Ostensibly one of a number of commentaries on Deng Xiaoping's *Selected Works,* published that July, Huan's article was in fact written as a defense of the open door policy—salted with quotations from Deng for added authority—in the face of the budding campaign against spiritual pollution. The polemical tone of his argument reflects this:

> As a major strategic principle . . . the open-door policy has become our unswerving national policy. . . . In the course of implementing this policy, we are bound to encounter many new circumstances and problems [but] what we need is the pioneering spirit and the attitude of seeking truth from facts. We must not try to make petty reforms or stick to old ways and conventions; still less must we backtrack. . . . We must not set the principle of adhering to self-reliance against the open-door policy. . . . Even if we let foreign businessmen run a number of enterprises on a sole proprietary basis, it will not change the socialist economic nature of China. . . . We cannot set the development of foreign trade against protecting the national industry. . . . We should not regard advanced science and technologies and scientific managment methods as capitalist things and discard them. . . . Decadent capitalist things have no intrinsic connection with the open-door policy.[23]

In his article, Huan Xiang tried to inject a powerful sense of urgency into the need for reform by demonstrating the inevitability of China's involvement with and competition in the global capitalist market. He explained that a new technological revolution was brewing that would come into full economic play in the twenty-first century. He also warned that if China remained indifferent or tried to remain outside the system of an international division of labor, the gap between China and the advanced world level would widen.

During 1983, Huan also worked with other senior advisers to protect those who had been introducing such concepts to China. As specialists in U.S. studies had expanded their knowledge of the West, they had begun to question dogmatic notions of the nature of capitalist states. Specialists in political philosophy, supported by Su Shaozhi at the social science academy's theoretical institute, had also begun questioning orthodox methodology and dogmatic assertions regarding the flaws of capitalism and the superiority of socialism. These changing perceptions of the world had profound foreign policy implications that Huan was in the best position to explore openly and to raise at higher levels.[24]

Those under attack included researchers at the social science academy, the science and technology commission, and the technical economic center who found their orthodoxy being questioned because of their involvement in the China futures society, headed by Yu Guangyuan and Tong Dalin. The society had sponsored a lecture series by Alvin Toffler in Beijing and Shanghai in January 1983. As preparation for his visit, researchers had translated and summarized futurist works similar to and including Toffler's *The Third Wave*. But Hu Qiaomu had protested against any discussion of a new industrial revolution or of a postindustrial society because this called into question orthodox views on the proletarian socialist revolution as the final act of history and on the preeminent political role of the proletariat and its vanguard, the Communist party. Hu insisted on very small, restricted audiences for Toffler's lectures in order to limit the influence of Toffler's claim as a lapsed Marxist that both socialism and capitalism were outmoded. In mid-1983, the translations of his book were taken off the shelves.

Huan Xiang, in an effort to break through such strictures in the oppressive atmosphere of mid-1983, sent the translations and analyses of these researchers up the line to Hu and Zhao; they in turn requested more information. Both Huan's work and Zhao's October 1983 instructions made use of this material, thus giving the authors immunity from political attack. In early November, Hu Yaobang wrote a letter endorsing Zhao's October instructions and quite pointedly said:

> An ever increasing number of our cadre are earnestly studying new, modern science and trying to apply it to solve China's current problems. This is very encouraging news. However, we must seriously note that at the present moment more leading cadre, particularly responsible cadre in the economic field, basically take little interest in modern science. Some of them, posing as experts, pay no attention to the new developments in the world. Some even regard the new achievements made by mankind in our time as heresy and capitalist sugar-coated bullets. In educating cadre in the economic field, whether the main task is to struggle against ignorance or so-called liberalization is a question worth seriously considering.[25]

These directives by Hu and Zhao prompted a series of special policy research meetings on the subject, one at the end of October, one in November, and one in April 1984.

Hu and Zhao may have focused particularly on third-wave themes as part of their preparations for planned visits to Japan and the United States. Their exposure to the accomplishments of advanced capitalism during these visits and the plans for President Ronald Reagan's return visit in April 1984 in turn may have fortified the leadership's resolve to give priority to science and technology despite ideological considerations. In January, immediately upon return from the United States, Zhao visited a Shanghai exhibit on microelectronic technology. In February, Deng Xiaoping gave his all-important endorsement to a new policy and propaganda focus on the technological revolution when he and Wang Zhen, a venerable military figure on the Politburo who had helped launch the campaign against spiritual pollution, visited the same exhibit and stressed China's growing need for advanced technology. Shortly thereafter, two other conservative party elders, Chen Yun and Peng Zhen, gave their blessing as well. These developments signaled both Deng's support for Hu and Zhao and the willingness of the elders to tolerate heterodoxy in the name of technological progress.

Shift in Propaganda

The propaganda apparatus dropped its diatribes against spiritual pollution and geared up for a mass campaign to spread awareness of the technological revolution that quickly drowned out more conservative themes. The press was flooded with articles popularizing the computer, and a series of workshops on the technological revolution between March and October 1984 were attended by more than two thousand top party and government officials. Among them were members of the Politburo and the Secretariat and top military officials. Speakers introduced their illustrious audiences to a basic description of the technological revolution, trends in specific areas such as microelectronics and biotechnology, and ideas on how to make use of modern management principles such as systems engineering. The speakers also discussed new strategic problems—for example, how to coordinate development of China's economy, technology, and society as well as to adopt and develop in China the new field of studies that overlapped the distinction between natural and social sciences (the science of sciences or the comprehensive study of science and technology).[26]

The effect of the instructions by Zhao and Hu and of these workshops was apparently extensive. Zhang Jingfu, a state councillor and minister of the economic commission, reported that Zhao's directive had prompted a change in the 6th FYP such that three thousand items of advanced technology would be imported by the end of 1985 (compared with only a few hundred items in 1982 and 1983).[27] Zhang and other reform officials liberally cited Toffler and other futurists in their speeches. Industrial and commercial banking cadre began work on a multilevel bank computer system plan; the ministry of chemical engineering imported 146 microcomputers; and the drafting committee in the planning commission began to gear the 7th FYP draft to the demands of the new technological revolution, especially in the areas of technical transformation and product development. In June 1984, the State Council began sending the managers of China's three thousand largest state enterprises to special computer familiarization courses, and there was a plan to set up twenty training centers around the country. By July, the Central Party School was holding meetings on how to restructure high-level cadre education to "face the world and the new technological revolution."

During this flurry of activity, one emerging theme—the potential for China to industrialize quickly through adoption of high technology— smacked of the old utopian hopes of finding a shortcut to catch up with the West. Fang Yi, the Politburo member responsible for science and technology, in introductory remarks to the lecture series, for example, urged that "we must seize the opportunity offered by the new world-wide technological revolution; only thus will it be possible for us to skip certain stages and quickly achieve our strategic objective by making use of new technological results."[28] Articles such as Huan Xiang's spoke of a "window of opportunity" that was open to China but that might close in the future, thus leaving China forever lagging behind. In the spring of 1984, a Chinese economic official visited Toffler in New York to discuss whether and how China could use advanced technology to skip or speed up stages of development.[29]

This new version of the old theme of skipping stages of development derived from Toffler's argument that the information societies of the future would have some characteristics of preindustrial society and that developing countries, by taking advantage of modern technology, could combine the best elements of agrarian society (such as a strong community life) and postindustrial society (advanced technology) and avoid the worst of the industrial revolution. In particular, the Chinese were interested in the potential for using new technology to develop production and jobs in the countryside and avoiding one of their worst nightmares—massive urban migration and slummization of China's already overcrowded cities.

Clearly, the new technological revolution was an idea whose time had come in China, for both intellectual and political reasons. The "third wave" became a powerful emotive symbol of a large groundswell of support for reform. The lessons of the ideological conflict in 1983–1984 were clear: Orthodoxy was more easily challenged in the name of science than in the name of humanism or democracy. Political theorists such as Su Shaozhi, who strongly supported these latter themes, readily integrated them into writings focused on the importance of science, education, and rationalist development planning.[30]

Attacks on reform were thus overcome by leaders and intellectuals committed to bringing China into the twentieth century before it became the twenty-first. The growing support base Zhao Ziyang had built within the economic and scientific systems of the bureaucracy, buttressed by the new research institutions serving them, was able to counter the bastions of orthodoxy in the party and military propaganda/personnel systems with which Hu Yaobang was struggling. Out of the victory came political gains for both Hu and Zhao. Hu's chief deputy in the Secretariat, Hu Qili, replaced Deng Liqun as head of the propaganda and ideology leading group, and in mid-1984 a new campaign began to "thoroughly repudiate the Cultural Revolution." Zhao was assured dominance in economic and science and technology work for the first time and also obtained new indirect influence over policy in other arenas as the imperatives of economic reform were given priority over all other concerns.

New Policy Guidelines

Following the 12th Party Congress of September 1982, Deng Xiaoping had attempted to enter semiretirement; he had left more and more decisionmaking to Hu and Zhao. But as a result of the political confrontation between the two men and the conservatives in late 1983, Deng Xiaoping reasserted his authority as paramount arbiter. Throughout 1984, he personally intervened repeatedly, using the new sense of urgency regarding international competition to cut through the fog of ideological questioning that threatened to obscure his program. Deng's strategy was to play his long suit—his role as senior statesman and the evidence of international approval of his program. When speaking to a succession of distinguished foreign visitors throughout the year, Deng introduced a new informal ideology of long-term "peaceful coexistence" as the pragmatic umbrella for reform. In essence, he was repudiating Mao Zedong's philosophy of struggle at home and abroad. Without overtly abandoning the long-term goal of communism, Deng nevertheless projected a lengthy period of domestic and international peaceful cooperation between socialism and capitalism, plan and market, Communist and non-Communist for the sake of Chinese modernization. Deng insisted that ideology and policy alike be judged by a single utilitarian criterion: Would it serve the cause of economic development?

Deng set forth new general guidelines in a series of cumulative speeches and remarks in 1984; their importance as a new legitimating policy framework was made evident in December, when they were published together as a volume, *Build Socialism with Chinese Char-*

acteristics.[31] Regarding domestic policy, Deng introduced a second-stage goal beyond that of quadrupling GNP per capita by the year 2000. He proposed that China spend the first thirty to fifty years of the next century developing its economy so as to approach (not surpass) the level of the advanced countries. Regarding reunification, Deng echoed this extended time frame for modernization by offering Hong Kong at least fifty years of autonomy beyond the 1997 date of its reversion to the mainland and by emphasizing that gradual peaceful reunification and autonomy were the only possible solutions to the Taiwan problem as well. His new reunification policy of "one nation, two systems" mirrored the concept of peaceful coexistence. Regarding foreign affairs, Deng sought to create an international framework that would support his other policies. He endorsed the aim of global détente, which for decades had been repudiated by Chinese leaders as merely a cover for superpower domination, and gave priority in China's diplomacy to problems of peace in East-West relations and development in North-South relations. This accompanied efforts to move Chinese-American relations to a higher level of cooperation and open up new possibilities for Sino-Soviet détente.

Deng's immediate aim was to shape the outcome of a party plenum scheduled for late 1984, which was to endorse a blueprint for economic reform. His intermediate aim was to influence the drafting of the 7th FYP and the twenty-year outline plan. His long-term aim was to use these planning documents as the economic basis of the political program for Deng's successors and thereby provide staying power for his vision of China's future.

Hu Yaobang and Zhao Ziyang worked in tandem to flesh out Deng's general framework in programmatic reform documents and specific concrete policies. In order to bypass the obstructionist politics of the elders in the Politburo, their strategy was twofold. First, they drafted policy documents and vetted them at lower levels before presenting them for review by the Politburo, thus in effect presenting a fait accompli. Second, they organized widespread implementation of reform experiments in the localities to give credence to the success of reform and create lower-level support for reform.

The complex linkage between China's domestic and international concerns was evident in the policy breakthroughs of 1984. Aims to create a new spurt of development and reform by 1990 required immense resources marshalled more effectively at home and abroad. Meanwhile, the good prospects for technology transfer from the United States, détente with the Soviet Union and Eastern Europe, continued prosperity in Hong Kong, and incipient indirect trade with Taiwan, combined with bumper harvests and a generally good economic picture at home, gave Chinese leaders confidence to try new measures.

Opening the Coast

Deng Xiaoping chose to intervene in the political dispute raging in late 1983 by going to the heart of the debate—whether to continue and expand the SEZ policy. Here, the issues of domestic systemic reform, reunification, and the open foreign policy were conjoined. He pushed through a policy decision to open coastal cities to direct foreign investment and trade; this breakthrough was rightly described by the Chinese press as a strategic decision that marked a turning point in the reform program. In the short space of one year following his intervention in January 1984, the concept of a city-centered regional approach to development, with a priority on developing the east coast first and then moving gradually westward, was drafted into policies, which then gave a major impetus to urban reform as a whole.

This second wave of reform was a response to the concrete interests of the localities; by offering them greater control over their resources, the central reformers strengthened their base of political support. Many localities in late 1983 had been lobbying for their own special economic zones, and according to insider stories in the Hong Kong press, Deng Xiaoping himself wanted to open more than a dozen new zones and allow them considerable leeway in experimenting with capitalist methods. He endorsed reformist conceptions of the SEZs not merely as local export processing zones, to be quarantined from the rest of the economy, but as windows on the world for all of China. They could be used to introduce to the interior foreign knowledge and management skills as well as technology, while enhancing China's influence in Hong Kong, Taiwan and abroad.[32]

Deng visited the SEZs as well as Shanghai from late January through mid-February 1984 and gave them his personal blessing. In Shenzhen, he wrote the inscription, "The development and experience of the Shenzhen SEZ prove the correctness of our policy to establish special economic zones." He especially praised the Shekou industrial zone and endorsed its controversial slogan, "Time is money; efficiency is life." In Zhuhai, he wrote, "The Zhuhai SEZ is a success." In Xiamen, the newest zone, he equivocated a bit regarding its success thus far: "Run the SEZs with better and faster results." But he also resolved a dispute among local and central officials in favor of those who wanted to expand the Xiamen zone to include the whole island; he recommended the gradual introduction of free port policies.[33]

Upon return from the south, Deng called a high-level meeting to recommend the creation of a number of open cities along the coast, specifically mentioning Dalian and Qingdao. (That is, they would be opened to a limited amount of direct foreign investment, allowed to offer special tax and other arrangements to attract foreign investors, and permitted to retain some of their foreign exchange profits.) Officials scrambled to clarify and act upon this unexpected pronouncement by Deng. A forum was convened by the State Council and Secretariat, attended by officials from the SEZs, localities, and economic departments, to recommend the specific open cities and their governing policies. At the beginning of the meeting, only five cities were assured of inclusion on the list—the two provincial-level cities of Tianjin and Shanghai, along with Guangzhou, Dalian, and Qingdao. After all the lobbying was done, however, the number of cities had grown to fourteen, including the five earliest treaty ports of the nineteenth century, and the Politburo endorsed the outcome reportedly only after "heated discussion."[34]

This decision only encouraged massive lobbying from the excluded cities and provinces, including those inland that feared they would be left far behind. By August 1984, thirty cities had been given various degrees of expanded authority over investment decisions and use of foreign exchange, although their privileges fell short of those enjoyed by the SEZs. The thirty cities included twenty-four inland cities and almost all provincial capitals. The reform commission also added more cities to the small select list of those that were listed under the national rather than provincial plans and were permitted to experiment with domestic economic reforms, such as in taxation or commercialization of housing.[35]

In the fall of 1984, Zhao Ziyang made several lengthy visits along the coast from Liaoning in the north to Shanghai and south. In Shenzhen, he introduced a new and radical concept for the SEZ development strategy that complemented and expanded Deng's window analogy. They would become two-way fans radiating both outwardly and inwardly. Whereas the zones were supposed to have been largely quarantined from inland areas, seeking foreign investment and technology for their own use and often processing imports for reexport, they had in fact already begun to absorb domestic investment from other regions and develop domestic products from all of China for export.[36] They were now also to sell products on the domestic market, transfer technology, and introduce management experience inland. Inland provinces quickly moved to set up representative offices in the SEZs. These links to the interior were partly an effort to salvage some of the idle industrial capacity of the third front.

Zhao for the first time also endorsed the idea of eventually opening the whole coast by forming much larger open zones around the three deltas of the Pearl, Yangzi, and Min rivers and the two northern peninsulas, Liaodong and Jiaodong. In late January 1985, at a national conference on the open regions, the delta zones were formally approved.[37] Thereafter, a media blitz touted the virtues of the Shenzhen model for the rest of the nation.

The new coastal development strategy appeared to be inspired by the Japanese model and reflected new attention to the fact that Japan was the only developing nation that had managed to catch up with the developed world. Hu Yaobang and many young researchers had found much food for thought in reading *Japan's Decisive Century: 1867-1967*, by former prime minister Shigeru Yoshida, which stressed the importance of welcoming and absorbing Western technology, knowledge and culture.[38] In Deng Xiaoping's comments to high-level leaders upon return from the south early in 1984, he recalled advice he had been given while visiting Japan in 1978. To modernize, China ought to develop energy resources and then transportation, communications, and information while encouraging high wages and high consumption. Although Deng stated that China was not in a position to adopt the latter suggestion as national policy, he implied that the coast was an exception—an increase in income there could lead to higher consumption. "Since conditions for the country as a whole are not ripe, we can have some areas become rich first. Egalitarianism will not work." For this reason, Deng emphasized the importance of opening Dalian and Qingdao, which were intended to orient the development of the whole northeast to Japanese resources and trade.[39]

Readjustments in Foreign Policy

A major focus of Deng Xiaoping's initiatives in 1984 was the fine-tuning of China's foreign policy to better serve the development program. Deng sought a more creative approach to the management of foreign relations, particularly with the superpowers. The earlier exploration in economic theory now surfaced in theories of international relations. Gradually, the foreign policy stance of strategic independence proclaimed in 1982 was refined to encompass the realities of international economic interdependence.

In 1984, Deng was trying to correct the drift in Chinese foreign policy evident since 1982. China's retreat from a proto-alliance with the United States and its initiation of contacts with the USSR had been paying fairly low dividends. Despite successful negotiation of the August 1982 communiqué reaffirming the basic principles of U.S.-Chinese relations, there was a frost in the air. The United States was aggravated by renewed Chinese charges of U.S. "hegemonism" and by the PRC's oversensitivity to a series of bilateral issues. In January 1983, the United States imposed restrictions on textile imports from China, to which China responded with a ban on imports of U.S. cotton and other products. Shortly after Secretary of State George Shultz's disappointing first visit to China in February, the Reagan administration began stressing the central importance of Japan to the United States and depicted China as a regional actor, thereby implicitly playing down its global role. Shultz also showed a lack of concern about the warming trend in Sino-Soviet relations.[40]

Improvements in relations with Moscow, meanwhile, had been glacial in pace. Rounds of political consultations, resumed in October 1982, had produced few results, in part because of Soviet preoccupation with its series of successions to General-Secretary Leonid Brezhnev; the Soviet Union had begun to deploy SS-20 medium-range missles in its Asian region, which alarmed both China and Japan.[41]

There were pressures within the Chinese leadership to adopt a policy of equidistance from the superpowers. Many veterans in military and diplomatic circles retained a traditional suspicion of and hostility toward both superpowers and sought to use each relationship tactically against the other. Chen Yun and his supporters, however, saw advantages to lowering Sino-Soviet tensions to keep the military budget low and make gains in terms of trade and technology. They also wanted to rebuild China's ties with the socialist world as a matter of legitimacy. Both goals would require distance from the United States. Civilian and military reformers, on the other hand, most notably Deng Xiaoping, argued that improving Sino-U.S. relations was necessary for both security and development purposes and that Sino-Soviet détente must be managed carefully so as not to jeopardize these ties.[42]

Beijing's policy since 1982 had been to avoid total equidistance but to pursue a balancing strategy to maximize China's flexibility and keep pressure on Washington to address the Taiwan "problem" and on Moscow to remove the "three obstacles" to normal relations (Soviet forces on the border, presence in Afghanistan, and support of Vietnam's occupation of Cambodia). The one to three ratio of concerns implicitly justified closer Sino-U.S. ties. This continued lean to the West was exemplified in Zhao Ziyang's denial of an equidistant policy on the eve of his visit to Washington in January 1984. He went on to say: "We are willing to establish a steady and lasting relationship with the United States. We are willing to conduct a dialogue with the Soviet Union and normalize relations."[43]

During the summer and fall of 1983, the United States relented in the stalemate over trade and technology transfer, and the PRC revived the military exchange relationship.[44] Secretary of Defense Caspar Weinberger visited China in September; Defense Minister Zhang Aiping made a return visit the next spring. Several teams of Chinese military experts made low-profile visits to the United States to explore the possibilities for military trade and assistance. The exchange of visits between Premier Zhao and President Reagan in early 1984 cemented the Sino-U.S. reconciliation, opened the way to an intimate partnership, and gave China new diplomatic strength and flexibility to deal with whatever leadership emerged in Moscow.

These developments helped dissolve some of the ideological strictures on Chinese foreign policy. Several concepts seemed out of date and unproductive: neo-Maoist assertions that China should align with the Third World to weaken the superpowers; antihegemonism premised on the Leninist and Stalinist concept of a global political-military struggle between socialism and capitalism; and the traditional view that China had no permanent friends, only permanent danger and temporary and untrustworthy allies. A foreign policy premised on struggle rather than cooperation did not position China to take full advantage of its international opportunities and kept Chinese diplomacy on the defensive.

Interdependence and Multipolarity

On 22 February 1984, shortly after Deng returned to Beijing from his southern trip and two days before he recommended the open city policy, he met with former U.S. national security adviser Zbigniew Brzezinski for a tour d'horizon of global trends. In this conversation, Deng revealed a desire for a more creative diplomacy that would actively serve China's development program. His comments reflected and served to legitimize new thinking by Chinese specialists about international trends and about China's proper approach to the outside world. Internal discussions had long been hindered by Leninist dogma regarding the nature of imperialism and the inevitability of war between the two polarized camps of imperialism and socialism.

But Deng now exuded a new sense of urgency about China's need for a peaceful environment for development and for a peaceful accommodation with Taiwan, Hong Kong, and Macao. He set forth a new one nation, two systems approach to reunification and then linked it to larger global issues by saying:

> Over the years, I have considered how disputes could be solved by peaceful means, rather than by war. . . . If opposing sides are locked in

> stalemate, sooner or later they will come to conflict. . . . [Peaceful coexistence] can help stabilize the situation, and for a long time too, and is harmful to neither side. . . . I have also considered the possibility of resolving certain territorial disputes by having the countries concerned jointly develop the disputed areas before discussing the question of sovereignty. New approaches should be sought to solve such problems according to realities. . . . We must rack our brains to find ways to stabilize the world situation.[45]

Deng's comments, which supported the view that war was neither inevitable nor desirable, were fleshed out further by Zhao Ziyang at the National People's Congress in May, at which he first set forth global détente as an important national goal. In May, Deng further expanded his views on peace and development as the focus of Chinese foreign policy.[46]

Reformers used the thirtieth anniversary in July 1984 of the origin of the "five principles of peaceful coexistence"—respect for sovereignty and territorial integrity, noninterference in internal affairs, equality, mutual benefit, and peaceful coexistence—to revamp China's foreign policy priorities along these new lines. (The principles had been formulated by Zhou Enlai and Nehru.) A speech by Premier Zhao Ziyang and a speech and an article in *Renmin ribao* by senior national security advisor Huan Xiang emphasized peace and cooperation with all countries and revealed how far some leaders and advisers had advanced in rehabilitating old concepts of competitive coexistence and accepting new principles of interdependence.[47]

Huan Xiang and others still active as advisers had been actively involved in formulating the original coexistence principles for Zhou Enlai's visit to Bandung in 1954 and in trying (unsuccessfully) to revive them in the early 1960s. Now for the first time since the 1950s, the realistic views held by policy researchers for decades regarding the advantages of friendly neutrality for China were showing up in the policy realm.[48]

This time, however, neutrality was refined to include concepts of interdependence. Huan, in *Renmin ribao,* gave full credit to the coexistence principles of the 1950s, which stressed competition between socialist and capitalist countries, for serving as a weapon against superpower dominance in the cold war era. He called for a redefinition of these principles, however, to suit a new era with a greater variety of social forms but only one world market and interdependence among all nations. Zhao Ziyang in his speech emphasized the need for all countries to build mutual confidence and pursue friendly cooperation, not merely competition, for the sake of co-prosperity.

Other major speeches and articles during the anniversary celebrations took a more traditional approach to the concept and context of coexistence, thereby suggesting a lack of leadership consensus. President Li Xiannian implicitly countered Zhao's focus on peace and mutual prosperity when he told a visitor that the basic guideline of China's foreign policy was independence. As one diplomat, tutored by Zhou Enlai during the Bandung era, later explained it privately, the main intent of the celebration was to reassert the preeminence of national interest over ideology in determining foreign policy. In his view, China's old policy of self-reliance—properly defined to exclude total self-sufficiency—was still compatible with this approach. As he put it, China still could not trust the superpowers—"can a tiger change its stripes?" Perhaps the developed nations were turning to tactics of peaceful cooperation and assistance to the Third World, but only because they recognized they must do so in order to maintain a favorable balance of power.[49]

Despite such resistance, there were intellectual forces pressing against the forbidden zones of ideology. Area specialists had reached more realistic conclusions about the nature and relative strength of the U.S. and Soviet socioeconomic systems. The work of economists and younger researchers, void of the old dogmatic biases, kept pushing forward the frontiers of research. The more influential older advisers such as Huan Xiang then played a key role in protecting them and repackaging their views in ways more understandable and acceptable to officials of the older generation.

Huan and his associates at the social science academy seemed to play a unique role in taking the new thinking about global economics and the new technological revolution among economic advisers and science administrators to the rather insular foreign affairs community and in applying that thinking to international relations theory. An example of the more far-reaching analyses was a paper presented at a symposium in March 1984 by two young academy analysts who boldly posited a global trend toward economic specialization and interdependence, peace, and cosmopolitan culture and recommended that China join in wholeheartedly. Circulated internally in China, the paper sparked tremendous controversy.[50]

Huan Xiang shortly thereafter touched on some of the underlying ideological issues that had been debated by scholars in internal journals and meetings for years.[51] Huan blamed the Stalin-Mao dogma that every country must choose between two exclusive, competing international systems of socialism and capitalism for China's disastrous seclusion. He also questioned the orthodox Leninist view that Western capitalism was moribund and that capitalist countries in their death throes continually would spark new world wars out of competition for foreign markets. Citing the new technological revolution as evidence both of capitalism's resilience and its capacity for multilateral cooperation, Huan predicted that at least until the end of the century there would be a period of peace.

By limiting his discussion to the next several decades, Huan avoided addressing even more sensitive issues, such as whether the nuclear era had permanently changed the nature of war and peace and whether world communism would ever come onto the horizon. He presented what had become a politically convenient consensus view among disagreeing specialists—that from a long-term point of view, socialism would inevitably take the place of capitalism but that at present, capitalism and socialism could coexist for a fairly long period of time.

Throughout 1984, Huan Xiang further reconceptualized the global power equation in ways that challenged Leninist beliefs in a hostile, bipolar world and broke new ground by publicly and realistically discussing China's future capabilities and stance in the world. He sparked another major controversy in a report that boldly claimed that the development of global politics was primarily determined by a "great triangular relationship" (U.S.-USSR-PRC) and was secondarily determined in Asia by the relationships among China, the United States, the USSR, and Japan and in Europe by the relationships among the United States, USSR, Eastern Europe, and Western Europe.[52] This thesis overtly challenged the dogma that China by itself could not be called a great power because this might imply that China had hegemonistic ambitions in Asia.

Chinese officials had looked favorably on the prospect of a multipolar world since the early 1970s because China might gain flexibility and influence. But earlier foreign policies intended to foster multipolarity had always tied China's interests to those of other powers, whether the Third World in the early 1970s or the Third and Second Worlds as well as the United States in the late 1970s. Huan Xiang, on the other hand, predicted a trend whereby the two superpowers would gradually be dealing more as equals with three other strong, independent powers, one of which would be China.

My review of Huan Xiang's speeches and articles shows a major shift in his thinking in 1983–1984 that grew out of his immersion in writings about the new technological revolution. He developed a greater appreciation for how far behind the United States and its allies the Soviet Union, Eastern Europe, and other developing countries really were in all but purely military terms. He saw an opportunity for China to surpass other developing countries and become a power in its own right; this depended, however, on a decisive turning away from the Soviet model and on China's integration into the Western-dominated global economy, no matter how difficult that might be.[53]

Huan's advocacy of balance-of-power politics was hardly new or incompatible with more conventional thinking. Rather, his more complex conception of national strength, which gave greater weight to economic influence and scientific and technological strength and less weight to purely military power, was the new element. One impetus for the reconceptualization of power, of which Huan's thinking formed a part, was the emphasis the Nakasone and Reagan administrations placed on Asian-Pacific trends. Chinese leaders were struggling to define China's future role in a region that might grow in strategic and economic importance in the twenty-first century and that might therefore become the focus of superpower contention. At the National People's Congress in 1984, Zhao Ziyang gave new attention to Asia, stating that "China places special emphasis on developing relations with the Asia-Pacific region, to enhance the security and development of China and peace and stability in the region."[54] After Huan Xiang attended a conference on the Pacific region in Hawaii, he promoted a proliferation of research projects and discussion sessions to consider trends in Asia.[55]

Peaceful Reunification

Sino-U.K. negotiations over the future of Hong Kong were another impetus to new foreign policy thinking. Again, Huan Xiang, as a former ambassador to the United Kingdom, provided advice. Prior to preparations for Prime Minister Margaret Thatcher's visit to Beijing in late 1982, public Chinese statements had implied that the Hong Kong and Macao issues were expected to come onto the agenda only after progress was made toward reunification with Taiwan.[56] The British, however, were feeling pressure from Hong Kong interests to work out a resolution well before the 1997 date when, by treaty, the New Territories were due to revert to the mainland. Thatcher's visit, which prompted a harsh exchange of rhetoric on the issue of sovereignty, moved Hong Kong up the list of Chinese priorities.

Throughout 1983–1984, a flurry of intensive research, on-site observation, and rethinking about Hong Kong occurred among researchers and officials in China. The leadership quickly rejected two options—allowing British administration to continue beyond a nominal change of sovereignty in 1997 or giving Hong Kong de facto independence under PRC suzerainty—but the actual means of exercising Chinese sovereignty were still to be explored.

According to one urban planner, Hong Kong had a shock effect on influential mainland visitors. The dynamism of the island compared with dilapidated Shanghai stimulated thinking about the economic functions of China's cities; investigation into what made Hong Kong work and what was necessary to maintain its stability and prosperity broke through old habits of thought. In 1984, Hu Yaobang encouraged Dalian to become a "Hong Kong in the north," and Zhao Ziyang relaxed the central government's hold on Shanghai's finances in order to foster its development. The liberalization of SEZ policy and the opening of coastal cities and deltas to foreign investment were intended, in part, to create a socioeconomic bridge between the mainland system and those of Hong Kong and Taiwan. China had very immediate as well as long-term matters at stake—annual earnings from ties with Hong Kong were in the range of $7 billion.[57]

It was during the delicate period of final negotiations in 1984 that Deng spoke with a number of visitors about the one nation, two systems approach to the Hong Kong issue that promised fifty years of autonomy beyond 1997. He used the Hong Kong issue as a springboard to woo Taipei into contacts and to reassure both Hong Kong and foreign investors of the long-term nature of Chinese policy. In speaking to CEOs from dozens of the world's largest corporations, who were attending China's first symposium on foreign investment, Deng made it clear that the fifty years of postreversion autonomy for Hong Kong would coincide with a general open door approach and that the period was actually open-ended. "By then, prospects for changes in the policy will be even slimmer. . . . If [complete reunification, including Taiwan] cannot be accomplished in 100 years, it will be in 1000 years. As I see it, the only solution lies in the implementation of two systems in one country."[58]

This statement strongly implied that China would never use force to reassert sovereignty over Taiwan, a pledge the PRC had always refused to make. At the same time, Chinese leaders began to make the unprecedented suggestion that the United States could somehow be positively involved in fashioning a peaceful settlement with Taiwan, although they never spelled out how except to say that China would welcome U.S. pressure on Taipei's leaders, similar to British pressures on Hong Kong parties, to accept talks largely on China's terms. Ironically, to avoid such a role, Washington found itself using the former PRC argument that outside powers should not become involved in internal Chinese disputes.

Nonetheless, these shifts in Deng's thinking reflected a more flexible view of the exercise of national sovereignty in an interdependent world. In celebration of National Day in October 1984, the newly signed Hong Kong agreement—in which Hong Kong was promised a considerable degree of self-governance backed by law after 1997—was touted as a major triumph for world peace and a model for other international problems (including, by implication, the divided Koreas and Germanys) as well as for reunification with Taiwan.

Sino-Soviet Détente

In 1984–1985, after several years of watching, researching, and debating the possibilities, Chinese leaders extended foreign policy changes to relations with the USSR. In March 1982, as the Soviet succession got under way, Brezhnev gave a speech that mentioned China with a conciliatory attitude. This prompted Chinese leaders and researchers to consider the implications of possible future change in Soviet policy toward China. Thus, through the transition period to Yuri Andropov in November 1982, to Konstantin Chernenko in February 1984, and then Mikhail Gorbachev in March 1985, Chinese leaders had a strong incentive to keep the door open for eventual improvements, albeit in a manner that would strengthen rather than jeopardize their primary interest in expanding relations with the West and Japan.

Throughout this period, the question of how to deal with the Soviet Union took on a growing importance for China for several reasons. First, a general relaxation of both international and internal tensions was needed to shift attention and resources away from Mao's wartime communism toward civilian economic development; Sino-Soviet tensions were a major obstacle to such a trend.

Second, bilateral state trade on a barter basis could diversify economic relations and save valuable foreign exchange. China's new development strategy, which focused on regional specialization and the greater involvement of local governments in creating their own economic plans, encompassed the advantages of resuming once vital cross-border trade between China's northeast and Siberia. Improved relations with Moscow also were integral to China's hopes of increasing economic cooperation with Eastern Europe, which Moscow would monitor and control.

Third, Sino-Soviet relations affected the reform of the army. Since 1975, Deng had worked to restructure the command system, while improving the education and training of soldiers, in order to shift strategy from the use of massive conventional forces to the use of a modernized, upgraded, combined force.[59] Professionalization of the military leadership would take the army out of high-level politics while partial demobilization, retirements, and reduction of waste would allow cuts in the defense budget and the use of financial and other resources for civilian economic development. Such changes in the military, however, required a low-tension international environment.

In early 1984, having restabilized relations with the United States, China became the suitor in Sino-Soviet relations. Vice Premier and Politburo member Wan Li led an official delegation to attend Andropov's funeral; Soviet deputy prime minister Ivan Arkhipov was invited to visit China.[60] Chen Yun, who rarely met with foreigners, made public his interest in meeting with this old friend, who had been responsible for Soviet aid to China in the 1950s and had worked closely with China's economic leaders. This gave the invitation special symbolic value.

Once Chernenko took power in late February, however, the positive momentum came to a halt. The fourth round of consultations on normalization of relations, held in Moscow in March, achieved nothing. Arkhipov's visit was postponed indefinitely on the day before his scheduled arrival in May, and speculation about the reasons focused on Soviet pique at the warm welcome given President Reagan and/or the Chinese shelling of Vietnamese border forces, both in April. In any event, the new Soviet leadership did not seem committed to serious pursuit of normalization of Sino-Soviet relations. Nevertheless, the Chinese took the initiative to show their continued interest in dialogue; Vice Foreign Minister Qian Qichen embarked on a hastily planned goodwill visit to Eastern Europe and the USSR. In September, at the U.N., the foreign ministers of the two sides met for the first time in decades, and the Chinese urged the Soviets to reschedule Arkhipov's visit.

In October and November 1984, to underscore his intention to improve Sino-Soviet relations, at least in the economic sphere, Deng proclaimed that China's opening to the outside did not extend solely to the developed countries of the West, although they constituted China's chief source of foreign funds and technology, but also to developing countries, the Soviet Union, and Eastern Europe. He endorsed the pursuit of commercial transactions, technology exchange, and joint ventures, specifically with regard to the 156 projects developed with Soviet help during the 1950s.[61]

Finally, in December 1984, the Soviet deputy prime minister arrived in Beijing and met with Chen Yun, Peng Zhen, Zhao Ziyang, and Yao Yilin. Officials signed a number of bilateral economic and scientific agreements, including a trade pact covering the 7th FYP period. A joint commission on economic and technological cooperation was organized, and the number of cross-border posts opened for trade and family visits in late 1983 was expanded. Regional planning in the northeast was refocused to encompass stepped up trade with the Soviet Union. Reconstruction and completion of the northern Xinjiang railway, left unfinished when the Sino-Soviet split occurred, was included in the 7th FYP budget. When completed, this railway will tie the Western European coast to the east China coast.[62]

The close link among the new propeace foreign policy, economic development, and Sino-Soviet détente was captured in an 8 October 1985 Hong Kong press report of a conversation between the two military commanders whose troops originally took over Xinjiang in 1949 and who later served as leaders of the province. When they were laying the foundation stone for the new railway link in 1985, one jokingly asked the other, "Are you not afraid that it will be easier for the Soviet Union to invade our country?" The answer was negative.[63] According to the report, the Soviets had requested that the line be completed, and after considering the matter and realizing that it would not cause a political or military threat to China, Chinese leaders had agreed.

In the course of 1984, Deng's views were presented formally as a foreign policy of "peace and development." The policy did not overtly abandon former themes of Third World alignment, independence, and opposition to hegemonism, but it did place them in a new light, as means to an end. Whereas Mao Zedong's Third World alignment had aimed at weakening the superpowers and restructuring the global system, Deng's nonalignment and rejection of power politics were aimed at enhancing the stability of the international system.

Blueprint for Reform

Deng Xiaoping's steady policy interventions in 1984 were intended to break through the ideological and political wrangling that had delayed the next stage of rural reforms and the launching of urban reforms. Deng and his supporters were aiming for a major political victory at the 3rd Plenum scheduled for October 1984, whose importance also contained symbolic aspects: The plenum would mirror the 3rd Plenum (1978) when Deng gained preeminence; and 1 October would be the thirty-fifth anniversary of the founding of the PRC. Deng's accomplishments in 1984—from the visit of President Reagan to the signing of the Hong Kong agreement—all gave him added political capital. This momentum helped Deng and his protégés put reformist pressure on the contentious process of drafting a blueprint (spelled out in three party documents) for future integrated reforms in management of the economic, science and technology, and education sectors. This momentum also enhanced the chances for major personnel and organizational changes that would benefit the reformers.

The party's official economic reform decision, "Decision of the Central Committee of the Chinese Communist Party on Reform of the

Economic Structure," adopted at the 3rd Plenum in October 1984, explicitly stated that the purpose of the plenum was to unify thinking and expand consensus about urban reform, just as the historic 3rd Plenum of 1978 had launched rural reform and the open door policy.[64] The document emphasized the importance of commercializing the urban economy to compete in the global economy, to handle expanded rural production, and to meet the needs of rural consumers.

The centerpiece of the document was its proposal that China construct a "planned commodity economy based on public ownership. . . . The full development of a commodity economy is an indispensable stage in the growth of society and a prerequisite for our economic modernization." This new formulation broke through the ideological barrier that had constrained the reforms for so long—endless debate about whether a socialist society could or should allow commodity exchange and whether a planned economy should make use of market regulation. The document's authors avoided the buzzwords "market economy" or "mixed economy"; this avoidance reflected the hard-fought and carefully crafted nature of the compromise. Apologists for the document went to considerable lengths to explain to the still unconvinced that a commodity economy was not the same as capitalism, the essence of which was private ownership, not markets.[65]

The decision to commercialize the urban economy was sound, claimed the document, because it was based on a positive assessment of the current political and economic situation and of the successful experience thus far in rural structural reform. Expectations were for a good harvest, and the 6th FYP targets had just been fulfilled two years ahead of time, a fact to which Deng and other leaders often referred with pride in 1984.[66]

At the same time, the economic reform decision also solidified the legitimacy of the rural reforms, thus officially ending disputes over whether the contract responsibility system (an admittedly effective means of increasing output) was properly socialist. The plenum called for increased specialization and large-scale commodity production in the rural economy.

The economic reform decision also defended the controversial concepts of international interdependence, domestic competition, inequalities of income, and expanded consumption by stating bluntly that "whether a reform facilitates the development of productive forces should be regarded as the most important criterion for assessing the success or failure of all reforms."

The economic reform decision document adopted in October was only one part of a broader reorientation of the Chinese management structure to improve methods of administrative control and to introduce new elements of market competition and regulation. The other two documents that constituted the new reform blueprint were officially endorsed in a March 1985 party decision on reforming the management of science and technology and in a May 1985 decision on reforming the management of education. The three documents provided a framework for new organizations and policies intended to foster integration of scientific and technical training and research and development with economic production. Taken together, these policy documents constituted a repudiation of the Soviet model and its variations that had been pursued for three decades. The Soviet-style compartmentalization and centralization of work in these arenas, disrupted by Maoist mass campaigns but rebuilt in the 1970s, had led to technological stagnation in the civilian economy. The new judgment that China must leave behind its own past models and concepts while avoiding the adoption as a whole of any particular contemporary foreign model reflected the recommendations reached by 1984 in the development strategy seminar and in a revised target model study.[67]

The Drafting Process

Key reform theorists had long been convinced that China should avoid ad hoc reformism and should spend several years carefully planning a package of reforms to be introduced in a sequenced and coordinated manner. But as of 1984, these desires had been continually frustrated by serious disagreement, which resulted in ongoing experimentation. In August 1980 and in the summer of 1983, draft plans for introducing economic reform had been derailed by leadership conflict. Finally, in February 1984, following Deng's visit to the coast, a new drafting group under the supervision of a leading group headed by Hu and Zhao began constructing a general blueprint for reform intended for approval by the October plenum.

Input from specialists in quantitative modeling may have helped produce this decision to move ahead. The reform commission in 1983 had tasked the Beijing information and cybernetics research institute, founded by science commissioner Song Jian, to research the issues of subsidies, prices, and wages and to compare the advantages and disadvantages of one large adjustment versus several smaller, phased adjustments of the economy. Their conclusion, reported in August 1984, was that China was already capable of adjusting prices, wages, and subsidies. The institute recommended rapid adjustment beginning in 1985 instead of 1986 (with the next FYP). This evidence sounded scientific and no doubt gave reformers the edge.[68]

The drafting group's original intent was to provide in one document the guidelines for reforms in management of the economy, science, and education. This document's mutual policy design would enable the economic system to provide incentives for technological progress and the educational and scientific systems to serve the needs of economic development; these goals accorded with a request by Deng and Zhao for such a policy.[69] To this end, the drafting group reviewed regular local reports on the progress of the current FYP and then collected information on ongoing research projects by five hundred institutes affiliated with the nation's science, education, and industrial organizations. After the group came to some preliminary understanding of the issues, it held a national conference to discuss them as well as several small symposia of experts in all related fields to glean new ideas. A number of drafts for the reform decision were produced and discussed within the small circle of drafters and members of the leading group.

During these proceedings in early 1984, however, participants soon realized that the document was becoming too simple and general on key issues, and senior leaders decided to concentrate only on the economic issues prior to the party plenum in October and to draft separate documents on science and education thereafter.[70] This decision probably also reflected the high level of disagreement over basic economic reform policy. One foreign economist with many connections in the bureaucracy said that "there was blood all over the floor"; disagreement resulted in the patchwork character of the final compromise document.

There is some circumstantial evidence that the drafters of the 1984 economic reform decision attempted but failed to resolve several sensitive ideological disputes. Hungarian specialists visiting China in October 1983, in the midst of the campaign against spiritual pollution, were told that delay in creating the document was due partly to disagreement over what stage of political development China had reached. Critics of reform charged that expanding the nonstate sector would regress the economy to the presocialist era of the 1950s, which was characterized by a semicapitalist economy. Most reformers were not prepared to argue that China was not or should not be socialist, and they were hard put to defend expansion of the market in some other ideological framework.[71]

The temporary solution was to bypass such problems by stressing the distinctions between a capitalist economy and a commodity economy and by postponing a more thorough ideological discussion. Nevertheless, the bold endorsement of a commodity economy set a precedent for freer theoretical exploration by implying that Marx was wrong in suggesting that commodity markets and money exchange would cease to exist under communism. This willingness to challenge orthodoxy, which Yu Guangyuan and others openly praised, elicited much foreign speculation that China was going capitalist.

Science and Education Reform

Once the economic reform decision was approved by the party's Central Committee, documents on reforming the management of science and education to better serve economic development were created. One participant in the drafting emphasized that the three documents should be viewed as a "bird [economics] with two wings [science and education]."[72] The science document also represented an important effort to reorganize military science and technology research and development assets to help develop the civilian economy.

The same leading group that monitored the drafting of the economic reform decision document, which included senior leaders responsible for economics, science, and culture, continued to monitor the two drafting groups working on the new documents. The science drafting group was headed by Song Jian, newly promoted from deputy to full director of the science and technology commission, and the education drafting group was directed by the minister of education.[73]

In mid-November 1984, Hu Yaobang met with the leading group and discussed his initial design for the two documents. By May 1985, this group had met twice more with Hu or Zhao presiding to discuss various drafts. The two groups proceeded in ways similar to the earlier economic reform decision drafting group. Members collected information, made investigative trips, and held small symposia with central administrators, leaders, and Chinese and foreign experts. Both drafting groups sat in on each other's sessions so that the two documents were intimately related. After drafts were discussed and approved by the State Council and the Secretariat, they were circulated more widely for feedback from experts.

The main aim of the science document was to reorient research to production needs and then to get the results out of academic ivory towers and laboratories and into the factory. An equally important aim was to reduce the burden on the state for funding research and development. To that end, the document encouraged research institutes and production units to engage in cooperative work through contracts and scientists to engage in consulting and moonlighting. The document outlined a system for awarding research funds based on peer review that was modeled after the U.S. National Science Foundation and the document indicated that the personnel system would be overhauled to allow more labor mobility as well to grant respect and rewards to scientists. Research organs, both civilian and military, would be reorganized to serve better the technological upgrading of state enterprises in the basic industries and the creation of new industries based on new technologies, especially in microelectronics and information, biology, and new materials. (Basic scientific research was given short shrift.) At the same time, development of appropriate technologies for local economies and their transfer to local enterprises would take place. This document essentially called for a massive internal technology transfer program, "from the laboratory to production, from the coast to the interior, and from exclusive military use to joint military-civilian use."[74]

In early March 1985, the State Council held a national science and technology work conference to discuss both of the documents underway and to review the science document before it was submitted for comment to the science academy and party and government organs at all levels. At this meeting, Deng Xiaoping gave a two-part speech on management reform and on the importance of developing qualified professionals. He said, "We should truly solve some problems each year for the intellectuals. We should create an environment in which talented persons can display their gifts. . . . We should not stifle real talent just because talented people may not be versatile, or lack party membership, a good educational background, or qualifications and record of service."[75]

From March through May 1985 the education reform drafting group worked on a document to be submitted to the Politburo for discussion and final approval.[76] The aim of educational reform was to revive the role of universities in scientific research and to upgrade the quality of education. Press reports emphasized that top leaders were paying close attention to the problems of education but also revealed the difficulties they were having in determining how and where to commit scarce resources in order to foster the spread of research and to improve the quality and scope of education outside the small number of elite institutions.[77] Leaders and officials examined how to introduce mandatory national requirements for education given that it would continue to be locally funded and how to deal with the reality of regional disparities in resources. The leadership decided that requirements should be introduced gradually so that subsidizing poor regions for the sake of uniformity on the matter could be avoided. On the issue of funding, the leadership seemed to be passing the buck, an approach that would bring regular complaints from intellectuals and educators.[78]

The conference emphasized the need for a wholly new approach to education that would create the kind of flexible, independent-minded citizenry interested in lifelong learning and retraining that China would need in order to cope with the information revolution of the twenty-first century. There was lengthy discussion of how to revamp the curriculum to teach students creative thinking rather than blind obedience and rote learning. Hu Qili stressed the importance of changing traditional thinking, which scorned vocational and technical education in favor of a university degree. He also pointed out that to better match education with production required changes in the labor assignment system, particularly in the enrollment and postgraduate work of college students.

The reform decisions in education and science led immediately to changes in management as well as policy. Shortly after the conference, the education ministry was upgraded to a commission headed by Vice Premier Li Peng. Experiments were launched in key universities that allowed the president rather than the party secretary to take responsibility for personnel, administration, and academic affairs and to replace student subsidies with a system of tuition charges, competitive scholarships, and work-study grants designed to induce better student performance.[79]

The science and technology commission under Song Jian and his deputy, Wu Mingyu, immediately began to create a new science development strategy, which was later published as a white paper, as well as detailed and concrete science policies for a dozen economic sectors, which were later circulated internally as pamphlets known as blue books. All were to be used in the drafting of the 7th FYP.[80] The national research center for science and technology development (hereafter S&T development center), which Wu Mingyu supervised, gained much power and prestige because of its role in creating these documents.

Setting the Stage for Institutionalizing Reform

The accelerated opening of coastal China to foreign economic ties enhanced the support base for reform, and the three policy documents of 1984–1985 on economic, science, and education reform, despite flaws, provided the legitimacy and direction for transforming the basic Chinese political-economic system. The basic aim of the documents was twofold: to introduce more scientific and efficient means of central policy guidance and to allow greater financial and decisionmaking autonomy based on market indicators for units of production, teaching, and research. The exact balance to be struck between state authority structures and market dictates was to be explored experimentally.

The economic reform decision listed a number of specific policy measures that would naturally flow from the mandate to develop a planned commodity economy: enterprise autonomy and management reform through adoption of all advanced (including capitalist) management methods; a shift to indirect macroeconomic regulation through pricing, taxation, and credit policies; reform of the government planning apparatus and personnel system; new economic legislation; and contract leasing of state-owned enterprises. The reform document announced that a plan would be drawn up to establish the order of importance, urgency, and feasibility for the gradual introduction of comprehensive reforms. These reforms were to be basically accomplished during the period of the 7th FYP.

Deng Xiaoping wholeheartedly praised the reform decisions and their formulators, and he defended the new stage of reform in meetings with party and army veterans who feared China was abandoning socialism.[81] Deng's primary message was that it was time to let a new generation take the reins. That Deng was also giving the strongest possible mandate for drafting a 7th FYP that would introduce comprehensive urban reform was made evident later. A press article cited his comments to veterans and linked them directly with his injunction to Zhao and Vice Premier Tian Jiyun when he met with them to discuss the plan: "The purpose of the reform [in the next five years] is to lay down a foundation for steady development in the next 10 years and the following 50 years. Therefore we must carry on with the reform." And at another (unspecified) meeting, Deng said, "We have to seize this best opportunity for reform and persist in it; otherwise we would be hopeless in the next 10 years."[82] By building on the hard-won victory of late 1984 (despite economic problems that required a miniretrenchment in 1985), Hu Yaobang and Zhao Ziyang were able to make much progress during the next two years not just in enlarging policy and personnel gains but in strengthening institutions and procedures that provided the political base for the reform program.

Notes

1. Xinhua, 20 January 1983, in Foreign Broadcast Information Service China Daily Report [FBIS], 21 January 1983, pp. K1–2.

2. Xinhua, 13 March 1983, in FBIS, 14 March 1983, pp. K1–16.

3. For detailed analyses of this conflict, see Stuart R. Schram, *Ideology and Policy in China Since the Third Plenum, 1978–1984* (London: Contemporary China Institute, 1984), pp. 42–56; and David Kelly, ed. and trans., "Wang Ruoshui: Writings on Humanism, Alienation and Philosophy," *Chinese Studies in Philosophy* 16:3 (Spring 1985), pp. 71–88.

4. Deng Liqun in an interview with Stuart Schram, cited in Schram, ibid., p. 56.

5. For the titles and dates of key documents on rural policy, including sequential annual no. 1 central directives, see Robert F. Ash, "The Evolution of Agricultural Policy," *China Quarterly* 116 (December 1988), pp. 529–555.

6. Report on Zhu Muzhi's announcement, Xinhua, 1 June 1983, in FBIS, 3 June 1983, p. K16. Minister Zhu warned that, of course, profit-seeking should be second to education as a goal, and party leadership and socialism must be upheld. Chuang Ming, "Zhao Ziyang Receives Instructions in Time of Danger to Save a Desperate Situation," *Ching Pao* (Hong Kong) [Mirror] 2 (10 February 1987), pp. 26–29, in FBIS, 12 February 1987, p. K6, claimed that in 1983 Hu Yaobang put forward twenty-three proposals for political reform at a national congress of workers, but the leadership immediately rejected them. I have not been able to confirm this.

7. Interviews with officials and researchers, Shenyang and Dalian, May 1986.

8. George T. Crane, "China's Special Economic Zones: The Political Foundations of Economic Performance," (Ph.D. diss., University of Wisconsin, 1987).

9. Christopher M. Clarke, "Reorganization and Modernization in Post-Mao China," in John P. Hardt, ed., *China's Economy Looks Toward the Year 2000, vol. 1. The Four Modernizations: Selected Papers Submitted to the Joint Economic Committee, Congress of the United States* (Washington, D.C.: GPO, 21 May 1986), pp. 100–101. By the end of 1983, 35 prefectures had been abolished, 22 counties had been completely absorbed by cities, and 368 counties had been placed under the administration of nearby cities.

10. Shanghai radio broadcast, 18 August 1983, in FBIS, 29 August 1983, pp. 5–6. David Chu, in personal communication, mentioned to me the advice from the Japanese.

Xinhua, 16 June 1983, in FBIS, 17 June 1983, p. K5, revealed that the Shanghai region would include nine other cities (Suzhou, Wuxi, Changzhou, Nantong, Hangzhou, Jiaxing, Huzhou, Ningbo, and Shaoxing) and fifty-seven counties in Zhejiang and Jiangsu comprising 50 million people, one-fifth of China's industrial output, and one-quarter of its revenue. Cooperation was to begin with foreign trade ventures, and major regional joint projects were to include a nuclear power plant in Zhejiang, hydroelectric and thermal power plants to relieve the energy shortage, and new ports along the coast to relieve congestion in Shanghai harbor.

11. Shanghai radio broadcast, ibid. In status, these offices were directly under the State Council; they were managed by the State Council's foreign investment leading group, but the planning commission was also given some oversight responsibilities. In 1984, a more informal southwest China economic coordination organization was also approved for cooperation among Sichuan, Guizhou, Yunnan, Guangxi, and Chongqing. These budding economic regions had precedent in administrative regions in the 1960s and were rooted in China's natural geographic divisions, as G. William Skinner and his associates have shown during the years. Reformers may also have drawn on Soviet experience with regional zones, judging from an article on the latter by Li Jun of the reform commission, *Shijie jingji daobao* [World Economic Herald], 22 August 1983, p. 9, in FBIS, 8 September 1983, p. C2.

12. Report on Tong Dalin's idea, *Shijie jingji daobao*, 1 August 1983, p. 1, in FBIS, 24 August 1983, pp. K9–10.

13. Huan Xiang, "Try Hard to Catch up Rather than Trailing Behind," *Jingji ribao* [Economic Daily], 18 February 1984, pp. 1, 3, in FBIS, 29 February 1984, pp. K9–14.

14. Propaganda department circular, "The Practice of Communism and Education in Communist Ideology (study outline), revised," *Jiefang ribao* [Liberation Daily], 9 October 1983, p. 1, in FBIS, 21 October 1983, pp. K26–46. (The first draft version was circulated for discussion on 1 March.) Also see Secretariat policy research center and the propaganda department, "Views on Strengthening Propaganda and Education on Patriotism," Xinhua, 15 July 1983, in FBIS, 18 July 1983, pp. K1–9. These study materials, which were prepared by fall 1983, insisted in rather strident tones that the policy of reform and opening required increased efforts to maintain the purity of communism. Engels and Lenin were cited to reinforce the warning that "we must not seek temporary gain at the expense of our fundamental plans and must not sacrifice the future for the sake of the present."

The inspirations for this neo-Maoist approach were the pre-1957 works of Mao and the writings of Chen Yun, Liu Shaoqi, and Zhou Enlai as well as the biographies and reminiscences of party and army veterans recalling historic episodes of military heroism. Besides churning out books of this sort, which for the most part sat gathering dust in the bookstores, the propaganda apparatus tried several Lei Feng–type campaigns promoting model youth who sacrificed personal interests for the good of the collective. These, too, were largely met with a yawn.

15. Reformers had fought unsuccessfully to remove this language in 1982, arguing that it was ultraleftist given that China was merely in the stage of socialism, not communism. They worried that this language would invite more Maoist Communist winds and leaps forward in social and economic policy. In 1982, Hu Qiaomu mediated between the two groups by drafting compromise wording; but in 1983, he used the slogan against Hu Yaobang.

16. Texts of decision on party consolidation and communiqué adopted by the 2nd Plenum of the 12th Central Committee on 11 October 1983, Xinhua, 12 October 1983, in FBIS, 13 October 1983, pp. K2–17.

17. For an accurate and detailed analysis of the campaign, see Thomas B. Gold, "Just in Time! China Battles Spiritual Pollution on the Eve of 1984," *Asian Survey* 24:9 (September 1984), pp. 947–974.

18. For a discussion of the literary disputes, see D. E. Pollard, "The Controversy over Modernism, 1979–84," *China Quarterly* 104 (December 1985), pp. 641–656.

19. Commentator articles in *Renmin ribao,* [People's Daily], 23, 30, and 31 October, and 9, 12, and 16 November 1983; editorial, 8 November 1983.

20. Interviews with several graduate students, writers, and theoretical researchers involved, Washington, D.C., 1985–1987.

21. Deng Xiaoping, *Build Socialism With Chinese Characteristics* (Beijing: Foreign Languages Press, 1985), p. 22.

22. Zhao's directive was cited in Ma Hong, "Toward an Overall Development Strategy for the Economy, Society, Science, and Technology," *Jingji*

wenti, (Taiwan) [Economic Issues] 1 (25 January 1984), pp. 2–9, in Joint Publications Research Service China Report [JPRS CEA] 84–059, 19 July 1984, pp. 13–26. Ma's article originally was a speech given in October 1983, which was intended, in part, to publicize and explain Zhao's directive to continue research on the new technological revolution as the "major guiding ideology for the study and formulation of China's long-term development strategy." Ma called for "preventing" spiritual pollution in the course of such study, thereby suggesting that there was none at the moment.

Zhao's directive helped defend Su Shaozhi and the Marxism-Leninism institute, among others, from criticism in the ideological campaign, according to a researcher there, interview, Boston, May 1985. The institute's very existence had been a burr under the saddle of conservatives at the central party school both because the institute was a new source of competition for authority in the field and because it implied that Marxism was a field for critical research and revision, not a set of eternal truths needing only to be taught. Su's speech at the symposium on Marx in March 1983, "Developing Marxism under Contemporary Conditions," published in Su Shaozhi, Wu Dakun, Ru Xin, and Cheng Renqian, *Marxism in China* (London: Spokesman Press, 1983), pp. 13–52, cited Daniel Bell's theory of postindustrial society and the theories of Ilya Prigogene and Alvin Toffler as examples of ideas that must be addressed in updating Marxism.

23. Huan Xiang and Dai Lunzhang, "Unswervingly Implement the Open Door Policy—Learning from the *Selected Works of Deng Xiaoping,*" *Shijie jingji* [World Economics] 2 (10 February 1984), pp. 1–8, in FBIS, 5 April 1984, pp. 5–14. Interview with Huan Xiang, Washington, D.C., 1987, confirmed both the motive and impact of his article.

24. Information about criticism of researchers and Huan's role in protecting them comes from interviews with several of those who came under attack, Washington D.C., 1985–1987.

For an excellent study of the largely unknown academic debate in internal publications on the nature of capitalism and imperialism and the debate's important foreign policy implications, see David Shambaugh, "The Erosion of Ideology in Post-Mao China: The Chinese Polemics on Imperialism and State-Monopoly Capitalism, 1978–1984," (Ph.D. diss., University of Michigan, 1988), Chap. 3. I am grateful to David Shambaugh for sharing his ideas and material with me. Shambaugh indicated that economists usually went further in critiquing orthodox views than did political theorists or area specialists (p. 109). He also showed how more objective analysis of the role of the state in the West opened the door to new thinking about the role of the state in China (p. 111); this thinking blossomed in 1986.

25. This part of Hu Yaobang's letter was quoted in Xinhua, 24 June 1984, in FBIS, 25 June 1984, p. K17. The date of it was cited in Chen Tuguang, "A Big Event in Science in China 1984," *Kexuexue yu kexue jishu guangli* (Tianjin) [The Science of Sciences and the Management of Science and Technology] 12 (12 December 1984), pp. 13–15, in JPRS CST–85–021, 8 July 1985, pp. 8–12.

26. Information on the workshops is taken from Chen, ibid.; Xinhua, 9 March 1984, in FBIS, 12 March 1984, p. K14; and Xinhua, 24 June 1984, in JPRS CST-84-023, 13 August 1984, pp. 1-2. The China association of science and technology, whose president Zhou Peiyuan was once a student of Einstein, organized the lecturers under the supervision of Politburo member Fang Yi and Wang Zhaohua, deputy director of the party's organization (personnel) department. Attendees included Vice Premier Yao Yilin, Secretariat member Hao Jianxiu, and future defense minister Qin Jiwei. In Beijing, the twenty star speakers included Huan Xiang, famous U.S.-trained cybernetics specialist Qian Xuesen, his protégé Song Jian, and the key backers of the China 2000 study: Ma Hong, Wu Mingyu, and Lin Zixin (newly appointed secretary-general of the science commission).

In conjunction with the workshops, an exhibition of information technology opened at Beijing's Science Hall in October. Similar workshops were held in the provinces. Yunnan, for example, held a forum for seven hundred cadre on the use of the microcomputer.

27. Zhang Jingfu, "Create a New Situation in Importing Technology to Transform Existing Enterprises," *Guoji maoyi* [International Trade] 12 (27 December 1983), pp. 3-4.

28. Cited in Chen, "A Big Event."

29. Alvin Toffler, personal communication, 1986.

30. Su Shaozhi and Ding Xueliang, "Marx's Predictions on the Era of Information," *Renmin ribao*, 24 August 1984, p. 5, in FBIS, 14 September 1984, pp. K12-18. In an interview with Ding Xueliang, Boston, October 1985, he told me that the article was written and published to signal that no limits should be set on the discussion of the new technological revolution and its implications, a matter decided by Zhao Ziyang and Wan Li.

Toffler's ideas, which had been circulating in very restricted circles in the form of selected translations from his book and a videotape of a U.S. television special, became more widely known in 1984 when the video was shown to high-level officials in workshops and to diplomats overseas and when translations of the book were released to cadre bookstores. Soon a "third wave fever" engulfed China's intellectuals, especially the younger generation. Other futures studies, such as John Naisbitt's *Megatrends,* and Ilya Prigogine and Isabelle Stengers' *Order out of Chaos,* which had also been circulating earlier at higher levels, became the rage. According to Xinhua, 26 March 1987, in FBIS, 2 April 1987, p. K45, in 1986, three of the six bestsellers in China were Toffler's, Naisbitt's, and a book titled *Toward the Future,* with which I am not familiar.

31. Deng, *Build Socialism,* introduced his views on domestic development goals and international peace and development (comments to the president of Brazil on 29 May, pp. 28-29); and on reunification and peaceful approaches to international conflicts (to a delegation from the center for strategic and international studies of Georgetown University, headed by Zbigniew Brzezinski, on 22 February, pp. 23-24).

32. *Cheng Ming* (Hong Kong) [Contending] 80 (1 June 1984), pp. 26-28, in FBIS, 7 June 1984, pp. W2-5.

33. Interviews with officials in Shekou and Xiamen, November 1985; and Deng, *Build Socialism,* p. 27. The Shekou slogan was imported directly from Japan, but at least the first half of the slogan originated with Ben Franklin.

34. The decision process is discussed in Zeng Jianhui, "The Birth of an Important Decision—A New Step in Opening the Country to the World," *Liaowang* [Outlook] 24 (11 June 1984), in FBIS, 18 June 1984, pp. K1–7. Deng Xiaoping's 24 February remarks were later published in *Build Socialism,* pp. 25–27; interview with SEZ office deputy director Zhang Ge, Beijing, May 1986. The fourteen cities were Dalian, Qinhuangdao, Tianjin, Yantai, Qingdao, Lianyungang, Nantong, Shanghai, Ningbo, Wenzhou, Fuzhou, Guangzhou, Zhanjiang, and Beihai. The treaty ports were Shanghai, Guangzhou, Ningbo, Fuzhou, and Xiamen. Zhang stressed that several of those cities added to the list were very weak candidates because they lacked physical infrastructure, including Fuzhou, Lianyungang and Nantong. Deng (pp. 25–27) also stressed the importance of developing Hainan Island, which had been given some vaguely defined autonomy from Guangdong province in 1983, but no new decision was made.

35. For a discussion of the complex variations in the privileges granted these several categories of cities, see Madelyn C. Ross, "China's New and Old Investment Zones," *China Business Review* (November-December 1984), pp. 14–19. The cities used as laboratories for domestic reforms in enterprise autonomy, commerce, foreign trade, machine building, construction, taxation, and planning included Shashi, Changzhou, Chongqing, Wuhan, Nanjing, Shenyang, and Mudanjiang. Except for Nanjing, these cities were given separate provincial-level status in the national plan, with the later addition of Guangzhou, Xian, Harbin, and Ningbo. This allowed them to negotiate directly with foreign investors. Just as each regional economic zone was represented in the State Council by an office and the SEZs by their office, so an economic development coordination group was set up in the State Council for each of these cities, according to a Hangzhou radio broadcast, 22 June 1987, in FBIS, 24 June 1987, p. Kl5. Xinhua, 18 February 1989, in FBIS-CHI–89-034, 22 February 1989, p. 29, announced that Nanjing, Chengdu, and Changchun had also been granted provincial-level status.

By 1987, pilot projects of one sort or another were under way in seventy-two cities representing one-fourth of China's urban area in terms of population, assets, and revenue, according to deputy reform commisioner Gao Shangquan, Xinhua, 26 September 1987, in FBIS 87–189, 30 September 1987, pp. 31–32.

36. Zhongguo xinwen she [China News Service], 12 December 1984, in FBIS, 13 December 1984, p. P1; interviews with Shanghai officials, November 1985, and with the social science academy's quantitative economics institute director Jiang Yiwei, the originator of the "fan" concept, Beijing, November 1985. Barry Naughton, personal communication, August 1988, mentioned the domestic investment in existence by that time.

37. *South China Morning Post,* 4 January 1985, p. 1, in FBIS, 4 January 1985, p. W3, reported that Vice Premier Gu Mu spoke to the fourth national congress of the Chinese Writers' Association and announced the opening of

four large regions: Pearl and Yangzi river deltas plus the Liaodong and Jiaodong peninsulas. But this was not reported in the Chinese press, and a State Council forum that met from 25 to 31 January decided to open only three, the first two plus one in Fujian along the Min River, according to Xinhua, 31 January 1985, in FBIS, 4 February 1985, p. K7.

Central directive no. 1 of 1985 on rural policy (see Note 5) was related to the coastal strategy. It called for new types of trade-industry-agriculture enterprises in the new open deltas and peninsulas. In effect, the booming rural enterprises along the coast were being encouraged to get into exports. See the report on an exchange between Zhao Ziyang and a local Shandong peasant entrepreneur in spring 1988, in *Liaowang* 22 (30 May 1988), pp. 4–6, in FBIS-CHI–88–119, 21 June 1988, p. 31.

38. Interview with a well-connected researcher, Washington, D.C., 1985. Yoshida's book was published by Praeger, 1967.

39. Deng, *Build Socialism,* p. 27; also see Deng's conversation with Japanese business leader Toshio Doko, Xinhua, 27 September 1986, in FBIS, 29 September 1986, p. D4.

40. For an analysis at the time of Shultz's speech, see Richard Nations, "A Tilt Towards Tokyo: The Reagan Administration Charts a New Course for Asian Policy," *Far Eastern Economic Review,* 21 April 1983. A later, fuller formulation of his views is in George Shultz, "New Realities and New Ways of Thinking," *Foreign Affairs* 63:4 (Spring 1985). For a more detailed analysis of Sino-U.S. relations in the 1980s, see Carol Lee Hamrin and Jonathan D. Pollack, "The Origins and Evolution of the Sino-American Alignment," in Harry Harding, ed., *Patterns of Cooperation in the Foreign Relations of Modern China* (forthcoming).

An unpublished interview with Huan Xiang in June 1983, kindly shared with me by Banning Garrett and Bonnie Glaser, revealed his skepticism at the time regarding improvements in either Sino-U.S. relations or Sino-Soviet relations. He was concerned about the new level of U.S. support for Taiwan and also said, "The Reagan administration says it will not consider China as a global strategic power. But it thinks Japan is. . . . As for China, we must wait and see."

In interviews with several foreign affairs specialists, Washington, D.C., 1985–1987, they indicated that in their view, China's behavior in 1983 reflected its lack of understanding about how the U.S. governmental system works. Two episodes served as valuable lessons: the rejection of Deng Xiaoping's personal appeal to President Reagan for the return of Chinese tennis star Hu Na, who defected to the United States in early 1983, and China's successful resort to court over a suit involving Qing Dynasty railway bonds.

41. Michel Oksenberg, in personal communication, May 1988, pointed out that the SS-20 missile deployment began earlier, but the Chinese raised the issue publicly in the context of Sino-Soviet bilateral problems only in 1983. See a *Renmin ribao* commentary, 17 September 1983, in *Beijing Review,* 26 September 1983.

42. Throughout the years, public comments by Li Xiannian, former foreign minister Ji Pengfei, and other veterans have consistently evidenced a

negative attitude toward both superpowers that seemed a residue of the 1970s policies they helped to formulate. Carol Lee Hamrin, "China Reassesses the Superpowers," *Pacific Affairs* 56:2 (Summer 1983), pp. 209–231, spelled out the position of Deng and his supporters and reviewed much circumstantial evidence indicating that Chen Yun, along with advisers close to Zhou Enlai such as Wu Xiuquan, Wang Zhen, and Liao Chengzhi, had long advocated reducing tensions with Moscow for economic development purposes, including reducing the military drain on resources. The prominence of Chen Yun and his protégé Yao Yilin in the development of Sino-Soviet détente in recent years tends to confirm this view. Interviews with several Chinese foreign affairs specialists, Washington, D.C., and Beijing, 1985, revealed that Chen was the central proponent of a more equidistant policy in 1982–1983.

43. Zhao Ziyang, cited in Banning N. Garrett and Bonnie S. Glaser, *War and Peace: The Views from Moscow and Beijing* (Berkeley: University of California Institute of International Studies, 1984), p. 81. Huan Xiang may have played an important role in forging the compromise. In the 1950s and 1960s, he was part of the Zhou Enlai–Chen Yun group advocating neutrality (see notes 42 and 48). Judging from his articles in the Chinese press and comments to U.S. academics, in the early 1980s, Huan maintained that China should make greater efforts to "play the triangle" by seeking "leverage" with the United States through an opening to the USSR. In the crisis of 1981, others were swayed to this view, including Zhao Ziyang, according to a foreign affairs specialist who is certain that Zhao came away from his first meeting with President Reagan at Cancun, Mexico, in late 1981 having decided to use Sino-Soviet ties to force the United States to pay greater attention to China's interests. But beginning in 1983, Huan's writings and comments become more slanted toward the United States.

44. See discussion of the U.S. part of the decision in an article on the role of the National Security Council, *Washington Post,* 6 January 1986. The Reagan administration decided to place China in the "V" category (along with NATO, Japan, India, and Yugoslavia) for case-by-case access to sophisticated technology, including military technology. Commerce Secretary Malcolm Baldridge first informed the Chinese of this in May, with formalities following later in the year.

45. Deng, *Build Socialism,* pp. 23–24. At the time, very little of this conversation was reported, which suggests Deng's views had not been fully accepted by the leadership. The importance of this conversation was highlighted only later. Interviews, Washington, D.C., April 1987 and May 1988, with two Chinese officials involved in the briefings and discussions of the visit stressed its influence on Deng's subsequent pronouncement that peace and development were China's main goals.

For a report on the discussions among Brzezinski, other scholars from the Georgetown Center for Strategic and International Studies, and senior Chinese specialists Wang Bingnan, Wu Xiuquan, and Huan Xiang, see Yu Jiafu, "Brzezinski Discusses World Strategy with Chinese Scholars," *Liaowang* 10 (5 March 1984), pp. 6, 7, in FBIS, 2 April 1984, pp. B1–2.

Deng's offers of autonomy for Taiwan were first mentioned to a visitor, but in a much less systematic fashion, in June 1983. The February 1984 conversation has been referred to as the origin of Deng's one nation, two systems formula for reunification, which he then fleshed out in June. Deng, *Build Socialism,* pp. 30–32.

46. Zhao Ziyang, report to the National People's Congress, 15 May 1984, in FBIS, 1 June 1984, p. K4ff; Deng, *Build Socialism,* pp. 28–29. For years, China had assumed that any improvement in U.S.-Soviet relations would work against China's interests; détente had been depicted as a "sham," a coverup for actual escalation of the strategic arms race and regional competition. But Zhao now stated that "China wishes to see a lessening of tensions between the U.S. and the USSR."

47. See the text of Zhao's speech at a forum marking the thirtieth anniversary of the principles, 18 July 1984, Xinhua, 18 July 1984; and the text of Huan's article, "The Five Principles of Peaceful Coexistence Are Principles for World Peace and Development," *Renmin ribao,* 18 July 1984, p. 6, both in FBIS, 18 July 1984, pp. A1–6.

In an interview with Huan Xiang, Washington, D.C., 1987, he confirmed that his 1983 article had influenced Deng's new views and that Deng's comments about peace and development in early 1984 had prompted Huan's "trial balloon" that summer. Several related themes stressed in the talks between the Brzezinski delegation and Chinese foreign affairs specialists began to be reflected in the Chinese media: that many tensions in the world were unrelated to superpower tension; that chances for a major global conflict were decreasing; and that the United States had a growing edge over the Soviet Union in the application of microelectronic technology to defense.

48. Huan Xiang was personally involved with both previous coexistence policies, in 1954 as an adviser to Zhou Enlai who accompanied him to Bandung and in 1963–1968 as assistant foreign minister in charge of policy research. Proposals for change in foreign policy in the early 1960s, attributed to the director of the international liaison department, Wang Jiaxiang, and linked indirectly with Chen Yun (see note 42), assumed that it was in China's interests to seek accommodation with the "revisionist" USSR as well as with the United States and other non-Communist states and to cease support for revolutionary movements. These were attacked by Maoists as an abandonment of revolutionary struggle. According to Doak Barnett, *The Making of Foreign Policy in China: Structure and Process* (Boulder, Colo.: Westview Press, 1985), note 32, p. 149, Chinese specialists now indicate that these were in effect a proposal for a policy of "three peaceful principles" (peaceful coexistence with Moscow, peaceful competition with the United States and its allies, and peaceful transition to socialism). David Shambaugh, "The Erosion of Ideology," p. 82 ff, recounted how the Maoists countered this trend by using public ideological polemics against the Soviet Union to put forth their policy of "no three peaceful principles." Maoists silenced the doubters such as Huan Xiang who throughout 1964–1965 were questioning Lenin's theory of imperialism. Beginning in 1980, a negative reappraisal of Kang Sheng, Mao's aide who supervised the Sino-Soviet polemics, reopened the debate.

49. Interview with former vice foreign minister Pu Shouchang, Beijing, November 1985.

50. Zhu Jiaming and Huang Jiangnan of the institute of industrial economics, paper presented in March 1984 at a symposium on world economic trends sponsored by the journal *Shijie jingi* and published in no. 4 (March 1984). For a conservative critique from scholars at the Central Party School based on Leninist ideological prescriptions, see *Shijie jingji*, no. 6 (June 1985).

51. Huan Xiang, "Viewing Wuhan's Development and Prospects from the International Political and Economic Situation," *Shijie jingji daobao*, 9 July 1984, p. 3, in FBIS, 26 July 1984, p. K11.

52. Ibid. For a glimpse of the ongoing internal debate on these issues, see "China Holds Symposium on Peace," *Beijing Review* 23 (May 1986), p. 25, which summed up the presentations by forty top scholars from diverse fields at a meeting in Shanghai from 20–22 May 1986, held to commemorate the International Year of Peace. Judging from the excerpts, the participants questioned every theory and assumption underlying Chinese foreign policy for the previous twenty-five years.

53. This interpretation of Huan is based on my analysis of dozens of his speeches, writings, and interviews. In 1982, Huan still seemed to think that the Soviet Union might get the upper hand in the 1980s, but in 1983 he stressed that the Western economy was entering a recovery phase that would lead to a major revival through the increasing influence of the new technological revolution.

54. Zhao, report to the National People's Congress, p. K17.

55. An interview, Boston, July 1985, with a specialist from Shanghai's institute of international studies, where Huan was an adviser, revealed that the new U.S. and Japanese interest in cooperation in the Asia-Pacific region spurred Huan and others to new thinking in the following ways. In April 1983, Pei Monong, Huan Xiang's deputy at the State Council's international studies center, spoke on likely Asian trends to the year 2000 at a conference in Japan. His talk foreshadowed Deng's 1984 themes of peace and development and stressed regional economic complementarity and cooperation. Pei also predicted China's complete reunification, including the recovery of the South China Sea islands. Huan attended a conference on the Asia-Pacific region in Hawaii in May 1984 and then organized a conference in Shanghai in November to pursue the topic further. This conference covered regional economic and strategic trends, the future of the region, and implications for China's development strategy; results were reported to the central leadership.

56. Hu Yaobang, interview with Parris Chang, "China's Party Boss Views the World," *Newsweek*, 4 July 1983, p. 19, indicated that the leadership first began to think about Hong Kong's reversion in 1980, and Pu Shouchang, interview, November 1985, said studies were being done in 1979. Frank Ching, *Hong Kong and China: For Better or For Worse* (New York: China Council of the Asia Society and the Foreign Policy Association, 1985), p. 80, said that Sir Murray MacLehose, then governor of Hong Kong, raised the issue of Hong Kong's future in Beijing in 1979, especially the matter of land leases expiring

in 1997. But both Ezra Vogel and I were told in interviews that until 1982, the leadership still planned to decide about Hong Kong matters after reunification with Taiwan. One explanation for the seeming anomaly may be that until 1982, China had hopes that a framework for reunification with Taiwan could be worked out fairly quickly; this possibility fit with Deng's listing, in a January 1980 speech, of reunification as one of three tasks for the 1980s. This list was only later revised to apply through the 1990s and was then usually omitted or given low priority in discussions of year 2000 and post-2000 goals.

57. Interviews with a senior urban planner, Shenyang, May 1986, and SEZ office deputy director Zhang Ge, Beijing, May 1986. On the value of Hong Kong to the mainland, see Christopher Howe, "Growth, Public Policy and Hong Kong's Economic Relationship with China," *China Quarterly* 95 (September 1983), pp. 512–533. By 1989, the interdependence had mushroomed. According to the deputy director of the Hong Kong economic and trade office, *Sunday Standard* (Hong Kong), 19 March 1989, p. 2, in FBIS-CHI–89–052, 20 March 1989, p. 84, Hong Kong was the largest source of investment in China, which was the third largest source of investment in Hong Kong; Hong Kong was the principal intermediary for trade between China and Taiwan (80 percent) as well as South Korea; and much of Hong Kong's industrial processing was being subcontracted to companies in the Pearl River delta that employed 2 million workers.

58. Deng, *Build Socialism,* p. 52; this official version omitted his generous timetable for Taiwan presented in the original press reports. Several studies have claimed that Deng's formulation of the one nation, two systems theory dated back to 1982, just prior to the Thatcher visit, when it was presented to the British as China's approach to Hong Kong. See Hsi Kuo-ch'iang, "One Country, Two Systems," *Issues and Studies* 23:3 (March 1987), p. 79; and Jurgen Domes, "The Impact of the Hong Kong Problem and the Hong Kong Agreement on PRC Domestic Politics," *Issues and Studies* 22:6 (June 1986), pp. 44–45. It is more probable that only the general concept of autonomy implicit in the original 1979 offers to Taiwan was applied to Hong Kong in 1982; Deng applied the concept even more flexibly to Taiwan in June 1983 in conversation with a Chinese-American professor, Winston Yang. But the exact formula for this concept seems to have been settled on only in 1984.

59. See Deng Xiaoping, *Selected Works (1975–1982)* (Beijing: Foreign Languages Press, 1982), pp. 11–13 and 39–46 for his views from 1975; pp. 73–79 from 1977; and pp. 127–140, 269–275, 372–374, and 386–390 from 1980–1982.

60. The following is from Richard Baum, "China in 1985: The Greening of the Revolution," *Asian Survey* (January 1986), pp. 47–48.

61. Deng, *Build Socialism,* pp. 67, 72.

62. See FBIS, 21–31 December 1984, p. C1ff for reporting on Arkhipov's visit.

63. *Wen Wei Po* (Hong Kong) [Literary Gazette], 8 October 1985.

64. Xinhua, 20 October 1984, in FBIS, 22 October 1984, pp. K1–19.

65. Both Doak Barnett and I have been told in interviews with economists that Guangdong economist Zhuo Jiong first began to discuss the continuing

importance of commodity exchange under socialism in the 1960s. See Zhuo's first article on the subject, which Barnett kindly shared with me, "To Expound on the Commodity Under the Socialist System," *Zhongguo jingji wenti* (Xiamen) [China's Economic Issues] (May-June 1961). According to economist Xue Muqiao, "Sum Up Experience, Deepen Reform," *Renmin ribao,* 30 October 1987, p. 5, in FBIS-CHI-87-212, 3 November 1987, pp. 35-38, the abortive 1980 draft reform document had pointed out that "China's current socialist economy is a commodity economy under the guidance of state planning and the predominance of public ownership of the means of production"; the draft proposed "combining planned regulation with market regulation and giving full play to the role of market regulation under the guidance of state planning." The report to the 12th congress, however, backtracked by insisting on the leading role of the plan and the supplementary role of the market. Meanwhile, no one dared suggest that China develop its commodity economy. "Outmoded views that set plan against market" prevailed.

66. The actual research for this assessment was probably done in the planning commission, whose normal duties included an ongoing review of the current FYP results. According to interviews, Beijing, November 1985 and May 1986, the judgment that the reforms thus far were successful came from a review done by a group of specialists, largely from the institute of economics, headed by Liu Guoguang and Dong Fureng.

67. The target model study was done by Liu Guoguang's task force, organized as a research group of the social science academy's economic institute. Interviews with some of the researchers involved, Beijing, May 1986, revealed that the group also included some from the rural development center and the reform institute and that their views were published in an article by the topic research group in comparative economic systems, "The Problem of a Target Model for the Reform of Our Country's Economic System," *Zhongguo shehui kexue* [Social Sciences in China] 5 (10 September 1984), pp. 37-54, in JPRS CEA-85-033, 4 April 1985, pp. 1-28; and Liu Guoguang, "Remolding the Model of the Economic Structure and Perfecting the Socialist System—An Understanding of the 'CPC Central Committee on the Reform of the Economic Structure,'" *Jingji yanjiu* [Economic Research] 12 (20 December 1984), pp. 16-24, in JPRS CEA-85-015, 11 February 1985, pp. 1-14.

The task force argued that the essence of socialism was public ownership and that within this context there were a number of alternative practical and theoretical models that could be adapted to create Chinese-style socialism. Whereas the 1982-1983 study was rather objective and historical in tone, granting that the Soviet model played a positive role in the 1950s, this was a more partisan version reflecting the freer atmosphere of May to August 1984. Researchers offered their recommendation to the drafting group that the Chinese-style socialism of the future depart radically from that of the 1950s.

For an excellent discussion of the failings of the Soviet and Maoist models in science and technology, see Denis Fred Simon and Merle Goldman, eds., *Science and Technology in Post-Mao China* (Cambridge, Mass.: Harvard University Council on East Asian Studies, 1989), pp. 1-68.

68. Wei Liming, "Burgeoning Soft Sciences," *Beijing Review,* 9–15 May 1988, p. 15. Information on the drafting of the economic reform decision is from an interview with deputy science commissioner Wu Mingyu, Beijing, May 1986.

According to interviews with Hungarian planners, Budapest, May 1986, members of a delegation from the reform commission visiting Hungary in May–June 1983 told their counterparts that they were then working on a statement of reform principles to be approved at the party plenum late that year. But according to an interview with a well-connected Chinese official, Beijing, May 1986, in September 1983 the 2nd Plenum of the 12th Party Congress again postponed action by putting discussion of guidelines for comprehensive urban economic reform on the agenda for the following fall. The decision was not made public, however, and drafting was delayed for months by the outbreak of leadership controversy over ideological issues at the turn of the year.

69. Interview with Wu Mingyu, ibid. The mutual design concept was originally put forth by Premier Zhao at a national science awards meeting in late October 1982, but at that point the concept did not yet include education.

70. Ibid.

71. Interviews with Hungarian specialists, Budapest, May 1986. A very small, select group of senior specialists was involved in drafting the document. Lin Zili, chief economist in the Secretariat's policy research center, mentioned his involvement to a group of foreign reporters in early 1985, according to Associated Press and Reuter reports of 4 January 1985. Judging from interviews and speeches they made shortly after its publication, the group probably also included Xue Muqiao, Ma Hong, Yu Guangyuan, Gao Shangquan (vice minister of the reform commission), Liu Guoguang, and Yuan Mu (spokesman and later deputy secretary-general of the finance and economic leading group). Others invited to review it may have included Dong Fureng, Su Shaozhi, Fei Xiaotong (China's famous anthropologist), and Xing Fensi (from the philosophy institute).

72. Interview with Wu Mingyu, Beijing, May 1986. The texts of the science reform decision and the education reform decision were in FBIS, 21 March 1985, pp. K1–10, and 30 May 1985, pp. K1–11, respectively.

73. Yang Ruiming, "Pointing the Way to Reforming the Education System," *Liaowang* 23 (10 June 1985), pp. 9–12, in FBIS, 26 June 1985, pp. K11–17. Hu Qili drafted the main principles for both sets of reform. The science drafting group was supervised by Politburo member Fang Yi, who was a member of the document leading group by virtue of his role as deputy head of the science and technology leading group. The education drafting group was supervised by Secretariat member Hu Qili. It is unclear whether Hu Qili was given his responsibilities by virtue of his general role as Hu Yaobang's top aide on the Secretariat or as head of a leading group in charge of propaganda and ideology (as reported in the Hong Kong press at the time).

According to the article by Yang, Hu Qili made a special tour of four provinces in late 1984 to investigate education work. Upon return, he made suggestions on the main principles of education reform, which were approved in principle by the Politburo standing committee; Deng gave his unconditional approval. The science group produced eleven drafts for discussion within the small circle of drafters and members of the leading group.

Xi Zhongxun, the Politburo member responsible for united front work with intellectuals, probably was also on the leading group, judging from his presence at a meeting involving a group of scientists, Hu Yaobang, Hu Qili, and Fang Yi, as reported in Xinhua, 13 January 1985, in FBIS, 14 January 1985, p. K12.

74. *Zhongguo kexue jishu zhengce zhinan* [China Science and Technology White Paper] 1 (August 1986), in JPRS CST–87–013, 2 April 1987, p. 6. See Simon and Goldman, pp. 69–198, for details. Denis Fred Simon, "The Evolving Role of Reform in China's Science and Technology System: A Critical Assessment," *Issues and Studies* 23:10 (October 1987), pp. 11–33, discussed how the science and technology reform proposed to reserve key areas such as large-scale integrated circuits for development under state grants but encouraged financing for other research through individual and institutional competitive contracting, whether for government or other funding. To back this kind of shift, the science reform document suggested creating high-risk investment corporations, developing a technology market, using patents and copyrights, creating joint research and production organizations, and developing a professional appointment system for specialists that would allow a freer flow of labor.

75. Deng, *Build Socialism,* pp. 6, 21. Deng also commented on the need for ideological education, moral discipline, and efforts to build socialist civilization in China's educational effort. Judging from Deng's restatement of a commitment to Communist ideals, the propaganda apparatus must have pressed its own pet project—education in communism and patriotism.

76. Yang, "Pointing the Way." In March, delegates to the annual sessions of the people's congress and consultative conference reviewed the education document. Nine Chinese-American scholars were invited to a forum in Beijing to discuss the topic of education, while the education ministry sent a team to the United States to consult with Chinese-Americans and Chinese students. In mid-April, the fifth draft of the education document was circulated to local levels nationwide and elicited three hundred proposals for changes. Hu Yaobang then presided over two sessions of the Secretariat, on 3 May and 13 May, that reviewed word by word the eighth and ninth drafts. A penultimate tenth draft was discussed at a national work conference on education shortly thereafter. Almost ten thousand people reviewed the document.

77. Xinhua, 15 May, 20 May, and 30 May 1985, in FBIS, 17 May (pp. K1–3), 23 May (p. K1), and 3 June 1985 (pp. K1–12), respectively. For the text of the education reform decision adopted on 27 May 1985, see Xinhua, 28 May 1985, in FBIS, 30 May 1985, pp. K1–11.

78. Education specialists complained that a mandatory education law was empty without a compulsory education fund because China's per capita expenditures on education—even with the increase in the 7th FYP—remained among the lowest in the world. Former education minister and well-known non-

Communist economist Qian Jiazhu took the lead in warning that only immediate and drastic correction in China's backward education system would avoid an economic and social disaster as great as that due to the wrong-headed population policy of the 1950s. Media articles suggested that an expected peak in school population, unrevealed illiteracy and semi-illiteracy, the loss of rural teachers and urban-rural inequality in education, the aging of intellectuals, and the obsolescence of current methods of training teachers, workers, and management were hidden crises waiting to happen. See quotes from Qian in "10 Crises in the Future of China's Educational System," *Qiantu yu fazhan* [Future and Development] (April 1985).

79. Interview with the president of Shenzhen University, Shenzhen, November 1985. The university president was to be accountable to a congress of teachers and staff, according to Xinhua and to interviews with university administrators during the 13th Party Congress, in FBIS, 30 October 1987, pp. 41–42.

80. Wu Mingyu, "Introduction," *Zhongguo kexue jishu zhengce zhinan* [China Science and Technology White Paper] (Beijing: State Science and Technology Commission, August 1986), published as a special issue of JPRS CST–87–013, 2 April 1987, pp. 1–17.

81. Deng, *Build Socialism,* p. 54. In emphasizing the importance of turning over responsibilities to capable younger leaders, Deng said, "Everyone says this [economic reform decision] is a document of historic significance. It's a good document, but I didn't write or revise a single word in it."

82. Zhang Zhichu and Lin Chen, "Report from Zhongnanhai: 'Concept of the 7th Five Year Plan' of the Chinese Communists," *Liaowang* 39 (30 September 1985), pp. 9–12, in FBIS, 21 October 1985, pp. K0–14.

5

The Second Wave: Institutional Changes (1985)

From the beginning, Deng Xiaoping viewed the economic reform program not only as a necessity for national well-being but as a survival kit for the Chinese Communist party and a means of ensuring his own personal imprint on history. These intertwined motives go far in explaining the growing urgency behind the reform drive after 1983. Deng and his chosen successors, Hu Yaobang and Zhao Ziyang, used every opportunity to speed up changes in policy, personnel, and institutions in order to expand their political coalition and cement its hold on power by the time of the 13th Party Congress in 1987. There were hints in statements by leaders and officials that at that point, Deng would retire, confident of a stable succession.

In this larger context, the 7th FYP's political importance came to outweigh its economic impact. The plan's political value had both tactical and strategic components. Tactically, because it was time to draft an FYP, the plan could be used as a political tool. Strategically, the FYP, through the drafting process—which involved an automatic review of the 6th FYP period and its accomplishments or failures and projections and an outline plan for the year 2000—provided a means of assessing the contributions of Deng, Hu, and Zhao since 1980 and of establishing the legitimacy of their long-term program. This was particularly important for Hu Yaobang and Zhao Ziyang, who could not fall back on their contributions to the revolution, as could Deng Xiaoping, but had to build legitimacy on very practical terms—that is, was China better off than in 1980?

The 3rd Plenum in October 1984, which adopted the economic reform decision, also decided to convene a national party conference the following September to discuss and adopt a party proposal (to be sent to the National People's Congress) on the essential elements of the 7th FYP and to elect new members of the Central Committee. When the conference convened in the fall of 1985, Hu Yaobang justified the special session primarily in terms of the importance of the economic plan. He reminded participants of the constitutional clause allowing such irregular meetings if a matter of sufficient urgency arose between scheduled party congresses. The only other party conference held by the Communist party, in 1955, similarly approved a party proposal for the 1st FYP, and the leadership considered the 1955 action a precedent for the 1985 procedure.[1]

Despite the issue of the 7th FYP, the personnel and institutional issues at the conference were paramount. The conference format allowed for a turnover of Central Committee membership and a reorganization of senior power organs several years earlier than the norm. (The 13th Party Congress, according to the party constitution, was scheduled for 1987, five years after the 12th Party Congress in 1982.) In 1955, Mao and Liu Shaoqi had used the conference of delegates, who exceeded in number the delegates to a normal congress, to stack the decks against several rivals. Deng and his protégés hoped to do the same in 1985. More than one-half of the 12th congress Central Committee members were replaced, which in turn allowed a similar turnover by half again in 1987. One outstanding feature of these changes was the mass retirement from senior party positions of prominent military figures, thus symbolizing the demilitarization of Chinese politics under Deng.[2]

There was an informal division of labor within the troika of senior reformers: Deng Xiaoping concentrated on the reforming and restaffing of the military, Hu Yaobang gave his attention to rural affairs and to the party's personnel and propaganda apparatus, and Zhao focused on the economic development sectors. The second wave of reform was most successful in consolidating the work already begun in strengthening the grip of reformers on the party and government organs responsible for the economy, science, and education, which before the 1980s were the monopoly of planning and propaganda officials who tended to be conservative, given their vested interests in the highly centralized Soviet system. The composition of the leading group responsible for the economic, science, and education reform was symbolic of the power shift. Hu and Zhao headed the group; their deputies were Hu Qili, the chief executive of a reorganized propaganda and ideology leading group in the party, and Vice Premier Tian Jiyun, the head of a new State Council economic reform working group. The more conservative propaganda department and planning commission thus played relatively minor roles.[3]

Deng Xiaoping made great gains during 1985 in national security and military affairs, with the help of Yang Shangkun, a close associate since the 1930s and now Deng's chief deputy on the military commission. In foreign policy, China's top economic officials, Zhao and Vice Premier Wan Li, increasingly exerted their influence through their involvement in the party's foreign affairs leading group. Although President Li Xiannian nominally headed this group, Zhao, who seemed to have been given authority by Deng over Sino-U.S. relations and foreign economic relations, increasingly set the group's direction. In the spring of 1985, the group's foreign affairs staff office in the State Council was upgraded. The need for foreign investment, trade, and technical advice began to weigh as heavily in the minds of foreign policymakers as did issues of war and peace. These economic needs were being articulated with new urgency through the foreign investment leading group and foreign expertise leading group, both headed by reformist officials close to Zhao.

Not to be outdone, Hu Yaobang appeared to expand his own foreign policy expertise beyond party relations to include relations with Japan and Eastern Europe. Foreign Minister Wu Xueqian, who was promoted to the Politburo at the party conference, was known to be Hu's associate. Hu also began to make significant changes in the control sectors whose interest in enforcing party monopoly traditionally conflicted with the need for greater autonomy in the development sectors Zhao supervised. Hu Yaobang's intent to make these changes was signaled in January, when the media gave widespread publicity to a press article known to be based on speeches by Hu.[4] This article complained that the bureaucracy was not fully supporting the reform program and singled out the party organization (personnel) and propaganda departments, the army's political department, and the organs responsible for public security and judicial work as particularly culpable. Officials in these organs were accused of fostering ideological campaigns to enforce orthodoxy instead of to increase productivity. The article indicated that the latter could be done only after major changes had occurred, including changes in method that would stress legal proceedings; revision of Marxist ideology to incorporate the findings of modern science, technology, and management; and adoption of democratic mechanisms to allow groups outside the bureaucracy to voice their opinions. In the summer, Hu Yaobang appointed two protégés to the propaganda department and the political and legal affairs commission; complementary changes in related party departments and government ministries followed the September party conference.

In general personnel work for which he was responsible, Hu made support for radical reform the main criterion for promotion to new jobs in the party, military, and government bureaucracies that were linked to membership in the Central Committee. Hu spearheaded media efforts to publicize the work of bold reformers as models for official behavior. In January 1985, the leadership revealed a new plan for recruiting, training, and promoting an elite corps of younger officials in which a strategic reserve of 1,000 would be groomed for ministerial-level posts and above, 30,000 for midlevel posts, and 100,000 for basic-level posts.

Clearly, China's reformers were playing for high stakes in 1983–1986, and as a means to their political and economic ends, they continued to make more radical departures from past ideological and institutional norms. In the search for quick economic and political successes, Deng and his protégés opened China's doors further to Western intellectual, institutional, and cultural patterns. In seeking to use all possible resources to strengthen their position, they turned to foreign capital, information, technology, recognition, and approval as important assets. In the process, outside actors became an indirect, informal political constituency with important influence on the Chinese political process.

Drafting the 7th FYP and the Year 2000 Plan

Zhao Ziyang's and Tian Jiyun's experiments in economic planning while creating the 7th FYP and the twenty-year (1980–2000) plan were one of the most effective reform efforts prior to the party conference.[5] Their experiments involved three simultaneous projects: a reorganization of the traditional planning organs and procedures; a second China 2000 study using quantitative modeling to project year 2000 trends; and a World Bank study of possible economic policy options for China between 1986 and the year 2000.

These projects all were intended to drastically revamp China's Soviet-style economic planning process, which was the prototype for administrative planning in all other sectors. (There were annual and five-year plans for everything, whether in social science research, job training and assignments, or ideological education.) Soviet-style planners emphasized nonmonetary exchanges of resources and quantitative production quotas at the expense of market rationality; they preferred top-down administrative commands at the expense of informational feedback to decisionmakers.

In formulating the 7th FYP, Zhao and Tian attempted to shift toward strategic policy planning based on signals from the market mechanism, expert advice, and grass-roots input. By legitimizing the airing of competitive views and the articulation of conflicting interests in the planning process, the reformers also aimed to create a greater degree of consensus and support that would then carry over into more effective implementation. (This reform effort had the potential to set a new paradigm for decisionmaking in other arenas.) A number of specific changes were made in the 7th FYP process to move in a new direction in planning.

Changes in Traditional Planning Procedures

Timing and Time Frame. The first major departure from past practice in planning was to start on time. Even before the 6th FYP was publicized in December 1982 (two years late), planners were beginning work on the 7th. A second departure was to better integrate short-term and long-term planning, something leaders and specialists had wanted to do so since 1978–1979.[6] From 1983 to 1986, planners concurrently drafted twenty-year outline plans for the year 2000, evaluated the implementation of the 6th FYP, and created the 7th FYP, for which research was done in 1983, consultations in 1983–1984, and drafting in 1984–1985.

Targets and Scope. Following the example of the 6th FYP, the 7th FYP set more modest and attainable goals in a number of areas. Realistic growth rate targets enabled planners to eliminate most of the gaps in materials allocation that formerly characterized the planning process. Enterprises thus were allowed additional production capacity for which they had to locate inputs and customers but for which they could also keep the profits earned at market prices. The number of commodities covered by the plan was also reduced over time; by 1985 only sixty (including most energy resources) were under the direct aegis of the planning commission. Fewer major projects were included in the plan; 60 percent of the remaining projects were in crucial bottleneck areas such as energy, transport, and communication. Resources for these could thus be assured, with more careful attention to major problem areas.[7] Overall, this left an increasing portion of the economy outside the plan and subject to new indirect instruments to guide production, such as taxation and sharing formulas for foreign exchange.

Shift to Strategic Policy Planning. In 1983, the central leadership launched two national-level studies to provide the planning commission with new perspectives and competitive views. Deng Xiaoping asked the World Bank for a study of China's long-term economic prospects, and Premier Zhao mandated a much-expanded and improved version of the preliminary China 2000 report done in 1981–1982. Similar competitive efforts were made in key localities such as Tianjin.[8]

One major intent of the studies was to improve the prospects for realistic and creative long-term planning. Another was to shift from simple material balancing to strategic planning based on the actual development needs and capabilities of the various localities and economic regions (the usual method had been to arbitrarily impose central demands based on material and financial balancing). In March 1983, Deng Xiaoping called for concrete local plans and approved setting up economic zones for planning purposes. Much energy was expended by local officials on this planning activity, with notable progress toward realism in at least some localities.[9]

The State Council's economic zone offices created regional plans focused on large-scale, long-term development projects. For example, the Shanghai economic zone office worked out plans to technically upgrade the textile industry, complete Yangzi River hydroelectric projects, and create a Silicon Valley by expanding the local electronics industry. The northeast economic zone office worked on energy, transport, urban land planning, and technical upgrading of heavy industry. The Shanxi energy base office planned for exploration, development, and transport for coal mining. A new planning office for restructuring the third-front industries, run jointly by the planning commission and the national defense science and technology and industries commission, investigated ways to coordinate development in eastern, central, and western China and planned for the upgrading and modification of military industrial plants. These regional plans then were used to shape local plans.[10]

In some localities, economic institutions were reorganized to facilitate the new planning duties. In 1983–1984, Sichuan and Jiangsu each merged their committees for planning, economics, finance, and agriculture. Officials hoped that the new economic planning committee would be better able to coordinate planning and regulatory functions, ensure that the annual and five-year outcomes meshed, and produce better-integrated sectoral plans.[11]

Premier Zhao recommended such mergers as an experiment for possible future use at the national level. In his former base in Sichuan, which first carried out this merger, disagreement continued as to whether the change would increase macrocontrol and decrease bureaucratism or would merely be inconvenient and slow down work. Delegations from other provinces thought the disadvantages outweighed the advantages, and few followed suit. Premier Zhao, despite earlier assertions that local decisions should be voluntary, intervened in favor of the merger during a July–August 1984 visit to Sichuan. Discovering that the organizations had merely been merged with no cuts in staff, he personally reorganized them, cutting staff by nearly half. The national press publicized this development in September, and five other provinces eventually imitated Sichuan.[12]

Broad Consultation. Planners were told in 1983 to elicit the views of academic and government specialists at each stage, something never before required. At the national level, the Secretariat, the State Council, and the party's finance and economic leading group held a series of meetings to elicit the advice of thousands of people, including central and provincial administrators, specialists, natural and social scientists, non-Communist officials, and economists who had worked on earlier plans. Along the way, China's five top leaders gave guidance to central planners, and Premier Zhao Ziyang met with visiting foreign business-people and overseas Chinese scientists and investors to solicit sugges-tions. Interviews at the local and national level tend to confirm the breadth of this consultative process as described in the Chinese press.[13]

Nevertheless, in some cases exchanges took the more traditional form of central intervention. Often, a visit by a central leader was needed to resolve an impasse in local decisionmaking. For example, Deng's visit to the coastal areas in February 1984 helped settle dis-agreements on the best size for the economic and technical development zone in Xiamen; visits to Dalian by Vice Premier Wan Li and state councillor Gu Mu in late 1983 and again by Vice Premier Li Peng in August 1984 enabled Dalian to gain status as a key experimental city as well as an open city.[14]

There were other cases in which the new-style deliberative process seemed to have little impact. Anshan steel mill, no doubt the archetype of old-style planning, created three successive FYPs aimed at quad-rupling output by the year 2000. All three plans were more heavily focused on purchasing new machinery and expanding capacity than on technically upgrading the existing plant. The planners' aim was to compete with the Wuhan and Baoshan steel mills for the market, partly by improving their product and partly by relying on Anshan's friends in the central planning apparatus to keep them in mind. There was no effort to set realistic goals based on consultation with specialists.[15]

Anshan's attitude was not uncommon. Officials in a number of localities complained that academics had no practical experience. Con-versely, specialists complained that although officials welcomed feasi-bility studies or survey work, they kept the decision process closed. Long-term forecasting too often amounted to simplistic pledges to quadruple or even quintuple everything from numbers of factories to tons of coal. This was especially true of the first drafts of long-term plans done in 1983. There were also too few trained specialists who knew how to do forecasting.[16]

In spite of these negatives, some positive impact on the decision-making process occurred at various levels. Officials were forced to think in a long-term framework rather than focus on short-term problem-solving. A more scientific decision process evolved, which helped create wider understanding and policy consensus and thereby enhanced the authority of the resulting plan. Researchers hoped the process would also contribute to greater policy stability and continuity, thus mitigating the tendency toward abrupt policy changes every few years.[17]

The Second China 2000 Study

Between 1983 and 1985, the State Council's technical-economic research center, headed by Ma Hong, placed top priority on completing a new, second China 2000 study to expand and improve on the first study completed in August 1983. Upon reading the first study, Zhao Ziyang had called for a second project of even higher quality, perhaps viewing it as an internal effort to parallel the external World Bank study commissioned by Deng Xiaoping that summer. (Chinese specialists emphasized the mutual data sources for the two studies and the regular exchange of ideas among the specialists involved to the extent that the studies were almost two halves of one whole.)[18] In October 1983, Ma Hong presented a report on the China 2000 study plans to a session of the development strategy symposium. He first explained the guiding ideology for the second study: realistic acceptance of a long development period and uneven regional development; creativity in finding a uniquely Chinese development path; priority to efficiency over speed in development; no sacrifice of long-term interests (especially in the environment) to immediate interests; the importance of cultural as well as material development; and the need to factor in the international economic environment.[19]

In directing the study, Ma Hong worked as the executive member of a special leading group set up to oversee the project; other members included officials from the social science academy and the commissions for science and technology, economics, and planning.[20] The prominence of the leading group, along with Ma Hong's own extensive personal ties throughout the bureaucracy, ensured that the study had a broad impact. Ma put his personal secretary and a top aide, both trained engineers, in charge as his deputies. With more than four hundred experts from the social science academy and the study's own working group, they oversaw the compilation of a report using data and supporting studies from throughout the State Council bureaucracy. In July 1984, one of the primary authors of the study's summary volume gave a report to a session of the development strategy symposium. This early report took the form of a Chinese megatrends and listed ten major trends for the 1980–2000 period:

- Urbanization involving industrialization and commercialization in both rural and urban areas with diversification in ownership and management forms and improvement of labor productivity
- Improvement in management of the environment and ecology
- Improvement in the economic infrastructure
- A shift of focus in investment and construction from high-technology industries and trade on the east coast (in the 1980s) to heavy industry, including defense in central China (in the 1990s) and then to natural resources in western China (after the year 2000)
- Simultaneous industrialization and broader, freer access to and use of information
- Increasing reliance on science and technology to spur economic growth
- A shift from shared sufficiency (equal distribution) in income to comparative (unequal) prosperity
- Increasing openness of the economy to the outside world
- Diversification of economic operation patterns
- A shift from administrative (plan directives) to economic (market, fiscal/monetary) means of economic regulation[21]

These general goals summed up consensus views achieved in the early part of the decade among China's senior economic advisers and provided guidelines for the drafters who were then putting together the party documents on economic, scientific, and educational reform as well as preliminary versions of the 7th FYP.

Policy Impact. It is difficult even for Chinese researchers to pinpoint what specific elements of the 7th FYP came from each study and planning effort in the 1983–1985 period, primarily because there was so much interaction among researchers and planners; certain ideas may have emerged from several different sources. Judging influence is doubly difficult for an outsider because only summaries of some sections of *China Toward the Year 2000* have been made public.[22]

The study team itself has claimed credit for shaping the following key section of the 7th FYP proposal of September 1985:

A comprehensive analysis and scientific estimate of the country's present economic and social conditions indicates that our economic and social development during the period of the 7th 5YP should be guided by the following four basic principles: (1) give priority to . . . comprehensive reform of our management systems for the economy, science and technology and education . . . (2) keep a basic balance between supply and demand in general, so as to maintain an appropriate ratio of accumulation to consumption . . . (3) give top priority to improving economic results . . . and (4) redouble our efforts to build a socialist civilization that is advanced culturally and ideologically as well as materially.[23]

Judging from this passage and also from a description of the twenty-five-point "policy system" recommended by the team to the leadership published later in mid-1987, there seemed to be less policy substance to the study than leaders may have wished. The policy system, like the preceding passage, amounted to a list of rather vague and general goals without a clear sense of priority or interrelationship. The study called for "appropriate" production, consumption, and foreign trade structures without specifying what those structures were. (In this area, analysts had identified the problem but were only just beginning to explore the complex art of industrial restructuring going on elsewhere in the world.) References to balancing and ratios were vestiges of the pseudoscientific Hegelian-Marxian dialectical method.[24]

The final 7th FYP echoed several other more concrete recommendations of the China 2000 study: maintaining a moderate growth rate target to avoid strain on the economy, to ensure genuine efficiency (not just rapid growth), and to create an environment conducive to system reform; using caution in introducing price reform; shaping consumption patterns in order to raise standards of living gradually and realistically without waste; and creating a network of supervisory measures to enforce strict economic discipline in the use of investment credit and foreign funds as well as in environmental protection.

The study team also recommended using a gross national product (GNP) target as well as the targets for gross value of industrial and agricultural output (GVIAO) and for national income.[25] This was done for the first time in the 7th FYP to facilitate international comparisons and to highlight the contribution of the commercial and service sector of the economy, which the other indicators slighted. The study stressed the importance of growth in services by projecting a rise from 16 percent to 26 percent of China's gross output value, which implied that China should drop its preoccupation with growth of material output and incorporate growth of services as a means of achieving per capita GNP targets. This would better suit the shift of goals from production for its own sake to increase in consumption (living standards); it would also help provide jobs for the expected 250–300 million new workers by the year 2000. The key importance of investment and reform in science, technology, and education were also stressed.

One of the most important differences between the earlier and later China 2000 studies was in population estimates. The first was optimistic, basing projections on a leveling off of growth at a 1.2 billion population by the year 2000; the second was more pessimistic, revising the projection upward by adding scenarios premised on a population of 1.24–1.28 billion, a difference with profound implications, especially for food and population policy. This probably led to the study's special investigation of consumption patterns, its call for continuing strict population control measures, and its recommendation of a flexible and open employment system that would help integrate rural and urban economies and provide the many new jobs required.

In regard to natural resources and ecology, the second report strained toward optimism in comparison with the first study's stark realism. Perhaps this was recognition of political reality; few politicians anywhere are willing to sacrifice current growth for future resources. This avoidance approach was evident both in the vague call for "practical effects" in environmental work and in one study organizer's careful wording when introducing the findings to an academic forum in 1985:

> If enough attention is paid to these [ecological] problems, and all the Chinese people are mobilized to plant trees and grass, China's forest coverage might possibly reach about 18% by 2000. Losses of natural pastureland may be stopped and the grasslands used more efficiently. Soil erosion might be allayed, and the ecological environment may gradually be able to regain a good cycle.[26]

Improved Analytical Capability. The second study helped further acquaint Chinese specialists with new methodology, which had an impact more far-reaching than policy recommendations. Quantitative forecasting was used in combination with traditional qualitative historical and comparative analysis to create mathematical models for looking at the economic system from different angles with different methods.

Two of the models went beyond the year 2000 to project trends to 2050 and 2080. According to its coordinators, the study aimed first to illuminate the operational interrelationships and mechanisms of the Chinese socioeconomic system and then to address more specific policy concerns by using computers to calculate the results of three optional plans as well as numerous simulated specific policies. This description of the approach clearly reflected the influence of the system dynamics national model developed at MIT by Jay Forrester.[27]

The MIT model explicitly set out to make policy-relevant insights into the business cycle phenomenon (three to seven year fluctuations causing recession), the Kondratieff long-wave cycle (forty to sixty year fluctuations in capital, technology, and productivity requiring industrial restructuring), transitions in energy sources, and problems of inflation and unemployment. For China to undertake a similar study, and to find its results highly relevant for policymaking, was an implicit admission that the distinctions between socialist and capitalist economic systems might be less than previously thought and that the overlap in categories and problems might outweigh them.

The experimental nature of the China 2000 study and the lack of precision in its conclusions must be underscored. Central participants emphasized that only a small percentage of specialists, even in Beijing, had the knowledge and skills to work on the quantitative aspects of the study. Local researchers and the bulk of Beijing researchers relied on old-style methods of investigation in which individuals, often retirees or young staffers, did the leg work of visiting factories and farms; collecting, collating, and analyzing scattered statistics of varying reliability; and soliciting public opinion.[28]

The China 2000 study was useful nonetheless in prompting large data-collection efforts, improvements in statistical collection and analysis, and new directions in research and training. The new focus on technical economics, broadly defined, served to counter the strong ideological component in previous Chinese economic analysis and gave a strong boost to the trend toward realism and pragmatism in economic decisionmaking.[29]

The continuing limits posed by ideological and political imperatives were evident, however, in the following effusive article published by the general report group:

> Our research shows that as long as we unswervingly follow the road determined by the Central Committee of the Chinese Communist Party, by the end of this century our country is bound to become a powerful socialist country with political stability, economic prosperity, solid national strength, and people enjoying peace and happiness. We shall present to the whole world a relatively perfect socialist mode full of creativity and vitality and with Chinese characteristics. . . . Our research also shows that in the middle of the next century our country might approach or attain the economic development level of the advanced countries, and that, by the end of the next century, we might even surpass them. Then, the long-cherished wish of numerous people with lofty ideals, and of the heroes and martyrs over the centuries, will be fulfilled. In this sense, the 21st century can be called a century of China![30]

Regardless of its limits, the efforts of the China 2000 team were appreciated and rewarded by reform leaders. In early 1985, Ma Hong's technical-economic research center was expanded to incorporate several other research centers, and its prestige rose greatly. Known as the research center for economic, technical and social development (hereafter development center), the organization was one of China's four most influential think tanks (the other three studied rural reform policy, urban reform policy, and science and technology development). Premier Zhao controlled and used them effectively in his various roles, which in combination made him China's senior economic policymaker.[31]

Foreign Advisers

A gradual shift from socialist to Western thought categories and methods in Chinese economic analysis was already apparent from 1978 to 1981; and this accelerated through 1985 and expanded to economic management as well. In the summer of 1983, the Central Committee and State Council issued the "Decision on Introducing Foreign Intelligence for the Four Modernizations" and set up a foreign expertise leading group.[32] This marked a turning point in Chinese thinking from a narrow focus on importing only foreign technology, equipment, and funds to a broader use of foreign technical and managerial expertise. This decision accompanied a major effort to enforce the policy of favorable treatment for China's own inadequate core of 15 million professionals, a policy that until then had been largely ignored.[33]

The ground had long been ready for the seeds of Western expertise; many of the older proreform researchers and educators in China were exposed to Western training in economics, science, or engineering, either in the West or in Western-style schools in pre-1949 China. Several of the most famous economists, for example, learned Western research concepts and techniques in the 1930s from Chen Hansheng, a U.S.-trained economist who in his nineties was considered a patron and model by younger, openminded policy analysts of the 1980s.[34]

Even the preoccupation in the 1979–1980 period with Eastern European development experience provided an indirect introduction to Western views and ways because socialist economists in that region were very much a part of the international dialogue on development. The growing involvement of Chinese economic units with those in Hong Kong, Singapore, and Japan also produced a number of informal advisers familiar with Western-style economies. These included frequent visitors to China who met with top leaders and gave informal personal advice such as Japan's famous economist, Saburo Okita, and the architect of Singapore's economic development program, First Deputy Prime Minister Goh Keng Swee.

During the 1983–1985 period, the door opened wider to Western expertise. A German technician, Werner Gerich, became famous for his work as the first foreign manager of a Chinese enterprise (a diesel engine factory in Wuhan), where he greatly improved both work efficiency and product quality. He wrote up his methods in a book that was then used to introduce similar reforms elsewhere.[35] After 1985, such cooperation was intensified with the formation of China's association for the international exchange of personnel. In two years almost three thousand foreign experts had been invited to China, and plans had been made to invite two thousand experts to China and to send abroad for training an equal number of Chinese technicians annually.[36]

In Premier Zhao's speech to the National People's Congress in March 1986, he thanked the pioneer foreign specialists, specifically the World Bank, for their contributions to the formation of the 7th FYP.[37] Advisory relationships were formalized as China belatedly recognized that knowledge had monetary value. The State Council engaged Goh Keng Swee, now retired, as a consultant on building tourism and developing the coastal cities and Hong Kong shipping magnate Y. K. Pao as an adviser (and financial contributor) on developing Ningbo, his hometown. The China Automobile Industry Corporation invited former Ford Motor Company vice president Harold MacDonald and ten other senior Ford experts to make proposals for the development of the industry in China.[38]

International Economic Organizations. A major factor in China's growing openness to Western economic management practices was its involvement with international economic organizations, which began in 1980 when China joined the International Monetary Fund (IMF) and the World Bank. This step was taken partly on the advice given by officials in Yugoslavia and Romania to senior Chinese economic officials during extended visits there in 1978 and 1979. Chinese leaders primarily sought access to new sources of funding and technical assistance, but it was evident from the start that Zhao Ziyang and others were also interested in advice on broad, strategic issues of economic development.[39]

Bureaucrats at first were quite reluctant to provide the required information and proof of technical feasibility for projects, but gradually the Western management practices of open competitive bidding and feasibility studies required for IMF and World Bank projects proved useful within China as they served to avoid waste and cut through bureaucratic wrangling. Eventually, experiments with international competitive bidding for Chinese projects were also begun.

Specific reforms made to facilitate cooperation with the international organizations included coal price reform (in 1983–1984) to obtain World Bank loans for mine development and changes in interest rates, data management, and currency devaluation on the recommendation of the IMF. Mutual adaptation between China and the international economic organizations took place in even more sensitive arenas, such as higher education. For example, the World Bank's first project in China was a loan approved in June 1981 to upgrade training in the sciences. Although the ministry of education wanted to spend the entire loan on equipment, it gradually acquiesced to some of the bank's priorities, such as increased manpower training and upgrading of university management.[40] Such intimate involvement with international economic organizations, while uncomfortable, was nevertheless more acceptable to the Chinese leadership than similar bilateral ties would have been because of the leaders' strong fear that economic dependence would impinge on political and cultural independence.

China's involvement with the international economy helped reshape its own decision process. Data supplied to the international organizations were made available to ever-widening circles of Chinese officials and specialists. In a sense, international economic cooperation forced the planning elite to bring into the policy process those specialists who could speak the foreign language of quantitative methodology, thereby accelerating a trend toward horizontal sharing of information and greater inclusiveness in the policy process.

Sharing of data between China and the organizations also raised Chinese understanding about how to handle statistics and measure economic change, including use of criterion like GNP, and thus enabled the Chinese to better comprehend their own economy and create more realistic policies. Press articles in the late 1980s provided long lists of Western methodologies new to China that were credited with improving China's management mechanisms and helping in the formulation of new types of socialist economist theory. These included consumption economics, theories of economic growth, the science of money and banking, international economics, the science of finance, and the science of marketing.[41]

Over time the whole range of foreign economic involvement in China—from international economic organizations to investing firms and political groups such as the North Atlantic Treaty Organization's (NATO) committee for deciding sensitive technology transfer policy—became an indirect, informal political constituency for the reform program, as Chinese reformers used outside financial and informational resources to strengthen their own political positions. For example, China's growing interest from 1984–1986 in participation in the General Agreement on Tariffs and Trade (GATT) was closely linked to the decision process on foreign trade reform and to institutional changes in the foreign trade system. To China's interlocutors, interest in the round of GATT negotiations scheduled to begin in late 1986 appeared motivated in part by efforts to involve China in international obligations that could be used to reinforce the economic reforms and make them irreversible.[42]

The World Bank. By the mid-1980s, World Bank loans to China averaged more than $1 billion annually (with projections of $3 billion annually in the 1990s). More than one-half of the loans went to support transportation and energy projects. But the value of the information and expert advice that were also being transferred was incalculable. Many Chinese officials stressed the usefulness of the World Bank's excellent analyses and suggestions regarding specific projects, such as industrial survey work, done in cooperation with the economic commission. Economic training programs were organized through the bank's economic development institute in cooperation with the United Nations Development Program, the central university of finance in Beijing, and the Shanghai institute of finance. These helped upgrade the abilities of midlevel officials and younger researchers.[43]

Meanwhile, the background information and general policy advice acquired through these cooperative relationships were increasingly valued. The World Bank functioned as a unique window on the world for China by introducing and comparing lessons from the global development experience. The bank's nonideological approach was especially helpful to reformers in bypassing or overcoming objections to non-Marxist economics. Bank reports were studiously neutral in discussing development stages and problems common to all countries and in providing information on the many alternative approaches to these problems. Authoritative evidence that all economies had to deal with commodities, markets, planning and economic cycles and that many more economic systems existed than the socialist/capitalist dichotomy suggested encouraged a more open atmosphere for policy research inside China.

The bank used a number of advisers and consultants of Eastern European background in its China projects; these advisers provided a personal bridge between more acceptable Eastern European and more suspect Western economic concepts and practices. An early influence of this sort, for example, was a paper presented by Bela Balassa of Johns Hopkins University at a Sino-U.S. conference on alternative development strategies in November 1980. Economists Xu Dixin and Dong Fureng were among those in attendance whose views were greatly shaped by his well-reasoned and fully documented view that countries adopting outward-oriented development strategies had a performance far superior to those that retained closed economies of the Soviet style beyond the first stage of import substitution. Using examples from Asia and Latin America, he sketched a picture (all too familiar to his Chinese audience) of the industrial structure created by closed economies—

small-scale production with inadequate specialization and outdated machinery that lagged further and further behind world standards. Hungarian economist Janos Kornai had special authoritativeness when in the mid-1980s he encouraged the Chinese to learn from Hungary's mistakes and move beyond the limits of Hungarian-style reform.[44]

The bank also provided a bridge between socialist China and the Western-oriented economies in Asia. Many of its studies either included success stories from these countries or focused on their economies.

In terms of Chinese general knowledge about development, then, the bank had a tremendous impact. Hundreds of its studies, especially the annual reports, continue to be translated and circulated internally as reference materials for China's top officials and researchers.[45]

The World Bank Study

In the summer of 1983, when Deng Xiaoping invited the World Bank to provide a study of China's economic options to the year 2000, the bank unexpectedly found itself in the new role of outside consultant to the Chinese government on the five-year and twenty-year plans just getting under way. World Bank president A. W. Clausen met with Deng and suggested that the bank begin work on a second assessment of the Chinese economy to follow up its well-received first overview (finished in 1981),[46] but Deng requested a more thorough study. (Normally, studies involving three to five-year trends were done every two or three years for members of the bank.) This invitation to become involved in China's macroeconomic planning process was a striking endorsement of the practical value of foreign information and knowledge and a vote of confidence in the bank.

The bank eventually responded with a series of analyses that began with nine preliminary studies of foreign experiences applicable to China, development of a quantitative model of the Chinese economy, and analysis of three major alternative projections to the year 2000 and ended with a written report, *China: Long-Term Development Issues and Options* (accompanied by six annex volumes). In the lengthy, interactive process through which Chinese specialists and officials and World Bank researchers worked on this report, there was great potential for influence on the 7th FYP and twenty-year plan then in draft. The bank research team visited China for four weeks in February and March 1984 and again for five weeks in April and May 1984. (These exchanges may have influenced debates over the economic reform decision.) A draft of the bank's study was given to the finance ministry in March 1985 for distribution to the large number of organizations that had cooperated with the teams. Preliminary drafts of the bank's nine working papers formed the basis for discussion at a series of seminars organized by the State Council in April and May. Both distributions resulted in valuable feedback for completion of the final report in May.

The Chinese-foreign collaboration and the resulting internal interaction and sharing of information within the highly compartmentalized Chinese bureaucracy marked this project as unusual. One Chinese economist who was involved termed the study "almost a mutual product," but it is impossible to determine whether the sharing was as equal as this statement implied. Several Chinese specialists who reviewed the report stressed the number of corrections they made in terms of facts, but the bank's contribution must have been heavy in terms of conceptualization, methodology, and recommendations.

The report did make a big impact on the leadership in the spring of 1985. Zhao Ziyang read the March draft, praised it highly, and circulated it widely for mandatory reading. In a speech to officials assembled to examine the science and education reform decision drafts, Zhao praised the study's recommendations on technology transfer and absorption, particularly that spreading commonplace technology, much of it already available in some Chinese factories, could aid considerably in renovating existing plants. Dissatisfied with the planning commission's current draft of the 7th FYP, Zhao set up a separate drafting group under the party's finance and economic leading group (headed by Zhao) to complete the plan proposal for endorsement by the September party conference. He told both this group and the planning commission to pursue their drafting with the bank report in hand.[47] Such a turn of affairs must have astounded China's insular bureaucracy and was perhaps the prime example of Zhao's openminded personal style of leadership.

According to officials at the planning commission, several recommendations in the bank report (resembling those of the China 2000 study) had great influence.[48] Among these were the call to maintain a steady pace with modest growth rates, to create a more balanced industrial mix by focusing on bottleneck areas (energy, transportation, communication, basic materials), to expand the tertiary sector, and to strengthen horizontal ties between and within sectors.

The most striking element of the bank's report was its stress on the service sector. The report recommended, albeit implicitly and politely, that China discard its year 2000 target of quadrupling material output and consider an alternative strategy for achieving its per capita income goals. This approach would be centered on development of the service sector and major systemic reforms to produce efficiency. The report stressed the advantages of this route for China: A greatly ex-

panded service sector would raise per capita income with less investment, would be less energy consuming and more efficient in transportation use, and would encourage rational urbanization with less
unemployment stress.

The 7th FYP did not adopt this recommendation overtly, however,
because even China's most reformist economists believed that the bank
overstated the potential for developing the service sector, given the low
level of material development in China. Nevertheless, the bank's advocacy of integrated market reforms and growth of services, coming
on top of similar recommendations from the China 2000 study, gave
cumulative weight to these arguments. The 7th FYP's eventual core
emphasis on reforms and on a city-centered regional development
strategy indirectly reflected this. Likewise, the influence of both studies
was reflected in the eventual goal of a nationwide, fully open, export-
oriented economy.[49]

New Trends in Planning

For more than thirty years, Chinese bureaucratic planning was
based on the Soviet model, which involved the planning commission
in almost every facet of the urban economy, from setting prices and
wages to determining personnel and education quotas. Theoretically
the planning commission was primarily responsible for creating annual,
midterm, and long-term plans, whereas the economic commission oversaw the implementation of annual plans. The nonstate sector was not
included in any planning, and consequently agricultural and service
sectors in which collective and individual enterprises were concentrated
lacked sufficient access to resources. Resource bias in favor of heavy
industry, both civilian and military, kept living standards static.

For years there had been great dissatisfaction not only with the
goals of planning but also with the actual planning process. While the
planning commission focused on the annual plan, which was in planning all year, it neglected the mid- and long-term plans.[50] It ended up
as arbitrary broker among special interest lobbies with little regard for
development priorities. Reformers wanted to shift from detailed annual
planning of resource distribution to macroplanning for long-range coordination and development. In their minds, such economic policy planning should integrate development planning with plans for reform of
the economic management system and for restructuring of the industrial
pattern among and within sectors and among and within geographic
regions.

A number of these concerns were on the agenda when the World
Bank, the reform commission, and the social science academy co-

sponsored a special seminar on macroeconomic management in early September 1985, in time to influence the final drafting of the 7th FYP. This Bashan Seminar, named for the Yangzi River steamer where it took place, was attended by several Nobel Prize–winning economists, including James Tobin (from the United States) and nearly all of China's senior economic advisers.[51] Chinese interest was particularly strong because of some serious economic imbalances that had emerged in late 1984. The seminar focused on China's management of the transition from command economy to indirect economic macromanagement, in particular the avoidance of runaway investment, inflation and foreign exchange deficit. Discussion by British, West German, and French participants of the shift from a wartime command economy to a peacetime market-regulated economy during the late 1940s and early 1950s proved surprisingly relevant to China. With this seminar, the World Bank redressed one complaint of Chinese specialists about the 1985 report—that it offered China only the experience of developing rather than developed nations for comparison.

There was a general consensus that China should retain use of administrative controls as long as market conditions remained underdeveloped while strengthening other management tools, such as monetary and fiscal policies. Three main objectives for macroeconomic management were suggested: maintenance of balance between total demand and total supply, primarily through control of the former; stability of the general level of prices; and stability in foreign economic relations. In the view of seminar participants, the government budget ought to be the most effective means of achieving these objectives, particularly in the short term.

Deficit financing and foreign borrowing were also mentioned in the seminar and perhaps influenced Premier Zhao's reference to plans for increased borrowing in his March 1986 speech to the National People's Congress. Discussion of the foreign exchange problem led to strong recommendations that China restructure its exports and shift gradually toward an export-oriented development strategy. These themes emerged in official statements and in the press in 1986, and so, too, did the general theme of the conference: "macroeconomic control, microeconomic enlivening."

Zhao Ziyang's efforts in the mid-1980s to reform the planning apparatus were not a smooth and steady process, however. On one hand, planning officials were able to point to some progress. They were limited to a strictly supervisory role more than ever before; to create the final draft of the 7th FYP, they relied on research documents done by other units on many issue areas. In a surprising reflection of new trends, one institute in the social science academy was even paid consulting fees by the commission for its contribution to a plan-related research project on rational industrial location. The commission claimed that although it had always listened to the views of key sectors and regions, it had worked harder to encourage full expression of all views.[52]

On the other hand, circumstantial evidence suggests that the planning commission moved in new directions with typical bureaucratic reluctance to accept painful reorganization. The 1984 economic reform decision called for planning reform, the chief responsibility for which was given to the planning commission, but most innovation was actually accomplished by officials and organizations outside the planning system.[53] For example, although the 1984 economic reform decision called for the use of forecasting in planning and the commission was the obvious unit to do medium and long-term modeling and forecasting, it was very slow to adopt quantitative methods. U.S. professor Herbert Klein was invited by the commission to present several lecture series on forecasting, yet the primary twenty-year forecasting was done by the World Bank and the development center. Initiatives to explore new concepts of development strategy likewise came from others. Only in February 1986, when the major 7th FYP and year 2000 plan projects were ready for final approval, did the commission announce that it would begin to use the China International Engineering Consulting Corporation (established in 1982) to evaluate and screen all applications for new large and medium projects.[54]

Meanwhile, important policy planning and regulatory responsibilities were being taken up by others. The reform commission and the State Council's economic legislation research center were the central actors in setting policy and legislation guidelines, respectively. The economic commission set up new groups to strengthen its regulatory role, and the ministry of finance and the People's Bank set fiscal and monetary policy.

At the party conference in September 1985, Zhao called for an acceleration of planning reform. Perhaps this was, in part, a late bid to affect the final drafting of the 7th FYP before its presentation to the annual session of the National People's Congress in early 1986. Shortly after Zhao's remarks were made, planning minister Song Ping published an article that ostensibly endorsed Zhao's approach but inadvertently revealed the complexity and slow pace of change.[55] Song identified five themes from the party's proposal for the 7th FYP that "made a breakthrough in the traditional ideology and method of planning and must be given particular attention in the final drafting of the plan itself":

- Changing the focus from setting quotas, listing items, and distributing investment and materials to strategic researching and planning of coherent sets of major principles and policies
- Shifting from increases in quantity to improvement of quality through enforced compliance, not mere exhortation
- Further integrating economic, scientific, technological, and social development with proper budgetary attention to each
- Incorporating the needs of foreign economic activities into planning
- Further reducing the scope of mandatory planning and expanding the scope of guidance planning and market coordination

In each of these areas, Song confessed, only some recent progress had been made, and he still did not stress the importance of forecasting.

Reform leaders took special measures to force a more rapid pace of planning reform during 1986, even though the 7th FYP was complete and presumably the next plan was not urgent. This move was probably prompted more by hopes of reformist gains in personnel and organization than in policy. In May, a scandal broke when six of the planning commission staff, all party members, wrote to higher levels complaining about the slothful and power-hungry behavior of bureaucrats in their unit. Vice Premier Wan Li later took credit for commenting on the letter and sending it to *Renmin ribao* for publication. According to Xinhua, the commission's party core group (no doubt headed by Song Ping) was shocked and moved to reorganize its staff and draft a new set of regulations to improve the situation. Reportedly, on the very day the letter was published, one bureau managed to approve a document in a half day that previously would have taken two weeks.[56]

Throughout the rest of 1986, heated debate continued over what ought to be the specific role of planning in directing China's economy. At a national symposium on economic management in September, one participant argued that the market should be allowed to assume most functions in regulating the economy, with great restraint on the part of the state. Others insisted that the state should retain dominance even in the market sector through guidance planning and direct control over some key sectors. Some argued for what was essentially a compromise through ambiguity—that the plan and market regulation should be mixed together. There was consensus, however, that earlier planning reform efforts, based on decentralization of power and administrative streamlining, were a failure. Participants concluded that "it is necessary to separate economic management from administration promptly."[57]

During 1987, preparations were begun for a major shake-up in the State Council planning apparatus. Zhao Ziyang skillfully used the potential benefits for China in joining GATT to press forward with the market reforms required for its members. When meeting with the GATT director general, Zhao told him that China would gradually expand the proportion of market regulation until the planned economy made up "only a very small proportion of the economy. . . . In two or three years only about 30 percent of the entire economy will be controlled through central planning" (a proportion already reached in the coastal areas).[58]

National Security Review

In 1985, important foreign policy and budgetary decisions affecting the military were made that were closely related to new five- and twenty-year plan development goals. In early 1985, Hu Yaobang urged the military to complete dozens of major construction projects by the end of the century, and press articles claimed that the army's closer involvement in national construction could speed up development and enable China to achieve its goal of quadrupling output earlier than the year 2000. These hopes seem to reflect in part the influence of investigations into the history of U.S. economic development, which had shown how the rapid civilian application of military research was responsible for U.S. technological superiority.[59]

There was also a budgetary connection. China's senior leaders wanted to continue the overall downward trend in the military share of the state budget, but they had always had trouble holding this line in the face of an impatient military.[60] The military reform program appeared in part to be a new financial strategy that would allow renewed cuts in the military share of the state budget without necessarily postponing military modernization. The military establishment would be allowed to use the resources released by cuts in personnel and by other conservation measures to upgrade weapons and training. Profits from civilian-military joint ventures or contracting and from military sales abroad could also be used for military purposes.

President Li Xiannian confirmed the linkage between civilian and military planning at the national party conference in September, when in a list of major decisions related to the 7th FYP, he included military reorganization along with the decisions on management reform for the economy, science and technology, and education.[61] But events of 1985 were just the beginning of new directions for the military. In March 1986, the army chief of staff called on researchers and planners to work out a new general target for defense development, intermediate and long-term plans, and development strategies for specific operational work. This major effort was to include a new look at the field of defense economics and a military 2000 study inspired by China 2000 and similar U.S. military studies.[62]

Meanwhile, the rethinking of foreign policy underway earlier entered a new stage. Themes of global economic interdependence were officially endorsed for the first time, and plans were introduced for reforming the foreign affairs sector to strengthen China's economic diplomacy. Economic development imperatives were being used to make personnel and organizational changes in the national security apparatus that would strengthen the reform program and politically benefit reformers.

Deng Xiaoping and the Military Commission

During the period of most intense drafting on components of the 7th FYP, several military commission meetings discussed the need for a major reform of China's armed forces. There were two stated goals for this reform: to enhance the resources available to the civilian sector in the short term and to prepare the organization and personnel foundation for military modernization in the long term. These reforms were premised on an official shift in the military's strategic stance from that of war preparedness left over from the Mao era to that of peacetime construction. An editorial in the army's daily newspaper underscored the epoch-making and historic nature of this change by comparing it to a 1975 military commission guideline that called for preparations for an early, global, nuclear war, the official line for the decade that followed.[63]

In November 1984, military commission chairman Deng Xiaoping set the rather adversarial, scolding tone of this series of military meetings when he commanded the army to "do nothing harmful to the general interest and work in compliance with it and in subordination to it." He told the air force, the navy, and the national defense science, technology and industry commission to speed up efforts begun earlier in the decade to make military technology and industry serve the civilian economy. Deng demanded greater effort in opening up to civilian use China's best science research and development facilities, as well as strategic airfields, coastal ports, and rail lines previously used exclusively by the military.[64]

His tone of urgency strongly suggested that efforts along these lines since 1980–1981 had been slow and desultory. In early 1983, at the start of the 7th FYP planning process, steps had been taken to better coordinate military and civilian technological development—the central units in charge of military industries and military research and development were merged, and the director became a member of the party's science and technology leading group.[65] Deng now renewed demands for rejuvenation of the military command and asked that military training programs consider giving soldiers training (such as raising pigs and driving cars) that would make them easily assimilable into the civilian economy upon demobilization.

Results were immediate. In December, forty senior officers of the general staff retired as an example for others. In January, there were further substantial cutbacks in budgets and personnel, and some security troops and the railway corps were placed under civilian control. The official press reported that new uniforms and ranks were forthcoming as part of the trend toward professionalization.[66]

Deng repeated and expanded upon his military reform themes in meetings of the military commission in January–February and late May–early June 1985. The commission decided to improve the pension system and then retire 10 percent of the officer corps by the end of 1986, followed by another 5 percent by the end of 1990, as well as to demobilize 1 million soldiers (one-fourth of the troop level). The command structure was reorganized to consolidate the eleven regional commands into seven; several powerful commanders were retired in the process. By the end of the summer, one-half of the regional senior officers and one-fourth of the central command senior officers were out.[67]

Deng Xiaoping had some personnel goals in mind that affected the very highest levels. These retirements brought one step closer the retirement of Yang Shangkun and other superannuated leaders, including Deng himself, in the military commission. Since 1980, Deng had been trying to set the stage for turning over his position to Hu Yaobang in order to cement him in place as successor. Hu's high profile in the military meetings of early 1985 indicated a connection.

Many of these changes promised to enhance China's defense readiness and capability once they were in place. Nevertheless, the Chinese press publicized demobilization as China's contribution to international disarmament and the resulting troop drawdowns in the north as a sign of sincerity in the context of Sino-Soviet rapprochement. The ensuing changes also gave concrete witness to the peaceful reunification policy because they included abolition of the Fuzhou military region, for twenty years known as the frontline force; the cessation of "shelling" by propaganda leaflets from Xiamen to the Taiwan-held offshore islands and the expansion of the Xiamen SEZ in preparation for creating a free port; and the withdrawal of naval forces from

Dongshan Island—the historical staging point for invasions of Taiwan—as it was opened to joint ventures and tourism.[68]

Foreign Policy Debate

To justify this major decision to shift to peacetime military construction, to accord defense low priority on the budget for at least five years, and to put the military through a wrenching overhaul, Deng Xiaoping told an enlarged military commission session in July 1985 that large-scale world war would not break out for a relatively long time because the forces for peace in the world had grown. Hu Yaobang, in commenting on Deng's June announcement of a change in threat assessment and strategy, stressed that it had been made after two years of repeated deliberations and a "cool and objective analysis of the international situation and China's own defense capabilities."[69]

As Hu implied, China's fear of the Soviet threat had gradually diminished in the 1980s, and there was a new degree of confidence that no major military conflict would arise in the near future. Specialists have emphasized in private, however, that Deng's decision emerged primarily from a more realistic understanding of China's own needs and capabilities rather than from a major change in the global situation.[70] Public comments by one of Deng's senior foreign affairs advisers, Huan Xiang, seemed to support this conclusion:

> Deng Xiaoping's peace thoughts are based on China's economic development and the political and economic reforms, which form the core of Deng's thought. . . . The basic things that China relies on in order to safeguard peace are political and economic reforms and development. I think that this is Deng's thought. Of course, living in today's world, we cannot completely abandon our armaments.[71]

There is evidence that Deng's new view of global trends caused some surprise and disagreement. In the months leading up to Deng's pronouncement, for example, even senior adviser Huan Xiang was warning that the arms race was intensifying and expanding into outer space, that the concept of a winnable nuclear war was a destabilizing one, and that the superpowers were extending their military contention to Asia and trying to reestablish economic hegemony through control of technology transfer. "The possibility of a new world war or nuclear war hangs over us all like the sword of Damocles."[72] Some media commentary in 1985 did begin to suggest that a strategic stalemate could lead to a period of no peace, no war. But throughout 1983–1986, there was still talk of growing international tensions. One influential military and diplomatic veteran, for example, continued to warn of

international problems and conflicts well beyond Deng's June pronouncement. "The danger of war and the expansion of war are just
below the surface. . . . Only when we attach importance to studying
warfare . . . and accelerate the modernization of the Chinese army will
it be possible for us to establish ourselves in an unassailable position."[73]

These conflicting views of international trends probably reflected
the military's reluctance to declare peace, which would weaken its claim
on scarce national resources and cause a major restructuring. But
conflicting views were also symptomatic of continuing strategic debate
in 1985 regarding trends in superpower behavior and China's appropriate military and diplomatic response. On one end of the spectrum,
according to knowledgeable foreign affairs researchers, Chen Yun and
Peng Zhen continued to favor greater efforts to normalize Sino-Soviet
relations and maintain a stance of equidistance. They argued that only
Cambodia should be considered an obstacle, perhaps as a match to the
single obstacle of Taiwan in relations with the United States. Chen's
group may have seen an opportunity to press its view again, now that
Deng indirectly acknowledged a diminished Soviet threat. On the other
end of the spectrum, the foreign affairs establishment continued to
adhere to the traditional self-reliant policy of distance from both superpowers, based on skepticism regarding their motives and the value of
East-West détente.[74]

Deng Xiaoping seemed able to use the 1985 debate to forge a
new level of leadership consensus regarding the shift in military strategy
and the positive appraisal of trends toward East-West détente. But the
new approach also involved greater impartiality toward the superpowers. Deng Xiaoping edged closer than ever before toward a policy
of equidistance. He secretly sent a message to Gorbachev through
Romania's President Nicolae Ceauşescu that either he or Hu Yaobang
would be willing to meet Gorbachev in Moscow if he were to use
Soviet influence on Hanoi to force Vietnamese withdrawal from Cambodia.[75] In April, a public misstatement by Hu Yaobang regarding the
impending visit to China by a U.S. naval vessel for the first time since
1949 led the United States to postpone the visit. (Hu implied the ship
would not be nuclear armed; standard U.S. policy was not to specify
which vessels were nuclear armed.)

In general, Beijing tried to play down the budding Sino-U.S.
military relationship. In his June speech to the military, Deng proclaimed that the independent foreign policy was a long-term one, whereas
earlier he had implied that it was a temporary stance subject to changes
in U.S. policy toward Taiwan.[76] These developments may have been
viewed by Deng as prudent positive signals to Gorbachev upon his
promotion in March. Deng and Hu probably hoped that a Sino-Soviet

warming trend would strengthen their plans for military reform and the military leadership succession.

In a major departure from the past, this time debate over international trends and China's best response was not limited to a tiny official circle. In the summer, international affairs specialists attended two conferences to explore policy options for the 7th FYP period.[77] One conference, the regular ministry of foreign affairs conference of ambassadors, was normally just a central briefing to diplomats rather than a policy discussion. The other, attended by a broad range of specialists, was convened by the institute of contemporary international relations under Huan Xiang's sponsorship.

These two sessions served in part as briefings to widen consensus on Deng's new strategic perspective and to elicit views on possible regional policies. But they were also used to speed up reforms in foreign affairs. Huan's conference was the first to allow specialists, including those outside the government, to recommend changes in foreign policy. Both Hu Yaobang and Zhao Ziyang addressed the ambassadors and emphasized the importance of economic diplomacy. They indicated a need to reform China's foreign affairs system to better serve the primary goal of economic development.[78] Around this time, the staff offices of the party's foreign affairs leading group were strengthened to better coordinate policy; representation on the leading group by economic officials was steadily increased.[79]

Both conferences concluded that earlier views that the international situation was quite tense should be revised. Huan Xiang and others at the conference of specialists predicted that the next five years and probably the rest of the century would witness a period of international stability for two reasons. First, the reemergence of a superpower dialogue would ease tensions and reduce the superpowers' intervention in local conflicts, even though their fundamental competition would continue. Second, the Soviet Union would be less aggressive, would not resume its southward thrust, and might even begin withdrawing from Afghanistan and reducing aid to Vietnam. Huan showed prescience in his address when he predicted a temporary partial compromise on strategic arms between the superpowers by 1987.[80]

Nevertheless, considerable room remained for debate over the length of time such a Soviet strategic retreat would last, whether it would evolve into a change of Soviet global strategy or would prove merely tactical, what U.S. staying power would be, and what China's international stance should be. Most specialists felt safe in predicting that the Soviet Union would focus on economic readjustment for at least five years, and some suggested it would be the end of the century before China and the United States would have to face a Soviet

comeback. But some thought the USSR would eventually emerge vic-
torious in the next century, while others predicted U.S. global domination. Many raised new questions about Japan's potential as a military
power, and this concern grew substantially in succeeding years.

Participants in both conferences found it especially hard to agree
on how China should deal with the superpowers. There was a standoff
in the ambassadors conference between those favoring equidistance and
those favoring a continuing lean toward the West. They finally recommended the latter, primarily because it was Deng's known preference.[81]

A New Understanding of China's Place in the World

Despite inconclusiveness in these debates, in practical terms considerable realism had been injected into China's view of its own place
in the larger international system. The new appreciation within the
political elite of China's basic weaknesses that had emerged from research on China's economic, science, and education needs led to a
greater willingness by the leadership to work within the international
status quo. For the first time, the right policy questions were being
asked of a broad range of specialists. Even though Deng Xiaoping still
personally set the policy parameters in the sensitive area of national
security, specialists had considerable opportunity to fine-tune his thoughts
in the ongoing policy process. Institutionally, the monopoly on policy
within the foreign ministry elite was being challenged, and the system
was facing pressure for institutional change.

In terms of policy, those who attended the specialists conference
thought its greatest contribution to the 7th FYP planning process was
the conception that a nation must be judged by comprehensive power
(technological and economic as well as military). This concept fortified
the leadership's decision to cut the military budget and reorient investment. Building China's basic strength would allow it to be prepared
for an eventual resurgence of Soviet power (and implicitly U.S. or
Japanese power as well).

Many of the specialists had already honed their new thinking
about power by participating in or reviewing the second China 2000
study, which was the first large-scale effort to forecast domestic trends
in relationship to broader international change. The focus of the study
on international economic-scientific rather than military-strategic trends
was still rather novel. In part this focus was a logical result of the
pursuit of a systems engineering approach, which addressed developmental policy concerns as a set of subsystems and placed China in its
full context—the international system, the social system, the economic

system, the science and technology system, and so on. But in part the focus also reflected a new determination in the leadership to understand and accommodate international realities so as to make the best use of international resources.

In the process of the China 2000 foreign economic review, a number of controversies had arisen.[82] Regarding the new technological revolution, some specialists had a Great Leap Forward mentality, hoping to use advanced technology to quickly close the development gap, but the study team stressed the importance of the long time frame required for China to catch up as well as the use of appropriate technology, except where high technology provided a clear advantage. Some analysts foresaw a rapid and fundamental technological and social revolution in the capitalist West, whereas others saw the change as important but not fundamental. The study team ended up following the unwritten official line of the moment by leaving the future of capitalism and socialism open and indefinite. "The time-frame for the advent of world socialism is much longer than previously thought," it stated.[83]

Analysts similarly disagreed as to whether and when the economic balance of power had shifted or would shift from Europe to the Pacific. Some argued that Pacific growth rates would slow because of dependence on an increasingly protectionist U.S. market and because of Japan's refusal to assist development in the region. They warned that Japan and the United States would control any Pacific basin economic cooperation organization. Public references to the study indicated that the final version was not as optimistic about the regional and global environment to the year 2000 as were views expressed by others. It spelled out the grave threat to Asia posed by Soviet and Vietnamese actions as well as U.S. deployments.

Pu Shan, director of the social science academy's institute of world economics and politics, whose staff helped conduct the research for this section of the China 2000 study, definitely thought that some of the public optimism about peace was unjustified. In his view, which was reflected in the study, China's integration into the global economy would not be a smooth process, given increasing protectionism and the troubles the world economy would face compared with the 1950s and 1960s. In fact, some countries might cooperate as economic blocs against the interests of others. Conflict among such blocs was just as likely as was global peace.[84]

Continuing Uncertainties

International developments in late 1985 to early 1986, as final changes in the 7th FYP were being made, were mixed in their implications for the foreign policy debate. Evidence of U.S. intentions to pursue a strategic defense initiative (SDI) and knowledge of ongoing Soviet space weapons research worried Beijing. These developments seemed to support the skeptics' view that superpower détente was merely a cover for an arms race and also greatly complicated long-term defense planning for China. Military and civilian specialists alike worried that these programs would increase the general technological gap facing China. In August and September 1985, Deng Xiaoping expressed China's opposition to such weapons programs because "the arms race will go completely out of control, thus increasing the factors for war."[85] When it appeared that the United States and USSR might reach an agreement that allowed the Soviet Union to keep its SS-20 missiles deployed in Asia or even shift those from Europe to Asia, China's traditional fears of superpower collusion against its interests led to a cooling of its relations with both powers.

But others held to a more optimistic view of trends. Toward the end of the year, Huan Xiang was tasked with summing up information and opinion on the global environment China faced during the 7th FYP period; some of his conclusions were published in January 1986. Huan spoke of a new era of global politics and economics during which all countries would concentrate on restructuring their economies to adjust to the fact that scientific and technological development was the dominant factor shaping both economic and political change at home and abroad. Huan viewed the U.S.-Soviet summit of November 1985 as the harbinger of this broader change, with profound and largely positive implications for the coming five years. A new superpower relationship characterized by both confrontation and dialogue would emerge, but competition would be more economic than military. The two powers would promote détente in order to gain time to work out their respective economic problems. Meanwhile, the shift of competition from military to technological and economic power would boost a trend toward global multipolarity because Japan, Western Europe, and China were all witnessing rapid growth. Huan was among those who thought China might be able to gain from the technological advances of the SDI program.[86]

The policy recommendations made by Huan Xiang emerged as a set of guiding principles for Chinese foreign policy discussed by Hu Yaobang in late 1985 and by Zhao Ziyang in his speech presenting the final 7th FYP the next spring. Half of these principles included some variant of the principle of strict independence and seemed a step back from the emphasis on interdependence in 1984, but the principles of co-prosperity and the open policy were endorsed. There was also a strong emphasis on building friendships based on principle and on not using one set of foreign ties for transient, tactical purposes in another relationship. Huan attributed this approach to the lessons obtained from an official review of China's diplomatic history.[87] Thus, regardless of the continuing problems of foreign policy management, Chinese leaders had begun to effect important readjustments in national security policy and institutions that buttressed the ongoing shift toward a fully open economy.

The Weak Institutional Base for Reform

In the several years leading to the party conference of September 1985, the reformers were intent on changing in their favor the institutions of power as well as policy and personnel. Under Mao Zedong, economic work had always been distorted by the dictates of military, security, and party work in the bureaucratic competition for prestige and resources. Under Deng Xiaoping, the imperatives of economic and technological development encroached on the old privileges, mentality, and institutional structure of the other policy arenas. Events during the second wave of reform gave a boost to this trend, although not without considerable policy debate and political competition.

The successes of the reformers by 1986 were notable but were limited largely to the economic and science and technology subsystems and the major coastal cities. Changes were just beginning in the foreign affairs, military, and security sectors and in the interior. There was constant political conflict for control over the party propaganda and personnel apparatus. There was no lack of opposition; rather, the opposition was ineffective in forging a coalition, coordinating actions, and posing alternatives to the reform program. This dynamic of reform success and opposition weakness was highly dependent on two factors: the economic situation and the personal proclivities and abilities of Deng Xiaoping as he sought to balance the interests of the conservative elders and the younger reformers.

Notes

1. Hu Yaobang's speech at the party conference, Xinhua, 18 September 1985, in Foreign Broadcast Information Service China Daily Report [FBIS], 18 September 1985, pp. K1–5. Wu Mingyu, interview, May 1986, explained how the leadership viewed the 1955 precedent.

2. See Richard Baum, "China in 1985: The Greening of the Revolution," *Asian Survey* (January 1986), pp. 32–35. The 1955 party conference witnessed the purge of Gao Gang and Rao Shushi, senior officials from China's industrial base areas in the northeast and Shanghai who allegedly were favored by Stalin,

who had gained influence through control of the central planning and personnel apparatus, and who were vying for top posts.

3. Yang Ruiming, "Pointing the Way to Reforming the Education System," *Liaowang* [Outlook] 23 (10 June 1985), pp. 9–12, in FBIS, 26 June 1985, pp. K11–17. By the end of the year, the new science commissioner, Song Jian, who headed the science reform decision drafting team, also became deputy head, under Zhao, of the science and technology leading group. The upgrading of the education ministry to a commission headed by a vice premier (Li Peng), with educational representation on both the finance and economic and science and technology leading groups, also helped to institutionalize the shift of control.

Zhao Ziyang's eulogy at Hu Yaobang's memorial service, Beijing television service, 22 April 1989, in FBIS-CHI-89-077, 24 April 1989, pp. 37–39, confirmed this division of labor.

4. Editorial Department, "How to Be a Thorough Dialectical Materialist," *Hongqi* [Red Flag] 1 (January 1985), pp. 1–4.

5. In an interview with Yu Guangyuan, Beijing, May 1986, Yu explained that following the October 1984 endorsement of a planned commodity economy as China's target model, reformers sought to shift the purpose and style of planning to serve the creation of markets.

6. Interview with Dong Fureng, Beijing, May 1986. Since 1979, the writings of Liu Guoguang, Sun Shangqing, and Dong had stressed the need to shift from detailed annual allocation planning to macroplanning.

7. Barry Naughton, "Industrial Planning and Prospects in China," in Eugene K. Lawson, ed., *U.S.-China Trade* (New York: Praeger, 1988), p. 189. Until mid-1984, according to interviewees at the planning commission, Beijing, May 1986, central planners concentrated on analyzing several major problem areas, including technical renovation of current enterprises using practical rather than advanced technology; improvement in the timing of major project construction; and the feasibility of the Three Gorges Dam project. On the latter, see Kenneth Lieberthal and Michel Oksenberg, *Policy Making in China: Leaders, Structures and Processes* (Princeton, N.J.: Princeton University Press, 1988).

8. According to officials interviewed in Tianjin, May 1986, two long-term plans were drafted in 1983, one by the planning committee and one by a new advisory group that included local science academy specialists who were doing research on local enterprises. This group also advised on annual plans and other economic matters.

9. Deng Xiaoping, *Build Socialism with Chinese Characteristics* (Beijing: Foreign Languages Press, 1982), p. 14. I base my judgment regarding local improvements on interviews with planning officials in Liaoning in May 1986. I thank Joe Fewsmith for providing ideas and excellent interpreting for me while in Shenyang, Dalian, and Anshan.

10. Report on a symposium on the work of the four offices, convened on 28 October 1985, *State Council Bulletin* 34 (20 December 1985), pp. 1131–1144.

11. Interviews with Liaoning officials, Shenyang, May 1986. According to Xinhua, 23 October 1986, in FBIS, 24 October 1986, p. K17, Shanghai set up

a new urban and rural planning and environmental protection commission "to better supervise city planning, construction and management." It drafted Shanghai's city plan for the year 2000, which was approved by the state council in October 1986.

12. Interviews, ibid.

13. Xinhua, 27 March 1986, in FBIS, 27 March 1986, p. K2.

14. Interviews with Dalian planning officials, Dalian, May 1986.

15. Interviews with Anshan planning officials, Anshan, May 1986. At Anshan, the same planning group first did the Angang 2000 study in 1983 and then began the evaluation of the 6th FYP before proceeding to the drafting of the 7th, all without outside advisers.

16. Local interviews with planners and researchers in Shenyang, Dalian, and Tianjin, May 1986.

17. Ibid.

18. Much of the following information comes from interviews with Wang Huijiong and Li Poxi, coordinators of the study, Beijing and Washington, D.C., November 1985, May 1986, and June 1988.

19. Ma Hong, speech on overall development strategy for the economy, society, science, and technology at a symposium on the subject held 21 October 1983, *Jingji wenti* [Problems in Economics] 1 (25 January 1984), pp. 2–9, in Joint Publications Research Service [JPRS], CEA–84–059, 19 July 1984, pp. 13–26. The following survey of the drafting process comes from Wang and Li, ibid. They began by setting up a preliminary design, which they presented to an annual meeting of the Society of Systems Engineering. (In 1985, they presented the final report to another annual meeting to compare start with finish.)

The thirteen sections of the main study included a summary, a description of the econometric models used, and an overview of the economy, as well as reports on trends in the key economic sectors (energy, transport and communication, agriculture), population and employment, consumption, science and technology, education, natural resources, environment, and the international economic environment.

Drafting of some sixteen second-level studies was done by specialists in the academies, universities, and related commissions or ministries. Nina Halpern was told in interviews with the study group that the science and technology section was done by that commission and the transportation section by the research institute of the economic commission in cooperation with design institutes of the railway ministry, for example. Twenty other third-level studies were divided among some one hundred professional societies belonging to the China Association of Science and Technology. Originally, the team planned to forecast economic trends by geographical region as well as by sector but was unable to do so in the time available.

20. Wang Huijiong and Li Poxi, "China Towards the Year 2000 and Her Impact on the Development of the Asian Pacific Region" (Hong Kong: Hong Kong University Centre of Asian Studies, 1987), p. 11.

21. Xinhua, 23 July 1984, in FBIS, 25 July 1984, pp. K17–19.

22. The following conclusions are based on interviews, news reports (Xinhua, 31 October 1985, in FBIS, 4 November 1985, p. K17; *Jingji ribao* [Economic Daily], 2, 6, 11, and 20 November 1985, in FBIS, 19 November 1985, pp. K12–20), and summaries of the study by Wang Huijiong and Li Poxi, *China in the Year 2000* (Beijing: Research Center for Economic, Technological, and Social Development of the State Council, February 1986 and April 1987). All of these sources are in English and have counterparts in Chinese, but the full study has not been released.

23. Zhao Ziyang, speech to the party conference presenting the 7th FYP proposal, Xinhua, 18 September 1985, in FBIS, 26 September 1985, p. K25. The text of the proposal is on pp. K1–24, and the *Renmin ribao* [People's Daily] editorial of 26 September is on pp. K30–31.

24. Wang Huijiong, interview, November 1985, expressed his view that systems theory could be used to develop Marxist dialectics. See an interesting article by Robert C. Hsu, "Economics and Economists in Post-Mao China: Some Observations," *Asian Survey* 27:12 (December 1988), on how the Chinese intuitive, nonquantitative, relational approach approximates Western general equilibrium analysis.

The policy relevance of projections may be too indirect to have impact. For example, the study projected rates of consumption much lower than had actually occurred in the post-1978 period and then recommended the "shaping" of consumption patterns to keep rates low and in balance with energy and supply shortages and investment needs. Stating the need to do so, however, is a long way from recommending how to do it. For a discussion of these and other projections on consumption, see Jeffrey R. Taylor, "Consumer Forecasting," *China Business Review* 14:2 (March-April 1987), pp. 22–25.

25. The latter two methods of measuring growth focus on output in material terms, reflecting ideological biases against commerce, and thus do not take into account the service sector.

26. Wang and Li, *China in the Year 2000* (February 1986), p. 16.

27. Details about the Chinese model are little known. According to Gerald Barney, it was developed by Wang Qifan, who studied with the MIT group in 1982–1983 and took back to China the basic papers on the U.S. national model. John Sterman from the MIT group later went to China to give a week of lectures and provided a copy of DYNAMO, the computer program used in developing system dynamic models. Shanghai's Jiaotong University and Shanghai Polytechnic University worked out two Chinese versions.

Six models of production structure were designed, based on the experiences and plans of others, including Taiwan, in industrial restructuring. According to Li Boxi, interview, Washington, D.C., 1988, as of late 1987 work had begun at the development center on a large-scale project to recommend a new industrial restructuring policy as the heart of national planning efforts during the 8th FYP period.

28. Interview with Lin Zixin, Washington, D.C., April 1987. The impact on Chinese policy of large-scale forecasting will likely be less pronounced in the future than in this early stage. As researchers and policymakers focus on

specific policy problems and fine-tune the reform program, they will need additional tools. Large-scale forecasts may also prove less helpful in an increasingly complex and unpredictable international economic environment.

Nevertheless, there are plans to continue with a "rolling" twenty-year forecast, such that each five-year plan will be accompanied by a new twenty-year outlook. Local-level analysis of optimal regional development strategies will be included. Throughout 1986–1989, Yu Guangyuan and other senior specialists continued to give advice to regional groups on local and regional development. In the 8th FYP process, provinces will have a special mandate to look at the problem of diminishing water resources. The China 2000 findings in this area were so grim that they have not been publicized for fear of the demoralizing effect. A special forecast will also be made to the year 2050, by which time, according to Deng's mandate, a second quadrupling of per capita income to $4,000 will have occurred. This will place China near the level of Hong Kong, Taiwan, and South Korea in the 1980s.

29. Hsu, "Economics and Economists," pp. 1215–1217.

30. General Report Research Group, "The General Strategy for Advancing Toward the Year 2000," *Jingji ribao*, 2 November 1985, p. 2, in FBIS, 19 November 1985, p. K18.

31. The others were the reform commission institute, the science and technology development institute, and the rural development institute. See Nina Halpern, "Scientific Decision Making: The Organization of Expert Advice in Post-Mao China," in Denis Fred Simon and Merle Goldman, eds., *Science and Technology in Post-Mao China* (Cambridge, Mass.: Harvard University Council on East Asian Studies, 1989), pp. 157–174.

32. *Renmin ribao*, 22 January 1987, p. 2, in FBIS, 2 February 1987, p. K16. Zhang Jingfu headed the leading group.

33. Xinhua, 14 October 1987, in FBIS-CHI–87–199, 15 October 1987, pp. 2–3.

34. Interviews with staff members of the *Shijie jingji daobao* [World Economic Herald], Shanghai, November 1985.

35. Xinhua, 19 November 1986, in FBIS, 21 November 1986, p. G3, reported on Gerich's background and praise for his work from Vice Premier Yao Yilin and state councillor Zhang Jingfu.

36. Interview with an official of the association who formerly worked with the state council's foreign experts bureau, Beijing, May 1987.

37. Zhao Ziyang, report to the people's congress, Xinhua, 25 March 1986, in FBIS, 28 March 1986, pp. K1–28.

38. Xinhua, 14 October 1987, in FBIS-CHI–87–199, 15 October 1987, pp. 2–3.

39. For an excellent study of this important topic, see Harold K. Jacobson and Michel Oksenberg, *Toward a Global Economic Order: China's Participation in the IMF, the World Bank, and GATT* (forthcoming). The following citations are from an earlier draft. For background on China's involvement after 1978 with the United Nations Development Program, which provided $93.5 million from 1979 to 1986 and allocated $162 million for 1987–1991, see William N.

Raiford, "Ten Years of Cooperation: UNDP in China," *China Business Review* 16:2 (March-April 1989), pp. 10–13. There has also been a large but undocumented contribution to China's development from foreign religious organizations, largely in the form of teaching personnel.

40. Jacobson and Oksenberg, ibid., p. 92.

41. *Zhongguo qingnianbao* [Chinese Youth Daily], 15 January 1986, p. 3, in FBIS, 29 January 1986, pp. K24–25; and *Guangming ribao* [Enlightenment Daily], 7 March 1987, p. 3, in FBIS, 24 March 1987, pp. K26–27.

42. Jacobson and Oksenberg, *Toward a Global Economic Order,* pp. 50–53. See Zhao Ziyang's comments to the director-general of GATT, Xinhua, 29 October 1987, in FBIS-CHI–87–210, 30 October 1987, p. 1.

43. Interviews with Chinese and U.S. officials involved in bank analysis and training efforts, Beijing and Washington, D.C., 1985–1986. Two seminars of the economic development institute in 1985 particularly reflected topics of great interest to those involved in the 7th FYP process at the time: economic development strategy and education management. The bank staff gave lectures in recurrent three- to eight-week sessions for high-level Chinese officials in the two Chinese cities. Since 1985, selected Chinese have joined other middle- and high-level officials from all over the world for three to four week programs in Washington, D.C. According to Jacobson and Oksenberg, ibid., p. 100, one-quarter of the institute's budget is devoted to China.

44. Interview with Dong Fureng, Beijing, November 1985, and interviews with a number of young and middle-aged economists influenced by Kornai's work, Beijing, May 1986. This select group also included Wlodzimierz Brus of Oxford, formerly from Poland. Yu Guangyuan, in an interview, Beijing, May 1986, relayed to me a conversation in which Brus asked how the Chinese dared to revise Lenin's definition of socialism to include a commodity economy. Brus said, presumably with tongue in cheek, "Only great men can sum up economics in a slogan." Yu replied, "The Chinese economy is great, so we dare."

45. All the economic specialists I interviewed acknowledged the intellectual debt.

46. The World Bank, *China: Socialist Economic Development. Volume I: The Economy, Statistical System, and Basic Data; Volume II: The Economic Sectors; Volume III: The Social Sectors* (Washington, D.C.: International Bank for Reconstruction and Development/World Bank, 1983); *China: Long-Term Development Issues and Options* (Baltimore, Md.: Johns Hopkins University Press, 1985), with six annex volumes and nine background papers published by the bank. The first study was finished in 1981, but the Chinese did not allow it to be published until 1983. This bent toward secrecy had been significantly modified by the time the second study was completed. The following account of the drafting process is based on interviews with a number of economists involved, Beijing and Washington, D.C., 1985–1986.

47. Interviews with an official who was present at Zhao's speech and with a senior economist, Beijing, May 1986.

48. Interview with officials at the planning commission, Beijing, May 1986.

49. Beginning in late 1985, Chinese officials and media began to stress the importance of strengthening horizontal ties among economic entities; the party's plan proposal stressed the need to expand the regional economic networks centered on major cities. A national symposium on economic theory related to tertiary industry was held in September 1985. Other influences included the recommendations that China create a social security system as part of its effort to delink enterprises and social services, investigate more carefully the implications of population age structure, and address the issue of rural poverty.

50. The following comes from interview with Dong Fureng, Beijing, May 1986. Reformers may have hoped to replicate the Hungarian planning office, which focuses on development strategy and theory, and its economic committee, which coordinates but has no staff and subordinate structure. By 1986, specialists and planners were discussing the advisability of adopting the Soviet-style "rolling" five-year plan in which each year planners plan for the sixth year. This would smooth a shift of focus in macroplanning to ten-year planning and twenty-year forecasting.

51. The following is from interview with Liu Guoguang, Beijing, May 1987; and Liu Guoguang, "Economic Restructuring and Macroeconomic Management: A Review of the International Seminar on Macroeconomic Management," *Social Sciences in China* 7:1 (March 1986), pp. 9–34. Other foreign participants included Michel Albert, France; Aleksander Bagt, Yugoslavia; W. L. Brus and Alec Cairncross, United Kingdom; Otmar Emminger, Federal Republic of Germany; Leroy Jones, United States; M. Kobayasu, Japan; and Janos Kornai, Hungary. Seventy Chinese economists participated, including a half dozen young people and Xue Muqiao, An Zhiwen, Ma Hong, Tong Dalin, and Gao Shangquan.

52. Interview with planning commission officials, Beijing, May 1986.

53. Interviews with economic commission officials, Boston and Beijing, May and November 1985. According to Xinhua, 9 October 1984, in FBIS, 11 October 1984, pp. K4–8, when the commission drafted the provisional state council regulations on planning reform in late 1984, the commission retained not only the control of resource balancing (including assignments of college graduates, expenditures, and wages) but also the primary responsibility for exploring the use of economic levers, introducing contract responsibility systems in key enterprises, building economic information networks and formulating economic laws and management regulations. The commission spoke rather vaguely about how it would shift from mandatory to guidance methods in its tasks. Although plans were discussed for merging the economic and planning commissions at the center, as had occurred in several provinces at Zhao's urging, these were not put into effect, ostensibly because of the continuing need for long-term planning of some key projects, such as railways.

54. Xinhua, in FBIS, 21 February 1986, p. K11–12.

55. Song Ping, "Important Changes in the Work of Planning," *Hongqi* [Red Flag] 19 (1 October 1985), pp. 45–49.

56. Xinhua, 28 May 1986, in FBIS, 29 May 1986, pp. K5–6.

57. Xinhua, 10 September 1986, in FBIS, 11 September 1986, pp. K8–9. One participant (possibly Liu Guoguang) recommended an approach that would eventually become official at the 13th Party Congress in 1987: "The state should regulate the market and the market should guide the enterprise."

In this fluid environment, the International Monetary Fund made a timely and important input by co-sponsoring a seminar with the People's Bank of China in November 1986, "Macroeconomic Management, Growth, and the Role of the IMF." Topics included the role of monetary policy and instruments and the formulation and monitoring of fiscal policy, as well as the phenomenally successful development policies pursued by South Korea from 1960 to 1985. During 1986, at IMF's recommendation, China had devalued its currency and increased its internal interest rates in an effort to improve its balance-of-payments situation. See Jacobson and Oksenberg, *Toward a Global Economic Order*, pp. 76–77.

58. Xinhua, 29 October 1987, in FBIS-CHI–87–210, 30 October 1987, p. 1. According to Zhao, nine years before, the proportion of the industrial economy under central planning was 100 percent; in 1987, the proportion was 50 percent. New thinking about planning by Zhao and others reflected many of the recommendations of the World Bank. According to Barry Naughton, "Industrial Planning and Prospects in China," in Eugene K. Lawson, ed., *U.S.-China Trade* (New York: Praeger, 1988), p. 181, the official number of important commodities allocated centrally was 256 for many years, although fewer than that were actually controlled. Beginning in 1980, no machinery products and fewer raw materials were allocated. Between 1981 and 1983, only 30–40 were actually allocated, and at the November 1984 national planning conference, only 27 were.

59. Hu Yaobang was cited in Xinhua, commentator article, 18 February 1985, in FBIS, 25 February 1985, pp. K20–21.

60. It is very difficult to estimate real defense expenditures because much defense-related spending is hidden in the civilian budget; foreign analysts judge that the defense budget amounts to approximately half the total spending. Christopher Clarke, "Defense Modernization: How China Plans to Rebuild Its Crumbling 'Great Wall,'" *China Business Review* (July-August 1984), pp. 40–45, estimated that expenditures fell from 17.7 percent of state spending in 1977 to 13.1 percent in 1984 and would be 11 percent in 1985, with exceptions in 1979 when China fought Vietnam and in 1982 when a slight rise occurred. Wendy Frieman, "China's Military R&D System: Reform and Reorientation," in Denis Fred Simon and Merle Goldman, eds., *Science and Technology in Post-Mao China* (Cambridge, Mass.: Harvard University Council on East Asian Studies, 1989), p. 269, charted declines in defense spending in 1980 and 1981 and then very slow growth since then: 2 percent in 1982, 0.4 percent in 1983, 1.8 percent in 1984, and 3.5 percent in 1985. She also cited the science and technology commission claim that one-half the national budget for science and technology in 1985 was for the military.

61. Li Xiannian's closing speech at the party conference, in FBIS, 24 September 1985, p. K2.

62. *Jiefang junbao* [Liberation Army Daily] 1 March 1986, cited in *Wen Wei Po* (Hong Kong) [Literary Gazette], 3 March 1986, p. 2, in FBIS, 6 March 1986, p. W4. Officials and researchers at the Beijing international strategic studies institute, interview, May 1986, showed great interest in the U.S. studies and spoke of their research plans along similar lines.

63. Editorial, *Jiefang junbao,* 13 June 1985, published the next day in *Renmin ribao,* p. 1, in FBIS, 18 June 1985, p. K15. See Commander Li Desheng's comments in February 1985 on the 1975 guideline, cited in *Ta Kung Pao* (Hong Kong) [Selfless Daily], 16 February 1985, p. 1, in FBIS, 18 February 1985, p. W12.

64. Deng, *Build Socialism,* p. 70ff.

65. "Chen Bin on the Development of the National Defense Industry," *Liaowang* 6 (11 February 1985), pp. 20–21, in FBIS, 28 February 1985, pp. K3–6; and Paul Humes Folta, "New Trends in the Chinese Defense Industry's Assistance to the Civilian Economy" (Dissertation research interviews with defense industry officials, Beijing, December 1986). I am grateful to Folta for sharing his research findings.

66. On retirements, see *Jiefang junbao,* 22 December 1984, cited in *New York Times,* 30 December 1984, and 20 April 1985; on reorganization, see *China Daily,* 3 January 1985, p. 2; on ranks, see *China Daily,* 13 January 1985, p. 1, in FBIS, 14 January 1985, p. K1.

67. Xinhua, 25 October 1985. There is little information on the early 1985 meetings, perhaps because of contention. This interpretation is strengthened by the many references to the degree of unanimity (belatedly?) achieved during the June meetings.

68. *Ta Kung Pao,* 25 August 1985, p. 1, in FBIS, 30 August 1985, p. W1, discussed the Fuzhou military region; Xinhua, 21 March 1986, in FBIS, 21 March 1986, p. K4, the shelling; Zhongguo xinwen she [China News Service], 11 December 1986, in FBIS, 18 December 1986, p. 1, Dongshan Island; and *Shijie jingji daobao,* 16 February 1986, pp. 1–2, in FBIS, 3 March 1987, p. K22, the Xiamen free port. Xiamen officials, interview, November 1985, told me that the free port concept was being discussed.

69. Deng Xiaoping, speech at a meeting of the military commission, Xinhua, 11 June 1985, in FBIS, 11 June 1985, p. K1; Hu Yaobang, Xinhua, 11 June 1985, in FBIS, 11 June 1985, p. H1. Officials at the Beijing international strategic studies institute and the contemporary international relations institute, interviews, Beijing, May 1986, confirmed that there was a long and thorough evaluation process involving a series of conferences and special studies as part of the 7th FYP drafting process (which took three years). The aim of these evaluations was to achieve a more realistic assessment of China's capabilities and resources.

70. Interviews, ibid.

71. Huan Xiang, interview with foreign reporters in Beijing, 21 June 1985, in *Wen Wei Po,* 22 June 1985, pp. 1, 2, in FBIS, 24 June 1985, pp. W1–6.

72. Huan Xiang, year-end review of international trends, *Renmin ribao,* 2 January 1985, p. 6, in FBIS, 8 January 1985, pp. A7–8. Also see Huan

Xiang, "International Conflicts and Our Choices," *Beijing Review,* 26 November 1984, pp. 16–24.

An official statement by senior military official Yang Shangkun on National Day, 1 October 1984, still stressed the inevitability of war just ten days before the first hint by Deng Xiaoping that this view was changing.

73. Wu Xiuquan, in an article in *Jiefang junbao,* 23 September 1985, cited in Zhongguo xinwen she, 23 September 1985, in FBIS, 24 September 1985, p. K22. See Deng Xiaoping, *Fundamental Issues in Present-Day China* (Beijing: Foreign Languages Press, 1987), pp. 116–117. Only a small exerpt from Deng's June 1985 speech was published in this collection, and the exerpt omitted his reference to a shift in strategy, another piece of evidence pointing to disagreement.

74. Interviews with several foreign affairs experts with family connections to senior international affairs advisers, Beijing and Washington, D.C., 1985–1986. One stated that the foreign ministry was divided and unable to advise on how to balance Sino-U.S. and Sino-Soviet relations until Deng's June speech clarified his preferences.

75. Foreign affairs specialists, interviews, Beijing, May 1986, revealed that Deng's June speech also included a lengthy overview of the international situation and defined China's independent foreign policy as evenhandedness, not equidistance, toward the superpowers; this part of his speech has not been published. His secret approach to Gorbachev was first revealed in *Ta Kung Pao,* 9 September 1986, and confirmed thereafter by Deng and other senior officials.

76. For an analysis of the Sino-U.S. naval issue and the generally lukewarm trend in Sino-U.S. relations, see Richard Baum, "China in 1985: The Greening of the Revolution," *Asian Survey* (January 1986), pp. 48–51.

77. The following information is from foreign affairs specialists, including those at the contemporary international relations institute involved in sponsoring the second conference, interviews, Beijing, May 1986. I want to express my gratitude to Bonnie Glaser and Banning Garrett for first informing me about the conference and then generously introducing me to officials and researchers at the institute.

78. Cited from interviews in Harry Harding, *China's Second Revolution* (Washington, D.C.: Brookings Institution, 1987), p. 242.

79. Current China's Economic Management Compilation Group, *Zhonghua renmin gongheguo jingji guanli dashiji* [Chronicle of the Economic Management of the PRC] (Beijing: China Economics Publishers, 1986), p. 614.

80. Interview with specialists at the contemporary international relations institute, Beijing, May 1986, and Huan Xiang's speech at the conference, published in *Xiandai guoji guanxi* [Contemporary International Relations] no. 1 (1986), pp. 1–4. The deputy director of Hungary's world economics institute, interview, Budapest, May 1986, said that he had found many of his Chinese counterparts at the world economics and politics institute and the foreign ministry's international studies institute in agreement with his view that the

next fifteen years would experience no major deterioration or improvement in the global situation and that China would be little affected. He found the Chinese increasingly interested in trends in Japan and western Europe.

81. Foreign affairs specialists, note 74.

82. The following information on controversies is from interviews with researchers involved, Beijing, November 1985 and May 1986.

83. From sources in note 22.

84. Interview with Pu Shan, director of the social science academy's world economics and politics institute, Beijing, November 1985. The foreign affairs section of the China 2000 study was coordinated by Pu Shan's institute at the academy in cooperation with four state council units, including Huan Xiang's international studies center and the development center.

85. Deng Xiaoping, interview with *Liaowang* 37 (16 September 1985), in FBIS, 6 September 1985, p. B1. For an excellent study of China's views, see Bonnie S. Glaser and Banning N. Garrett, "Chinese Perspectives on the Strategic Defense Initiative," *Problems of Communism* (March-April 1986), pp. 28–44.

86. Huan Xiang, interview given to a reporter from *Shijie jingji daobao,* 6 January 1986, pp. 1, 4, in FBIS, 24 January 1986, pp. A1–5.

87. Interview with a former assistant to Huan Xiang, Washington, D.C., 1987. These foreign policy principles already were evident in Huan Xiang, interview, *Wen Wei Po,* 22 June 1985, pp. 1, 2, in FBIS, 24 June 1985, pp. W1–6, in which he referred to a review of Chinese foreign policy, perhaps one that had been in the works for a number of years under the supervision of foreign affairs veteran Xue Mouhong. Hu Yaobang's list of principles, in *Beijing Review,* 21 October 1985, p. 7: (1) friendly ties with all countries on the basis of the five principles of peaceful coexistence; (2) an independent foreign policy— no alliance with any big power or bloc of powers; (3) work with others to oppose hegemonism and protect world peace; (4) an open policy with all countries; (5) support for the Third World; (6) no search for hegemony and no succumbing to its pressure; (7) good faith and no playing of "cards" at the expense of principle; and (8) treasuring of friendship but no sacrifice of principles for the sake of a relationship.

At the people's congress, Zhao Ziyang spoke of the international situation as "turbulent and disturbing" and the situation in Asia as "grim." He also reiterated strongly independent foreign policy principles. This emphasis suggested that the peace and development line of 1984 was still meeting with skepticism. Nevertheless, the endorsement of the open policy in all fields was strong. His list of principles in FBIS, 28 March 1986, pp. K24-25: (1) oppose hegemonism, maintain world peace, develop friendly cooperation, and promote common economic prosperity; (2) oppose hegemonism and support international equality; (3) make independent judgments on international problems, using (1) as criterion; (4) maintain strategic nonalignment but work for improvements in relations with both superpowers; (5) promote normal relations and friendly cooperation with all on the basis of the five principles, not on the basis of ideology; (6) support Third World solidarity; (7) oppose the arms race, including a race in outer space; (8) promote a long-term policy of opening to all countries; (9) support the U.N. charter; and (10) expand contacts and cooperation in all fields.

6

Crosscurrents: Problems of Systemic Transition and Political Succession (1985–1988)

The start of the second wave of reform in 1984 demonstrated the wisdom of the axiom that nothing succeeds like success. Record-breaking grain harvests, relative stability in prices and wages, and balanced growth among sectors of the economy had given reformers considerable political capital to push their program farther and faster. Beginning in 1985, the other side of the coin turned up. Economic imbalances undermined the legitimacy of the reform program and opened up widespread questioning about its relative benefits and costs, not only in economic terms but also in social and political terms.

Economic Problems Threaten the Reform Program

The wave of decentralization in 1984, which allowed local enterprises to retain more profits and permitted them as well as local banks to make key decisions about financial investment, triggered economic instability. Local enterprises used their retained funds to pay wages and bonuses unwarranted by any increases in productivity; local governments and their enterprises then conspired to force local banks (also under control of the government) to release loans to fund new investments; and the central government was compelled to issue new currency to cover the loans. Much new investment was in nonproductive projects, especially for housing for which there was tremendous pent-up demand or for light industrial projects that offered enormous quick return due

to price distortions. Long-term infrastructural projects so vital to development got short shrift, both in funding and in supplies of materials
and energy. Runaway local spending on construction and imports in
the last half of 1984 kicked off a general inflationary trend, an over-
heated industrial growth rate of 25 percent, and a drop in foreign
exchange holdings. The dual-price system, which allowed insiders with
connections to gain access to goods at low state prices and resell them
at higher market prices, also encouraged widespread corruption, smuggling and illegal foreign exchange trading.[1]

This type of instability automatically increased political pressures
for recentralizing administrative controls on the economy and threatened to produce a cycle that had become typical of Eastern European
reform efforts. Pent-up demand for consumption and investment was
endemic to Soviet-style economies characterized by severe shortages of
supply; periods of relaxed central control quickly led to rapid increases
in the rate of consumption and investment, which then intensified
sectoral imbalances and created inflation. But ensuing retrenchment
through government controls on credit and prices struck arbitrarily at
efficient and inefficient factories alike. As plants shut down capacity,
the growth rate slowed, resources were wasted, and government revenue
declined. This treadmill of reform continually hamstrung efforts to
introduce structural changes intended to break the cycles.[2]

The economic problems emerging in early 1985 raised serious
problems for reformers then attempting to create a major policy document—the 7th FYP proposal—to be presented for endorsement at the
party conference in the fall. The plan proposal was intended to establish
at the highest authoritative level the absolute priority of introducing
economic reforms during the 1986–1990 period and to set forth a basic
plan for comprehensive reform. Emerging economic problems threatened to undermine all the efforts and accomplishments thus far, for
they highlighted ways in which reforms tended to undermine rather
than enhance the more fundamental goals of long-term development
and rising standards of living. As a result, 1985 witnessed fundamental
questioning of the reform program by its critics; this questioning
sparked debate and uncertainty about reform that would continue
through the rest of the decade.

Reassessing the Economic Situation

Throughout 1985, how to evaluate the positive and negative aspects of the current economic situation, the causes for the latter, and
their solutions became a central issue. In early 1985, assessments were
quite optimistic regarding current trends and therefore regarding pros-

pects for rapid reform. In late January, the leadership announced its decision to create special economic delta zones along the coast. Zones were promised greater financial and planning autonomy, thus further reducing the scope of authority for the central planning commission and enhancing the responsibilities of the SEZ planning office, which was subordinate to the foreign investment leadership group headed by Gu Mu.

By mid-January, however, this budding reform drive was threatened by the evidence of serious economic problems. Throughout the spring, the reformers struggled to keep their program on track while getting the economy back under control. In speeches in March and April, Zhao Ziyang depicted current problems as minor and stressed the importance of moving ahead with comprehensive urban reform. He convened four conferences of provincial governors in the course of the year, urging them to control the excessive scale of capital construction without "slamming on the brakes." Deng made several important interventions through statements to visitors in April and May insisting that reform should and would not be set aside no matter what problems arose.[3]

Later, a Hong Kong journal cited knowledgeable sources who described the situation through mid-1985 as follows:

Inflation in 1985 made Zhao Ziyang alarmed and bewildered. He attended meetings day and night. Every day at 1600, after handling state affairs, he used to invite people from various fields to meetings. He invited those who knew something about economics to suggest ways and means. Two questions were raised: (1) What was the actual economic situation in China? Would there be an economic collapse? (2) If that happened, what should be done? What countermeasures should be taken? At that time, some people told Zhao: "You should persist in reform." But he replied: "If the inflation rate can be controlled within two figures, I will persist in reform. Otherwise, I dare not."[4]

The reformers did not duck the hard issues as difficulties mounted; they admitted to some blame for the problems and then sought to come up with new solutions to prevent a retrogression to old central command ways. Zhao used all his institutional assets to defend his record and strengthen his political position. In March, he assigned a drafting group to begin work on the 7th FYP party proposal in a quiet compound in Beijing's western suburbs. The group was supervised by Tian Jiyun acting on behalf of the party's finance and economics leading group, headed by Zhao. The group had the advice of a brain trust made up of some well-known senior specialists and scholars and a number of young and middle-aged theoreticians who had records of proven contributions to reform.[5] But ideas were fed into the drafters from many other channels as well.

A team of economists from the social science academy headed by Liu Guoguang, using the mandatory provincial-level reports on the implementation of the 6th FYP, were asked to reassess the economic situation for the 1981–1985 period as a whole.[6] Another group of twenty-one young researchers from the research institute of the economic reform commission were assigned a major quick action project to conduct surveys in the cities in which reform experiments had been conducted by the commission. These researchers were part of the group of friends who had been intimately involved in the reform program from its inception and had shifted from rural to urban research to further the cause. They organized more than four hundred other specialists from many government and academic institutions to do social surveys on the following topics: the relationship between reform and development; the functions of government in the economy; the aspirations of factory managers; the public attitude toward price reform; the trends and views among state workers regarding employment and benefits; and the views of youth regarding work and life. The researchers' mandate was to ascertain the nature and causes of the economic crisis as well as current social attitudes toward reform and make policy recommendations.[7]

The studies by the academy and by the reform institute both defended the urban reform to date, emphasizing the positive changes, but both also admitted to serious problems and the urgent need for a new stage of research, understanding and policy revisions. The institute surveys showed a trend toward rapidly growing public support for reforms once they were introduced and people became accustomed to them. Nevertheless, the institute study concluded that the strategy of decentralization required revision in order to create more scientific policy solutions for the transition from a command to a mixed economy. They argued strongly, however, that return to administrative controls should be temporary; China needed to push reform at the microlevel by creating markets and reorganizing government as the means to achieving a new type of indirect control at the macrolevel.

The reformist conclusions of the China 2000 study and the World Bank study, both of which became available to Chinese leaders and researchers in the spring, were additional timely voices in favor of using further reform rather than retreating to address current problems. There was much exchange of information and overlap in personnel among these various studies, all done by the new institutions set up to serve Zhao Ziyang, so that their similar conclusions were not surprising. One political journal later praised the 7th FYP proposal for its realism, claiming this was based on extensive evaluations of the domestic and foreign situation, including those made by high-level officials visiting localities in China as well as abroad. Zhao was clearly using scientific expertise as a major political resource in an attempt to buttress his policy proposals against ideological and practical critiques.[8]

Leadership deliberations at a work conference during the summer were critical in reshaping policies as well as the 7th FYP proposal, to redress immediate problems but at the same time salvage the heart of the reform program. According to the Hong Kong press, Zhao was subjected to harsh criticism for the country's poor economic performance.[9] Meanwhile, the FYP drafting process proceeded through several stages, all of them fraught with controversy. Several related sets of practical issues were thoroughly reassessed in the tense political atmosphere, including how to balance investment in capital construction with popular demands for an improved standard of living; what should be the appropriate growth rate; how to balance local economic initiative with central control; what should be the ratio of civilian to military expenditures; how to balance investment in the coast with the demands of the interior; and what was required to create favorable foreign trade conditions.[10] The two issues of most immediate importance to the future of the reform program were the growth rate (how to deal with the investment hunger) and the SEZs program (how to deal with demands for special treatment from China's poorer regions).

Debate over the Growth Rate

During December 1984 and the first quarter of 1985, the growth rate of the gross industrial output value approached and then passed 20 percent, largely because of uncontrolled credit for out-of-plan local investment, especially in the processing industry. Rising costs and prices and the resulting competition for scarce energy, supplies, and markets put considerable pressure on priority state enterprises in materials, energy, and communication whose goods were priced abnormally low. State income dropped along with the output from these enterprises.[11]

A major debate ensued in the leadership and among theorists regarding how serious the problem was and what to do about it. Some argued that state revenue had fallen only slightly short of growth in 1984, and thus there was no crisis. Others argued that this alleged gain in income was inflated and in any case could not continue because of shortages; they won the day. On a short-term crisis basis, the decision was made to reinstitute administrative controls on wages, supply of money and credit, imports, and foreign exchange. Although reformers avoided using the term *retrenchment* for these procedures and called for the use of new indirect methods of deflation, in fact, the growth rate plummeted throughout the year.

On a long-term basis, therefore, the debate was not really resolved. The real issue was how to avoid these economic cycles. Slow growth, such as that achieved by the end of 1985, was as great a problem as hypergrowth. Work slowdowns due to poor supplies and poor turnover of funds and goods hurt worker morale and allowed plant capacity to sit idle. Reformers found themselves caught between the demands for balance by the fiscal conservatives and the demands for growth by industrial planners. They also were caught between deflationary policies that strengthened the old system and created shortages and inflationary policies that forced delays in price reform and undermined popular support for reform. The reformers wanted badly to achieve a moderate and stable growth rate in order to facilitate reforms, but in fact those reforms, not yet in place, were the only sure means of achieving stability.

Given the countervailing pressures, the moderate target growth rate set for the next plan period was an important achievement—6.7 percent for GVIAO (industry, 7.5 percent, and agriculture, 4 percent) and 7.5 percent for GNP—although there were caveat statements by officials that these targets might well be exceeded. Officials also decided to retain 1985 rates for investment in fixed assets for at least 1986–1987.

China's Poverty Program

During 1985, criticism surfaced regarding new inequalities of income between geographic areas and between social groups rising from reforms. Some of this criticism was quite reasonable and was expressed in practical terms; unrealistic propaganda regarding the newly rich "10,000 yuan households" was raising popular expectations for instant, easy wealth and was leading officials to overlook the still impoverished rural majority. Conservative economic officials were legitimately concerned that national interests were being damaged by pursuit of individual or local interests.

Much of the criticism, however, was voiced in highly polemical, ideological terms by conservative propaganda officials and reflected the underlying political competition of 1985. By reminding the reformers of China's commitment to egalitarian socialist values, conservatives implicitly questioned the legitimacy of reform leaders and raised a banner that could rally political support from among those threatened by reform.

Two trends in particular were cited as evidence of the reemergence of capitalist exploitation and class-based disparities in wealth—the spread of private enterprises in the countryside and the increase in joint or solely owned foreign ventures on the coast. Thus, both the rural reforms and the open policy were attacked as nonsocialist in nature. In February 1985, chief propaganda official Hu Qiaomu visited rural Fujian and complained about speculators and about high rates of consumer spending by the newly rich peasants. He called for a new slogan—"Get rich through hard work"—an implicit correction of Hu Yaobang's 1983 call for peasants to "get rich as soon as possible." Again, Hu was the main target of conservatives who dared not directly attack Deng Xiaoping and his program.[12]

In fact, judging from statistics released only much later, there was a considerable and growing disparity in distribution between social groups and between geographic regions despite an overall doubling of rural per capita income from 1978 to 1986. Output in the ten eastern provinces and regions during the 6th FYP period increased so much more than output in the eleven western areas that the gap was almost equivalent to the gap in wealth already accumulated since 1949. One hundred million Chinese remained below the official poverty line of approximately $70 per year, most of them located in the northwest (Gansu, Qinghai, Tibet, and Xinjiang), with pockets in southern Guizhou and Guangxi.[13] Clearly, the inland provinces had reason to worry that with the new east to west development strategy, scarce investment funds in the next FYP would go disproportionately to the coast, and they were lobbying for redress.

Deng Xiaoping found it necessary to defend plans to expand the commodity economy. For example, in March 1985, following a formal speech praising the new directions in science and education, he felt compelled to make impromptu remarks reaffirming his dedication to socialism and to the eventual goal of communism. Deng admitted that concerns that China might go capitalist were not entirely without foundation, and in effect, he set some new limitations on reforms: the policy of getting rich must not lead to class polarization but to common prosperity; limits should be placed on individual wealth; prosperous regions must contribute to development of backward regions; and public ownership must remain dominant.[14]

Egalitarian political pressures had been there since 1978, of course, and they had already produced several stopgap welfare programs along the way.[15] At the same time, reformers were under pressure regarding problems with the thousands of small-scale, collectively owned, or family-run rural industries and services that had sprung up as a major part of the booming rural economy. Their output was growing at a rate of 20–30 percent, which was faster than in any other sector of the economy. But these industries tended to be inefficient, at the low end of the technology scale, and demanding of scarce resources.

Reformers thus were under pressure not to forget the poor interior and agriculture, but they were also determined to continue their new coastal strategy and were looking for new ways to address the fierce competition for funds. In their view, more subsidies for agriculture and welfare were not the answer; local self-development was.

Science administrators came up with a new program that promised to address both of these issues by promoting rather than crippling the growth of the market economy.[16] The new approach had its roots in a visit to Sweden by deputy science commissioner Wu Mingyu, who supervised both the commission's policy bureau and the science and technology development center. Wu and his colleagues were impressed by various venture capital programs in Sweden and were exploring ways of adapting them in China. They conducted experiments with technical training in selected rural areas. At first, they focused on upgrading rural industry in the relatively advanced areas along the coast where the agrarian sector was already commercialized; they only later applied their ideas to poorer inland areas. Even then, the plan's originator stressed that the goal was not to enforce equal distribution of income but to provide equal opportunity for poor areas so that the goal of common prosperity was a realistic one.[17]

By late May 1985, science commissioner Song Jian had endorsed the proposal for a new nationwide Spark Plan and forwarded it to Premier Zhao's office. (The name was taken from a Chinese proverb used as the title of Mao Zedong's famous 1930s article, "A Single Spark Can Start a Prairie Fire," but this time it referred to the spread of technology and development rather than revolution.) The plan proposed to mobilize the research and development resources of China's universities, government, and military institutions in a major rural development drive. Funding for the project would be shared, with the rural enterprises and local governments each paying one-third and state loans providing the rest. In case of success, the state would be repaid by installments; in case of failure, losses would be shared three ways.

By equipping rural enterprises of all types (including farming, fisheries, factories, services) with practical technology already available in China through a kind of internal technology transfer project, the plan promised to release material supplies for larger-scale, established Chinese industries; provide industrial employment for peasants leaving the land and improve rural living standards; and create small or medium-sized cities to prevent problems of overpopulation in the major cities. The program was especially shaped to address the overwhelming shift that lay ahead from the agricultural sector to other sectors. China faced the prospect that during the next five years, half of the farm laborers would turn to nonfarming work in either services or industry. By the year 2000, the urban population would grow from 200 million to 400 million.[18] Only if most of this shifting population established new small and medium-sized cities with industry and services supportive of the major metropolises could China's overburdened major cities gain breathing space to rebuild infrastructure and move up the technological ladder.

Premier Zhao's response to the plan's promise of a "short-term, inexpensive, and quick result" was predictably positive:

The development of town and township enterprises is indispensable in transforming the structure of our agriculture. If we do not rely on science and technology, there will be no future for the development of our town and township enterprises. By combining the two, we may chart a new path suited to China's national conditions. . . . In the future, we should, in the main, first popularize the application of scientific research achievements we have scored at home.[19]

In October 1985, Wu Mingyu convened a special symposium in Changzhou, an experimental city also known as China's electronics city. He used the meeting to get widespread support for his proposal. In December, Wu and his colleagues gave a briefing on the plan to Hu Yaobang, following a visit by him to poor areas. On that visit he was deeply disturbed by the severe material deprivation (including one family who shared a single set of clothes), cultural poverty, and mental retardation he saw. During the annual rural work conference that same month, Vice Premier Wan Li also backed the Spark Plan and wove it into the broader planning process. Following another round of conferences, in February 1986, Premier Zhao maintained that "now and in the future, the vitality of our rural areas comes, and will come, from the development of the commercial economy and the popularization of science and technology."[20]

The program reflected several new concepts summed up in a set of slogans: "Get out of poverty and get rich" (recognize that growing wealth will not automatically reduce poverty, which requires a special effort); "stop giving blood transfusions and start making blood" (change from giving welfare grants to fostering development); and "open up the poverty areas" (use an internal as well as the external open economic policy to overcome regional isolation). The first of the three clearly reflected a revision of earlier controversial calls for all to get rich as soon as possible, but it also avoided using the term *common prosperity* so as not to encourage egalitarianism.[21]

The science and technology commission pioneered this effort using funds from the 7th FYP committed to (1) developing 100 complete sets of appropriate technological equipment and putting them into production; (2) establishing 500 model enterprises; and (3) training local educated youth and cadre to take back and apply technical knowledge and management practices suited to their locality. The commission adopted the poverty-stricken Dabie mountain area in Anhui for its first efforts and sent special technical teams to do project feasibility studies, setting up technical advice and training programs, and encouraging young technicians to work in poor areas. Commissioner Song Jian personally led the first mission to the region in April 1986, and by mid-1987 the commission claimed to have raised 800 Anhui households above the poverty line while also making the program self-funding.[22] These efforts were pointedly contrasted with the Maoist "learn from Dazhai" approach that required all rural areas to grow grain and become self-sufficient regardless of local conditions.

Based on the commission's pilot projects, a nationwide program was launched in early 1986. It was under the guidance of a new leading group headed by the secretary-general of the State Council, who reported to Vice Premier Tian Jiyun. A vice minister of the science and technology commission provided coordination. Other central government organs chose individual poverty areas to assist, and local garrison troops were directed to set up village centers to aid the poor, propagandize rural policy, provide economic information, and run technical training programs. The military also provided free transport, technical assistance, and medical teams to poor areas.[23]

The project was aimed at ensuring basic subsistence within five years for the 120 million peasants whose income was below 200 yuan, in eighteen poor areas located in eighteen provinces. Many of the regional development strategy seminars convened during 1985–1987 by Yu Guangyuan aimed at giving advice to these areas. The China association for science and technology set up correspondence training courses that reached 80,000 students in two years.

This project came after party approval of the 7th FYP and obviously affected the FYP budget at a fairly late date. Following a visit by Premier Zhao to poor areas in Sichuan and Hubei, the leadership decided in early 1986 to provide more than $300 million per year in special low interest rate loans. The planning commission began drawing up a development plan for poor areas for the year 2000. The final draft of the 7th FYP added a program for mutual cooperation projects between eastern and western China. Personnel and technologies flowed west while raw materials and labor went east, and the projects were partly funded with monies earmarked for poor areas. Due to continuing inequities in prices, however, which meant that raw materials were greatly undervalued, western areas remained dissatisfied.[24]

Altogether, this episode was a good example of the intermixture of politics and economics during the five-year planning process, as well as the ways in which the midterm and even annual plans were continually revised in process. It revealed not only the fierce competition for scarce resources but also the ways in which ideological disputes masked very practical conflicts of material interest. The chronic tension in post-1949 politics between so-called socialist goals of equal distribution of wealth and capitalist goals of economic growth and development could be viewed in part as competition between the two Chinas—the relatively poor interior and the comparatively wealthy maritime provinces. The Soviet-style central planning apparatus was in fact a mechanism for redistribution of resources, not a mechanism for planning economic development. The reform in planning and the drive to introduce a market economy held out promise for the coast and threatened the interior. This conflict, which broke into the open in the final stages of planning in 1985, was also evident in heated debate over the SEZ program.

Revising the Coastal Development Strategy

Throughout 1984 and into January 1985, the second wave of reform kept building toward a major expansion of the open economic policy much beyond the SEZs and even beyond the coastal cities. A wide array of economic officials endorsed the idea of opening nearly the whole coast, thereby revealing their intent to use the SEZs as models of a national transformation to a mixed economy. In the political atmosphere of the time, these officials undoubtedly saw political as well as economic benefits. The strong demands from every city and province for special rights in foreign economic relations dangled the prospect of a greatly expanded reform coalition. The more entwined China's economy was with the international market, the less likely it was that the whole reform program could be reversed. Arguments by zone officials for the diffusion of the zone concept were given prominent national press coverage.[25]

One researcher from the People's Bank followed the logic of the open policy to its extreme conclusion—that every region of the country should be allowed to explore how to use its comparative advantage to attract foreign capital and join the international economic division of labor. This author was rather impatient with the SEZ approach; he

complained that the SEZs were undeveloped, involved peripheral industry, and were too restricted in scope. They could not attract foreign
capital and advanced technology because they could not offer highly
skilled labor and extensive access to China's domestic market. He
proposed that Shanghai and Guangzhou be given enormously extended
decision powers so that they could replace Hong Kong's function as an
international financial center for the mainland economy; he also proposed that foreign investment be drawn into the developed basic industrial centers of the interior.[26]

Others lauded the SEZs in order to lobby in an openly partisan
fashion for an extension of the policy to their particular geographic
area. Given the long lead time for funding and planning for basic
infrastructural improvements in transportation and communication,
many argued strongly for simultaneous development of the interior and
the coast, even though inland resources might not come into full play
until late in the century. Others argued convincingly for an opening of
inland ports and expanding the frontier cross-border trade, including
trade with the Soviet Union. Some argued for developing the northwest
first, others favored the southwest, and still others suggested that SEZs
be set up in the interior (one official toured Xinjiang to look at the
potential for establishing an SEZ there). National symposia discussed
China's ideal long-term regional distribution of productive forces and
various regional development strategies.[27]

During the spring of 1985, however, dissenting opinion arose, and
a round of serious disagreement broke out in the leadership over how
to pursue the open economic policy into the future. The timing of this
policy review was affected by: (1) a policy factor—the end of the original
five-year (1980–1984) grant of special authority in foreign economic
relations to Guangdong and Fujian, which required renewal or lapse;
(2) a cyclical factor—the need in the drafting of the five-year and
twenty-year plans for policy guidelines, clear lines of administrative
responsibility, and budgetary decisions affecting the two provinces, the
zones, the coastal cities, and the regions designated for special authority;
and (3) an opportunity factor—a drop in foreign exchange reserves
and a corruption scandal that justified critical review.[28]

A major policy debate ensued. It focused specifically on the value
of the SEZs but had wide-ranging implications for regional budgetary
priorities and foreign economic policy. Some critics also addressed
problems of smuggling, economic corruption, and social immorality.
The press reported that many enterprises kept their accounts in Hong
Kong to avoid the state auditors, cooked their books, or prepared two
sets of books for tax evasion purposes. Meanwhile, the recreation and
tourist business had begun to offer gambling and prostitution services.

Delegates to the National People's Congress and Chinese People's Political Consultative Conference in March voiced their concerns on these issues.

The most polemical accusations, however, came from the ideologues who suggested that SEZ political losses outweighed economic benefits. To them, the foreign privileges available in the zones—special tax and customs treatment and the leasing of land—echoed the nineteenth-century foreign concessions and threatened political sovereignty. Hu Qiaomu voiced such reservations during his February 1985 visit to Fujian and in official circles.[29] He reportedly also complained that party committees and trade unions were not allowed in foreign enterprises in the zones. The Hong Kong press speculated that he was indirectly criticizing other SEZ political experiments endorsed by Hu Yaobang, such as the establishment of a university in Shenzhen with no party committee. Mainland press articles raised a related argument that expanding the SEZ policy was tantamount to the Hong Kongization of China; according to this view, China was following the Hong Kong and Taiwan model, was therefore regressing to capitalism, and was suffering from the attendant ills of corruption, exploitation, immorality, and heterodoxy.[30]

Nevertheless, the economic problems of 1985, particularly the growing shortage of foreign exchange, were the key factors in allowing these grievances to resurface. The rapid expansion of consumption funds in late 1984 stimulated a boom in foreign imports. Loosened controls over foreign trade provided opportunities for corruption as well as profitmaking. Foreign exchange reserves fell by about one-third, from $16+ billion in September 1984 to $14+ billion in December to $11.2 billion at the end of March 1985.[31]

Leadership feuding was catalyzed by evidence of a foreign exchange scam on Hainan Island that involved many central and Guangdong officials and more than $1 billion of lost or misdirected foreign exchange. This scandal strengthened the opposition and put reformers on the defensive. The feuding was heightened when a practical cost-benefit analysis led even many former supporters of the zones to reassess the policy. Vice Premier Yao Yilin changed his tone regarding the zones from praise to blame in a few short weeks. Yao complained that Shenzhen made outrageous profits on sales to the interior instead of earning foreign exchange through industrial exports, while the state suffered losses subsidizing the zone.[32] Foreign exchange controls were recentralized nationwide. The zones were allowed to retain only 30 percent (instead of 70 percent) of their earned foreign exchange and therefore lost much of what made them special.

Criticism expanded quickly to encompass a general failure of the zones to meet their stated policy goals. Zone boosters now suffered the consequences of their rash promises in 1982 and 1983 that they would rapidly bring in foreign capital and advanced technology and quickly develop a capability for export. Shenzhen's medium and long-term plans in 1982 had projected a rapid annual industrial growth rate of 29 percent to the year 2000. When visiting Shenzhen in February 1983, Hu Yaobang had personally endorsed this calculated gamble.[33]

Into the policy crisis of early 1985 stepped the voice of reason and moderation. Liu Guoguang and other economists working with him in evaluating the 6th plan period took a special investigative trip to the zones from February through April. Working with local Shenzhen officials and researchers from the Shenzhen SEZ development strategy group, they concluded that "we should acknowledge both problems and achievements; problems are inevitable, but they can be overcome." They recommended a lowering of expectations and an adoption of a gradualist, cost-conscious approach to zone development and expansion. They tried to find a compromise position between the goal of a purely industrial export orientation for the zones and the current realities of Shenzhen, whose natural strength was in trade and processing.[34]

In its report, the group spelled out a three-stage approach to development of the SEZs: (1) construction of infrastructure, funded by profits from processing, compensation trade, tourism, commerce, and real estate; (2) development of low-grade products for sale on the domestic market as import substitutes; and (3) development of technology-intensive export industries. By these criteria, the report could pronounce the SEZs a success and praise them for their work in the first and second stage while urging them to move on to the third, basically outward-oriented stage. The report carefully insisted that although the SEZs should never become primarily free trade areas, they should always remain composite in nature—that is, combining the simultaneous development of industry and commerce. The report also pointed out that SEZ development was impossible without international and domestic sources for markets, materials, and funds.

Moreover, the report spread the blame for SEZ failures by detailing the flawed conditions with which the zones were forced to struggle, including faulty policies and lack of services, information, personnel, technology, and resources for production. Thus, according to the group, zone development could not proceed without improved administrative support from central and local officials, and the report held up Shekou as a model—this time of the political reforms necessary to support economic reform. A seminar on the open policy held by leading reform researchers and officials also followed up on this point by proposing a restructuring of the foreign exchange control system.

In early April, a forum reached conclusions on zone policy, and the leadership issued a central directive that reflected Liu's report and recommendations. For a time in May and June, this compromise seemed to be firmly in place, and the policy crisis seemed to be over. Gu Mu's public remarks suggested that the further opening of the coast could resume.[35]

In the summer, however, feuding heated up again as the leadership met for its usual summer work conference. The renewed feuding was catalyzed in part by first quarter 1985 economic statistics, which looked bad. On 29 June, Deng Xiaoping startled everyone at home and abroad by telling a visiting delegation that "the success of Shenzhen has yet to be proved. . . . We hope it will succeed, but if it fails we can draw lessons from it."[36] In striking contrast to his unqualified approval and optimism in 1984, Deng now strongly implied that the SEZ policy as well as the fairly recent decision to open other areas of the coast could be drastically changed or even discarded. This set off a flurry of foreign press speculation.

In early July, the State Council called a meeting of governors and mayors to discuss the issue again. A decision was made by participants to reduce investment in the zones for 1985 back to their 1984 allotment level. Gu Mu told reporters that a freeze was in effect on the opening of all but the four largest coastal cities (Shanghai, Tianjin, Dalian, and Guangzhou) so that the leadership could reevaluate policy and conserve resources.[37] The full report on the Hainan scandal was belatedly publicized for the first time, even though investigation into the scandal had been carried out between February and May. The delay and the stark differences among leaders in their assessments of the severity of the incident underscored the acrimony at the top.

The tenor of this whole debate changed, however, in September when several thousand student demonstrators in Beijing explicitly criticized the open policy and implicitly criticized Deng. Seizing on the anniversary of the defeat of Japan in 1945, the students complained of a current Japanese economic invasion. Demonstrators cleverly used this ostensibly patriotic theme to protect themselves from reprisal while still setting forth their unhappiness with economic trends. Students were among those civilians who were on a fixed income (state subsidy) and thus suffered most from inflation. Posters also complained, however, of official corruption and nepotism. Students began networking to plan a larger demonstration on another historic anniversary—the famous student demonstration in Beijing against Japanese encroachment in China on 9 December 1935.

This turn of events made it difficult for opponents of the open policy to continue their criticisms without appearing to encourage dissidence. Education officials hurried to the universities to dialogue with students regarding their practical complaints about housing and food. The leadership debate was muted, and the regime initiated a new propaganda effort to defend the open policy and thereby address public doubts and complaints. Senior central and zone officials submitted ringing defenses. They set out new detailed statistics to belie the charges that the zones were heavily subsidized by the state and had not increased exports. Zone leaders laid the blame for the worst offenses on state enterprises set up in Shenzhen by the central government. Specialists argued that a 100 percent export orientation for the zones was not wise or even possible.[38]

During the last quarter of the year, the leadership finally reached a compromise that affirmed the correctness of the decision to establish SEZs, preserved the heart of the open policy, but involved major concessions to critics. These latter apparently included stepping up efforts to develop zone exports in order to earn foreign exchange; halting illegalities; reexamining SEZ plans to cut waste and better coordinate with the national FYP; carefully screening investment projects; and placing a moratorium on expansion of the zone model, at least for the time being.

Reformers were able to make gains, however, by learning from the crisis. The shortage of funds prompted new research into foreign commercial loans; expansion of tourism, China's overseas construction projects, and joint ventures; and a policy that would allow foreign investors to remit foreign exchange abroad rather than having to use it in China. As Shenzhen avoided new projects for export processing, the nearby counties picked up the business. Soon Dongguang county was attracting investment from former residents who had escaped to Hong Kong in the 1970s, and residents from further inland were working in Dongguang and sending remittances back home. Guangdong became the Hong Kong of interior China, as the east to west development strategy took hold in the south.

Reformers also obtained a mandate to improve economic legislation and accelerate management reform experiments in the zones. They were convinced that abuse by local officials of the decisionmaking power they had obtained was at the heart of the 1984–1985 crisis. Gu Mu complained that localities had refused to cooperate in providing goods and allocating quotas and had competed in ruinous price wars. He concluded that "the experiences gained over the past few years have told us that opening up to the outside world must be carried out simultaneously with the strengthening of administration. . . . By no means does this mean returning to the old road. . . . The point is to establish a new system."[39]

The 7th FYP party proposal reflected this overall policy compromise when it reiterated Zhao's double track concept—which held that the zone economy was the pivot of a two-way fan radiating outwardly and inwardly—but stressed the importance of exports without clearly addressing the issue of SEZ ties to the interior. The proposal blamed faulty zone performance on individual local leaders, who lost their jobs, rather than on higher-level officials or on the open policy itself. Nevertheless, the loss of face for Deng, Hu, and Zhao had its effects during the next few years. They now had a greater understanding of the depth of opposition to the reform program and its vulnerability to local implementation. This seemed to prompt them to press on with changes of personnel and policy with even greater urgency when they next had the opportunity.

Compromise in Politics and Economics

At the party conference in September 1985, reformers did quite well considering the obstacles in their path. Their gains in personnel and policy suggested that Chinese politics had stabilized to the point where economic problems could be addressed without major swings in policy or abrupt changes of leadership. There was sufficient political capital from the economic and diplomatic successes of the second wave of 1983–1984 to carry the reform program through the trough of 1985. Critics of reform were too weak and divided to offer any alternatives. The stronger hold by Deng, Hu, and Zhao on the key institutional levers of power and their concerted efforts to forge formal policy decisions that gave them a mandate for further change paid off politically at the conference.

Although there were no retirements or promotions in the Politburo standing committee, leaving the elders in place, important changes were made at the next level down. Elderly veterans, especially military figures, retired to other bodies, and the younger, active executives of the reform program were rewarded. Hu Yaobang's chief aide in the Secretariat, Hu Qili, as well as Vice Premier Tian Jiyun and Foreign Minister Wu Xueqian all joined the Politburo; so did Vice Premiers Yao Yilin and Li Peng, who tended to side with more conservative views on economic matters but were not leftist ideologues. Li and Tian also entered the Secretariat along with newly appointed Vice Premier Qiao Shi and several others. These younger figures were then well placed for promotion to even higher posts by the time of the 13th Party Congress.

On economic policy the conference ended up in a situation similar to that at the beginning of the 6th FYP—affirming the need for reform and readjustment while leaving open the details to continual negotiation and experimentation. The plan proposal endorsed a slow growth rate and minimal budgetary resources for the military in order to create the best possible conditions for an eventual, comprehensive structural reform program, which pledged to address all the practical problems that had arisen:

> We must introduce a series of mutually reinforcing reforms in the planning system, the pricing system, the fiscal system, the banking system and the labor and wage system so that these mechanisms will function together, integrating planning with market regulation, and micro-flexibility with macro-control. Accomplishing this will lead to a satisfactory handling of various economic relations, making it possible to harmonize the interests of the state, the collective and individuals, to achieve greater uniformity in the speed, proportion and efficiency of economic development and to bring about self-sustained growth in our national economy as a whole.[40]

Precisely when and how to implement this program were left a bit vague, however. Reformers were given a yellow light for their program—that is, if and when they stabilized the economy, they could move ahead. Zhao suggested at the party conference that one year or two would be required to consolidate the reforms to date before moving on. By the next spring, in his speech to the people's congress, Zhao indicated that new reforms would not be introduced before the third year of the plan.[41]

There were degrees of urgency even among reformers regarding how long it would take to complete the reform package. Deng Xiaoping and Hu Yaobang had spoken of completing the reform in three to five years. Zhao said in late 1985 that China would lay the foundation during the next five years, but the next spring he flatly stated that "it will be impossible to complete the reform in all. . . . aspects during the 7th FYP." Hu Qili said that "it will probably take ten years or even longer to fully shift to the new structure."[42]

Despite the usual attempt to create a compromise document that would give the appearance of leadership unity, speeches at the party conference by Deng Xiaoping and Chen Yun revealed considerable and surprisingly public disagreement about future policy directions in a number of areas. Deng emphasized the gains made from reform; Chen harped about the problems it brought and emphasized that central planning should maintain a predominant role in the economy. (The plan proposal had skirted the issue of how planning related to market regulation.) Chen's sharpest criticism was aimed at the 1985 slowdown in grain production, when price disincentives for grain growing were exacerbated by the abandonment of monopoly procurement and sale by the state. Chen also complained that the authority and functions of the party's ideological and organizational mechanisms had been weakened and that work in this area required improvement.

In the sensitive area of social and cultural development, which had been included in the planning budget since the onset of the 6th FYP, budgetary apportionment was made, but very little was said about the direction of policy. Although Zhao Ziyang in his speech to the party conference urged improvement of the system of social science research and study of new branches of learning and frontier sciences, these recommendations seemed rather at odds with the focus of Deng and Chen, who spoke of the importance of studying Marxism and inculcating Communist ideals.

Overall, Chen Yun's remarks were a strong, albeit implicit criticism of the performance to date of Deng's two successors. Chen seemed to allow reformers their gains on condition that they work harder to ensure economic and social stability. By speaking out, Chen Yun spoke for and encouraged conservative critics of reform at all levels. By complaining of economic imbalances and inequalities, these critics highlighted the continued importance of redistribution through central planning; by complaining of corruption, social indiscipline, and ideological dissent, they underscored the need for strengthening control mechanisms.[43] Events during the next two years proved that the sharp differences between Deng and Chen were more telling than the surface appearance of compromise. The consensus that allowed the party conference decisions proved quite fragile.

Political Struggle Delays a Third Wave

The economic crisis of 1985 shook the confidence of reformers, and they came to realize that decentralization of power and simplification of administration—the heart of economic and political reform strategy to date—were inadequate and problematic. Local government officials had abused their new powers by putting the squeeze on enterprises instead of delegating power to them. Officials who had privileged access to resources had through bribery, speculation, and nepotism used their new economic authority and loopholes in the tax and price systems to line their own pockets. The irrational price structure still fostered low productivity and technical stagnation in enterprises. Egalitarian values and authoritarian/dependency attitudes toward authority led to widespread suspicion of reforms that introduced competition and promoted social and political pluralism.

These problems highlighted an urgent need for major political reforms and changes in political culture to improve decisionmaking and followthrough. Attention turned toward understanding the complex linkages among economic and technological change, political institutions, and cultural values and behavior. Comprehensive reform was redefined to include these noneconomic areas, but the fundamental question remained: What was the future role of the party-state in a modernizing Chinese society?

Even as reformers turned their attention to these problems, their mandate for change in noneconomic arenas was quite weak. Deng Xiaoping had called for political reform as early as 1980, and party rule had been regularized and rationalized in the years since, but the essence of the party's monopoly on the economy and society had scarcely been touched. Ideological issues had been so politically sensitive that reformers had avoided discussing them and had proceeded with reforms in the name of pragmatism and science. The leadership had little understanding of the rapid and vast moral and social changes underway in China. Now that these matters were coming to the fore, Hu Yaobang, as the leader responsible for party affairs, had to define a less interventionist role for the party in a manner that would strengthen rather than weaken its legitimacy and authority.

As reformers addressed the more complicated aspects of reform, they began to disagree among themselves over the direction and pace of economic and political reform. These differences were exacerbated by the pressures of succession politics; opponents of reform were able to take advantage of uncertainty and lack of coordination. Major attempts to create a third wave of advance for Deng Xiaoping's comprehensive reform program in 1986 and in 1988 were stymied by leadership fears of social instability and by dissent. Reform opponents used student demonstrations in late 1986 to remove Hu Yaobang from office and used panic-buying and bank runs brought on by economic inflation in mid-1988, and signs of local economic separatism, to attack Zhao Ziyang. The issue of social order moved to the top of the political agenda and was likely to remain there, judging from the experiences of other nations trying to manage the modernization process. A polarization of social forces emerged in China. The intellectual community pressed for democratization while local authorities pressed for more decentralization; the central control bureaucracies pressed for uniformity and recentralization. As a result, compromise approaches to China's serious problems were harder to achieve, and the future of Deng's program appeared increasingly uncertain.

As 1986 began, reform economists and officials were very much on the defensive. In speeches and articles, they countered arguments by unnamed critics that in practical terms the reform program was as reckless a failure as the Great Leap Forward and that in ideological terms it was a rightist turn toward capitalism. Reformers countered that on the average the previous five years had been the best in PRC history and that real income was still rising. They blamed the old economic structure rather than the new policies for current problems and argued that the solution was more reform, not less. This was the line taken by Liu Guoguang's group in its report on the 6th FYP period, which was included in the introduction to the 7th FYP when it was presented to the National People's Congress in March.[44]

Neverthless, the official statistics for 1985 showed a foreign trade deficit of $14.9 billion, a reduction in grain output by 28.33 million tons, and a rise in vegetable prices by 34.5 percent.[45] The official press announced in early January 1986 that stabilizing the economy, especially prices, would have top priority throughout the year and that any reform measures not conducive to this must be set aside. In particular, any reforms that might exacerbate unfair distribution of income or put the economy out of control would be avoided. Zhao Ziyang defended the price and wage reforms of 1985 but announced his intention to focus only on change in the monetary system and internal management of state enterprises in 1986.[46]

One reason for the slow comeback of reform in early 1986 was a growing disagreement among reform theorists and officials. They seemed genuinely surprised at the unexpected side effects and distortions of reform policies that in theory made a great deal of sense. Sympathetic Hungarian reformers had detected overconfidence when visiting China in 1984–1985. When they had asked Chinese reformers about their plans for handling errors in the program, they had been told, "We won't make any more mistakes."[47] The negative feedback of 1985 showed the reform leadership the strength of bureaucratic obstruction and also the fragility of support for reform among intellectuals, students, and the rest of the urban populace once inflation and corruption set in. This realization led to confusion and disagreement within the reform camp that proved to be a serious weakness during the next several years as the reformers sought to make further progress.

A 7th FYP for Economic Reform

Shortly after the 7th FYP was adopted in the spring, a new economic reform drafting group was established whose mandate was to create a detailed plan for introducing the reforms. The group was probably supervised by Vice Premier Tian and the economic reform office of the finance and economic leading group. In a sense, this was one more effort in a long series since 1980 to flesh out general slogans and policy guidelines.

The problem facing the reform drafters was something of a chicken and egg problem—which reform should come first. Reformers had fought for and won endorsement of a comprehensive set of coordinated reforms and had concluded that these must be introduced gradually in a stable economic environment, not in a single one-shot package. Yet this still left most of the key procedural questions unanswered. In one passage of the party plan proposal, the linkages among the reforms were explained in such a way that price reform would logically come first. Another passage, however, discussed three stages for implementation that did not seem to conform to the same logic and implied that price reform would come later. The statement that these stages of reform were interrelated and overlapping and the description of reform implementation as a "formidable and complicated problem of systems engineering," although true, also seemed handy euphemisms for not knowing how to proceed.[48]

Reform planners went back to the drawing board. As one specialist put it in January 1986, "The loss of economic control in the second half of 1984 and the results of implementing the ensuing control measures fully show the complexity and difficulty of restructuring China's economy. Complex reality will inevitably give rise to theoretical introspection . . . and a new round of theoretical probes." According to this author, there were two main schools of thought about reform. The majority of specialists argued that the incomplete nature of the reform, with irrational prices still making fair competition impossible, had fueled investment hunger and inflation. The solution was to introduce coordinated reforms in pricing, taxation, and interest rates in order to create the proper environment for competition. They also criticized basing taxation and foreign exchange earnings reform on bargaining over profit sharing between central and local authorities and argued that economic authority must be transferred to local enterprises, not local officials, in order to overcome local protectionism and pressure for higher growth rates.

A second, minority group agreed that the market environment was important, but these specialists argued that the issue of ownership and management rights was even more fundamental. So long as enterprises used state funds without well-defined authority for managing the funds, and so long as these enterprises functioned as social welfare institutions instead of businesses, they would continue to expand investment, wages, and benefits without linking these to rises in productivity. Ill-defined management rights just promoted the search for short-term gain and inhibited long-term and larger-scale (consortium or regional) investment. The solution, therefore, lay in creating a new interest structure by guaranteeing that enterprises will have sole responsibility for profits and losses and will have control over a defined portion of their assets. Eventually, this should take the form of stock ownership and enterprise groups.[49]

The first approach, which emphasized the central role of price reform, shaped both the 1984 economic reform decision and the 7th FYP proposal and has been identified strongly with Wu Jinglian, a senior economist at the development center. Wu was one of the chief members of Liu Guoguang's task force on alternative economic models and was highly critical of gradual, ad hoc reformism, which he believed would land China in the same straits as it had Eastern Europe. He warned, however, that the state had to be in good shape financially to protect society from the shocks of change, and this required a relaxed economic environment. Wu favored a strong central state to centralize resources and guide investment. His approach complemented the development center's interest in using new means such as the China 2000 and World Bank forecasts to improve central planning. Liu Guoguang of the social science academy generally shared Wu's views but was less optimistic that the proper environment—low inflation, consumption, and construction rates—could be easily and quickly created. Liu, like many of the older economists, viewed inflation as totally unacceptable.

The second approach, which emphasized the central role of ownership reform and implied that enterprise bankruptcy and worker unemployment should be permitted, was identified with Li Yining, an economist at Beijing University, and was close to that of Dong Fureng at the social science academy. The young researchers at the reform institute also tended to favor Li's approach, although they emphasized in their 1985 study that financial reforms as well as enterprise reform were essential.

Advocates of this second approach tended to view inflation and the corruption stemming from the dual-price system as necessary and acceptable costs of delaying price reform. Younger reformers favored continued rapid growth through consumption, perhaps partly out of a political desire to retain and expand support for reform. They also put a much higher premium on political reform, including legal reform, in order to cut the ties between the enterprises and the bureaucratic organs at all levels and to guarantee new arrangements by law. They were much more skeptical than the first group about the advantages of government interference in market operations.

By February and March of 1986, the tide was beginning to turn in favor of resuming reforms. Perhaps the results of the fourth quarter of 1985, which showed a drop in the growth rate to 4 percent, prompted the usual concern that economic stability merely meant stagnation. The reform drafting group was set up by Zhao to bring together the younger reformers from the economic reform commission's institute with the competing groups of older specialists. They drafted a full set of comprehensive reform policies, as called for by the 7th FYP, covering the price, tax, and fiscal systems as well as a bankruptcy law. Their bold program called for a large-scale, immediate adjustment of prices part of the way toward market prices during 1986, followed by a full release of price controls within one or two years. Clearly, the timetable followed Wu Jinglian's preferences and ignored the political compromise reached at the party conference that required two years of stabilization policies.

At first, the proposal appeared to win Zhao Ziyang's approval, but then he wavered, in part because of the inflationary environment that remained despite retrenchment efforts and in part because the plan called for very large transitional subsidies and the coffers were low. According to one specialist involved in the decision, despite the lack of major adjustments of state-controlled prices in 1985, the average price of heavy industrial products still rose by 11 percent because of the rise of out-of-plan prices. Increased costs of industrial inputs invariably were passed on as increased prices and/or reduced tax payments.[50]

After April, when Zhao Ziyang convened a provincial governors conference to discuss how to give factory managers greater responsibility, he decided to shelve the macroeconomic reform plan intended to create market conditions and concentrate on reforms in factory management and in government-enterprise relations, at least for the time being. This decision reflected a major change in Zhao's thinking about reform. He may have been partly influenced by political demands for increases in the industrial growth rate and state revenues. Controls on the money supply and credit were again loosened, perhaps at the encouragement of the younger reformers, who tended to argue that China's problems were due to insufficient demand not insufficient supply. To address the shortage of investment funds, renewed efforts were made to attract foreign investment and loans; pilot projects to reform the financial system were launched in twelve cities and in Guangdong province. These localities opened money markets, initiated capital lending among banks, and drew up draft plans for overall financial reform.

During the summer of 1986, expanded experiments in factory autonomy were conducted in the key experimental cities. Directors were allowed to employ workers by using contracts that allowed hiring and firing with less interference from the party committee. Directors were also given more control over production decisions and contracted tax arrangements with government authorities. These contracts were modeled after the rural contract responsibility system and were a half-way measure that still gave the state considerable influence. More radical measures were also tried. A number of state-owned enterprises were turned over completely to collective management, and a national symposium of experts discussed new ownership arrangements—joint stock enterprises—that would divide shares among the state, the enterprises, and individual workers. As political change moved to the forefront of the reformers' agenda, the State Council selected sixteen medium-sized cities as testing grounds for urban administrative reform.

A 7th FYP for Reform in Ideology, Culture, and Politics

During 1986, as Zhao attempted to set new economic policies in motion and explore administrative reform, Hu Yaobang tried to address the burning noneconomic issues, including political reform and corruption. Hu resumed aborted efforts of 1983 to introduce guidelines for political democratization. All his efforts in 1986 were undertaken with one eye to enhancing his prospects of succeeding Deng as China's paramount leader at the 13th Party Congress the next year. He began in January by launching a pair of complementary initiatives. One was the drafting of a formal document to guide social and cultural (spiritual) development and political reform for the 7th FYP period, to be endorsed nine months later at the 6th Plenum.[51] Hu used this opportunity to introduce revisions in ideology, policy, and political institutions that required a much less interventionist role for the party in education, research, the arts, and social organizations. Just as Zhao was drafting economic reforms that if carried out would revolutionize the way the planning apparatus worked, so Hu was drafting cultural reforms that suggested an overhaul of the propaganda and security apparatus. Both efforts by another name were major political reforms.

Hu's second initiative was a campaign against official corruption at the highest levels, which—according to Hong Kong rumors—resulted in the arrest or imprisonment of a number of offspring of high-level leaders, including those of Peng Zhen and Hu Qiaomu. Several characteristics of this campaign, however, raised the widespread suspicion that a personally motivated purge was under way. Hu assigned this task to Qiao Shi, thought to be a close associate, under a new leading group, rather than use the existing party rectification commission, which was heavily salted with conservative elders. Moreover, those families most affected were known to be Hu's opponents. This personal power aggrandizement probably galvanized opposition and undermined his other initiative, which required building leadership consensus behind an official document.

Both initiatives were launched at a meeting of central officials referred to as the 8,000 cadre conference, held in Beijing. In his keynote speech, Hu gave a ringing defense of the major programmatic innovations since 1978. He spoke of the need for a five-year effort to achieve new approaches to ideology, culture, and politics that would better serve the goals of the 7th FYP for the economy. Tian Jiyun backed him with a speech that put an optimistic gloss on current economic problems.

Parts of Hu's speech seemed almost like a pep talk to senior officials, urging them to overcome bureaucratism and set an example for the rest of the populace in pressing forward with the reforms. They were to be more efficient, knowledgeable, disciplined, and democratic in their work. Hu criticized cadre for corrupt, autocratic practices and for not implementing central reform policies when they were sent down. There was something of an archaic ring to this speech, in which Hu used old-fashioned moralistic political campaign methods to push progressive goals.[52]

The word got out that Deng Xiaoping had personally encouraged Hu's effort, and beginning in late March, Deng made a series of public comments in favor of speeding up reform and expanding its scope beyond the economy. In one meeting with foreign visitors, he said, "The 7th FYP . . . will be crucial to China's stability and progress for several decades. . . . During the next five years, comprehensive economic reforms will also involve politics, education, science, technology and other areas. . . . The reforms will not succeed if we lack determination, or if we are unwilling to take risks." Most importantly, Deng's comments singled out China's feudal culture, rather than new bourgeois influences, as the cause of official corruption and abuse of power. To emphasize his commitment, he even raised the spectre of another cultural revolution if China failed to carry out political and cultural reform. Both Hu Qili and Wan Li expounded on Deng's themes, and in May, the reform commission set up test centers for political reform in sixteen cities. None of the leaders' speeches was made public in China, suggesting strong opposition to this upsurge.[53]

Deng was motivated in part by concern that the slowdown in economic growth would complicate achievement of his long-term goals. He introduced the idea of a second quadrupling of per capita income in the first half of the next century from $1,000 to $4,000. Whereas in April 1984 Deng had spoken of reaching or approaching the most developed level in thirty to fifty years, and in August 1985 Hu Yaobang had hoped to achieve this by 2050, now Deng underscored the need for greater realism. "We do not hope to catch up with or surpass the developed countries. We will then [2050] be up to the medium level of development."[54]

The impact of Deng's interventions was quickly evident in intellectual circles. It helped turn around another outbreak of the perennial conflict within propaganda circles. Conservative media attacks on several openminded scholars in the social sciences academy early in the year were intended to set constraints on the new upsurge of policy research and drafting and to launch another campaign for orthodoxy. One target was a young economist who recommended adopting Western economic practices; another was a well-known cultural theorist, a strong critic of traditional Chinese culture. The attacks were now superseded by symposia clearly intended to defend them.[55]

Reformist intellectuals organized to float new ideas on ideological and cultural issues for Hu Yaobang's document-drafting group. They used the thirtieth anniversary of the 1956 post-Stalin thaw to widen the doors to freedom of thought and policy-relevant research. In May, to celebrate the anniversary of Mao's 100 Flowers speech, the social science academy held a forum on cultural and academic freedom. Shortly afterward, Shanghai convened a conference to discuss local cultural development strategies and plans that was attended by China's free thinkers and newly appointed reform-minded propaganda officials. Media reports proclaimed the meeting the start of a new May Fourth Movement of intellectual enlightenment.[56]

The implicit message of this celebration was that China should guard against any repeat of the Antirightist Campaign of 1957, which ended the post-Stalin thaw in China and led to decades of anti-intellectual leftism. China's new propaganda department director, its new minister of culture, and several prominent artists as well as a whole generation of newly appointed vice ministerial officials had been branded as rightists at that time and had been banned from politics for two decades. They had a personal political stake in reviving the 100 Flowers policy; their legitimacy and careers would be enhanced. These were the cream of the Hu Yaobang constituency.

The overt theme of these celebratory sessions was the need to reform China's autocratic political culture (and, implicitly, its political system) through the development of scientific concepts and democratic values and institutions. By summer, the intellectual ferment was moving discourse beyond previously acceptable concepts and standards, and senior reform officials signaled their support. Vice Premier Wan Li gave a major address at a national symposium on soft science (the multidisciplinary use of related natural and social science knowledge to improve decisionmaking). Science administrators who had long backed democratic reforms for the sake of freeing science and technology from the fetters of ideology, including Commissioner Song Jian and nuclear scientist Qian Xuesan, worked on the speech. Wan Li reaffirmed the prevailing official line (most often breached in practice) that the arts and academic research should be free of political interference. But he went on to say that policy research also must be liberated from its subservience to politics in order to create more scientific decisionmaking at all levels in China. Wan Li stressed the usefulness of soft science for updating old methods of party leadership, including mass campaigns, emulation of models, and heavy reliance on field investigations by officials.[57]

This speech turned out to be the boldest official statement during the discussion of ideological and political reform in 1986. Wan Li's speech, like Hu Yaobang's speech of March 1983, was a manifesto for creating a new type of party by bringing specialists into leadership positions and adapting new scientific approaches to making and enforcing decisions. The statement set the stage for moving concrete political reform policies onto the leadership agenda at the plenum. The Secretariat set up a political reform leading group to explore the issues. Headed by Hu Qili, it was dominated by Hu Yaobang protégés. Shortly after Wan's speech, however, there was an outbreak of major leadership disagreement over the plenum document being created by Hu Yaobang and Hu Qili, and the leadership made a decision to postpone discussion of political reform until the next year.[58]

The specific grievances against the treatment of ideology in the draft document were several, including the absence of criticism of bourgeois liberalism, calls for an ethic of competition and innovation to expand the socialist commodity economy, and a change of the 12th Party Congress program to delete the reference to Communist ideology as the core of China's socialist spiritual civilization. The document insisted that because China was only in an initial stage of socialism, only party members were required to believe in the ultimate ideal of communism. In the meantime, the majority of China's citizens who shared the common ideal of making China a modern, highly democratic, and cultured socialist country should be given political equality.

Clearly, the party was being asked to give up its role as a priesthood bent on transforming society through mass campaigns and to carve out a new role as a modernizing elite leading society by more technocratic and democratic means. More to the point, old revolutionaries were being asked to turn over the reins to the younger generation at all levels. One intended purpose of the document was as a basis for reformist criteria for cadre promotion and demotion during the last phase of the three-year rectification campaign at the grass-roots level.

Another purpose of the document was to require local officials to draw up five-year plans for social development with real backbone to them—more money for housing, education, health, entertainment, and other services. This they proceeded to do, but judging from complaints in the press, much of the activity was pro forma. In November, an official leading group for the social sciences set the priorities for social science research for the following five years, with an emphasis on research into comparative political systems, regional development strategies, and cultural development strategies.[59]

Politically, the 6th Plenum witnessed a stalemate. The title and phrasing of the resolution were watered down; its focus became developing socialist spiritual civilization rather than reforming the propaganda system. No personnel changes occurred. Zhao Ziyang was put in charge of a new political reform leading group. This suggested that Zhao was being favored over Hu and that political reform was to be limited largely to administrative restructuring.

Nevertheless, a media campaign to publicize the resolution encouraged a return to muckraking journalism and sensitive themes. Speeches and articles by leading intellectuals favoring liberal democratic reform grew surprisingly radical in their calls for human rights and democratic institutions.[60] When students in Anhui took to the streets in December to protest unfair state elections, the free-wheeling intellectual atmosphere contributed to the rapid spread of demonstrations to more than fifteen cities. Some posters declared support for Hu Yaobang against his critics. This provided the perfect pretext for a vengeful conservative counterattack on Hu Yaobang and a strategic decision by Deng Xiaoping in January 1987 to abandon him as a liability to the reform program. The ensuing campaign against bourgeois liberalism and total Westernization in the early months of the year, in which three prominent intellectuals close to Hu Yaobang were deprived by Deng of party membership, brought up all the old charges against the reform program as a whole.[61]

Hu Yaobang's Dismissal

Beginning in 1978, Deng Xiaoping had planned carefully and had used all his political skills to put Hu Yaobang and Zhao Ziyang in unassailable positions as his successors. His model appeared to be an old one, the Mao-Zhou relationship at its best. Hu, like Mao, would run party, military, and security affairs; Zhao, like Zhou, would be responsible for economic and foreign affairs. But in actual practice,

Deng kept the reins in his own hands; as paramount leader, he intervened wherever and whenever he chose. In particular, Deng had difficulty turning over military affairs. Ostensibly, the reason for continual delay in his stated plans for retirement was the refusal of other elders to do likewise.

In 1986, the de facto triumvirate that had worked together so successfully to create the programmatic basis for long-lasting reform fell apart. As the 13th Party Congress loomed on the horizon, the younger men's political interests diverged from Deng's because they had to plan beyond the Deng era. Whereas Deng sought to balance the interests of elders and his successors, Hu and Zhao sought to please Deng while building constituencies among a younger generation of officials whose views would be decisive in the long term. Hu Yaobang made politically fatal mistakes in trying to consolidate his power at the expense of the party elders and even of Deng and Zhao. Zhao Ziyang, having survived his own crisis in 1985, managed to turn his administrative responsibilities for the economy into political capital, at least for a short time.

The two men, while working closely in alliance to defend and strengthen Deng Xiaoping's reform program, had built different constituencies and had quite different relationships with the elders. Using shorthand, we might call Hu Yaobang's coalition the humanistic reformers—those younger cadre such as Hu Qili who had worked under him in the Communist Youth League and humanistic Marxist intellectuals such as Hu Jiwei and Wang Ruoshui involved in theory and propaganda work. Many in both groups had been labeled rightists in 1957 and had been on the fringes of power for two decades. They were not Western-style liberal democrats, but wanted to make the party accountable to the people within a single party system. Using his appointment prerogatives as general secretary, Hu gradually promoted these types within the Secretariat and party departments as well as to provincial posts, particularly in the interior provinces.[62]

In 1986, as he tried to swiftly promote followers in the sensitive arenas of propaganda, personnel, military, and security affairs, Hu explored a more democratic way of governing that included elections of party officials and appointment of younger intellectuals to party posts. Calls for change in culture and research were meant to justify a turnover in the propaganda apparatus. Hu Qili in propaganda, Wan Li and Du Runsheng and their followers in rural affairs and science and technology circles, and Yu Guangyuan and others (such as Su Shaozhi and Yan Jiaqi) at the social science academy were close allies in this endeavor. The reform upsurge of 1986 brought them into direct conflict with the orthodox wing of the party leadership, which retained strong influence through formal position and informal access to Deng.

The chief opponents of Hu Yaobang were National People's Congress chairman Peng Zhen (with clout in the political-legal sector), advisory commission vice chairman Bo Yibo (industrial planning and personnel affairs), Wang Zhen (military affairs adviser), and Hu Qiaomu and Deng Liqun (propaganda overseers). These men knew their personal positions and the future of their families were threatened by Hu, and they represented sectors of the bureaucracy that were losing out overall in the reform process.

Meanwhile, Zhao Ziyang's coalition of technocratic reformers had been growing. His constituencies included many central officials and researchers in economic development, trade, and science circles as well as local economic administrators, especially in Guangdong and Sichuan provinces (where at times he had been the leading official) and in the open cities and special economic zones. These were China's pragmatists; all of them had gained tremendously from the reforms. As premier, Zhao apparently had special influence in appointing mayors, governors, and State Council ministers. Zhao's primary critics were Chen Yun, Bo Yibo, and Yao Yilin, who spoke for central planners and were positioning Li Peng for the premiership.

Throughout the 1980s, the reform program expanded the influence of the State Council from purely economic administration to policy research, science and technology, and education affairs, to legislative matters, and gradually to military and foreign affairs that touched on economics. This growing imperialism of the economic bureaucracy steadily strengthened Zhao's personal power base. When Deng turned to Zhao in early 1987 as a replacement for Hu Yaobang in control of party affairs, he probably also had the support of Chen, Bo and Yao, who could then hope to gain control over economic affairs.[63]

Little is known about the relationship between Hu Yaobang and Zhao Ziyang, but there is some circumstantial evidence that differences between them helped open the reform camp to attack in 1987. In their years of cooperation, at least three areas of disagreement were discernible: the speed of economic growth, foreign policy, and the nature of political reform.

In the early 1985 economic growth rate debate, Hu Yaobang urged a double digit target and was active in the military demobilization and reform program. He argued that cuts in the conventional forces and reorientation of military industry for civilian purposes would allow China to reach its quadrupling of output goal earlier than the year 2000. This stance fitted with Hu's consistent demands during inspection tours that local officials, including managers of energy projects, speed up their quadrupling efforts.[64] He may have been appealing to the interests of central and local heavy industrial planners and military modernizers in the high-tech sectors (air and naval). Zhao fought off this speedup, probably with the support of Chen Yun, Yao Yilin, and others concerned about economic balances.

In foreign affairs, Deng Xiaoping seemed to be delegating some of his powers by dividing geographic regions between his protégés, but overlapping and competition occurred. Zhao was most active in economic, Sino-U.S., and Western European relationships. Hu encroached on these areas, however, by making comments in late 1984 and again in 1986 that threatened to upset Sino-U.S. ties. Hu Yaobang's party responsibilities naturally inclined him toward improving party relations and ties with other socialist countries. He had a personal interest in Eastern European reform experiences dating back to the 1950s.[65]

The one foreign affairs issue involved directly in Hu's fall was relations with Japan. Knowledgeable diplomats acknowledged that policy and personnel in this arena were overhauled in early 1987 to adopt a tougher stance on trade and prestige issues. Hu had developed a personal interest in the Japanese development experience and cultivated a special relationship with Prime Minister Yasuhiro Nakasone in order to cement close ties. During his visit to Japan in late 1984, Hu announced new principles to guide the relationship down through the generations that overshadowed those announced by Zhao while in Tokyo in 1982. Hu's invitation to thousands of Japanese youth to visit China caused logistical problems and appeared to many demeaning to China in comparison to the few hundred Chinese youth invited in return.[66]

A basic source of conflict between Hu and Zhao was the ambiguous institutional framework in which they worked. The interests of both lay in rejuvenating and democratizing the traditional Politburo-dominated approach to policy formation and implementation in order to give more influence to the views of younger officials they were wooing. They wanted to avoid vetting policy options in informal expanded Politburo meetings or work conferences dominated by the elders. From there, their interests diverged, however. Hu Yaobang sought to increase the power of the Secretariat in setting policy directions in all arenas and to hold party plenary sessions, congresses, and conferences that brought in central and provincial party officials. Zhao sought to enhance the power of the government to increase efficiency and rationality of policy planning (in part by reducing its involvement in economic administration). This aim implied a need for greater autonomy from the Secretariat for the party leading groups for economic, science, and foreign affairs that Zhao ran. He preferred to make policy through national conferences of officials convened by these functional groups or through meetings of governors, mayors, or State Council ministers.

In the early 1980s, the Secretariat at first played an equal or dominant role in all spheres of policymaking. This was evident in Hu's early involvement in SEZ policy and his co-directorship with Zhao of the leading group for the economic reform decision. Gradually, however, Zhao's leading groups and their offices and think tanks in the State Council played a larger role in researching, shaping, and coordinating policy. As economic development was given highest priority, these organs headed by Zhao were encroaching on matters that normally would be exclusively party affairs—from research to rural policy to science, education, and even national security matters. Indirect evidence of this conflict emerged after Hu's fall when the powers of the Secretariat were severely trimmed and functional party leading groups were strengthened.

Ultimately, however, although Hu's problems with Zhao made him more vulnerable to charges of factionalism, his conflict with the elders over the issue of social control and a falling out with Deng over the timing of Deng's retirement brought Hu down. Heated disagreement broke out between Hu and military veterans at a military commission meeting underway in December 1986 when student demonstrations were spreading. When Hu recommended a calm and measured response to the student demonstrations, he made it appear that at a minimum he was soft on anarchy or at a maximum was trying to use Cultural Revolution–style mass politics for his own political purposes. Yang Shangkun reportedly refused to support Hu's assumption of Deng's position as military commission chairman. Deng chose to abandon Hu to save his program and his own hold on power, despite a close personal relationship for more than forty years.[67] There is no evidence that Zhao played a hand in this crisis except that he was available as an acceptable alternative.

This political crisis was a natural outcome of Deng's decade-long strategy of liberalizing economic theory and policy while preserving Leninist political and ideological controls. Social groups promised more freedom and resources in the process of economic liberalization—especially the intellectuals—were not adequately accommodated by new political institutions and processes. Grass-roots efforts by groups outside the bureaucratic establishment to create new means of expression, ranging from unofficial media to house churches to entrepreneurs' associations, and the use of noninstitutional methods, including demonstrations and strikes, exacerbated leadership tension. Chronic student protest calling for democracy—encouraged by the teaching, publishing, and convening of salons and conferences of younger faculty, graduate students, and prominent party and government intellectuals (many of whom were adjunct professors)—provided evidence of the disaffection from the aging oligarchy of several generations within the elite.

The division of labor among senior leaders set up by Deng to prepare for the 13th Party Congress reflected his intent to pursue his dual strategy despite its shortcomings. Zhao supervised the drafting of the work report setting forth the main policy program for advancing reform in the future. He assigned each of several research institutions to draft a proposal for economic reform to be compiled into one by the reform commission; the head of the reform institute drafted a program for political reform. But a cabal of elders had primary responsibility for personnel and organizational changes, with military and civilian under separate groups, and the political reform leading group was reorganized to include conservatives.[68]

This reversion of key decisions to a tiny, exclusive elite of the revolutionary generation—Deng and those with access to him by virtue of seniority—marked a retrogression in Chinese politics. This was symbolized by the forum used to approve Hu's dismissal and Zhao's promotion as acting general secretary: A Politburo meeting was expanded to include the senior members of the advisory commission (who constitutionally had no right to vote in a Politburo meeting but whose opinion nevertheless weighed heavily). This development was a signal failure for Deng in his efforts both to regularize and democratize intraparty politics and to turn over his own power to others before death. Open conflict between the elders and Zhao's supporters was evident throughout 1987; the elders launched a campaign against bourgeois liberalization so as to expand the purge of reform-minded officials and limit reform policy initiatives. Zhao tried to shut down the campaign and limit the purge to retain a base of support and advance the reform program. The untidy and lengthy sorting out process beginning in mid-1986 lost China more precious years of progress. Clearly, the succession to Deng Xiaoping was going to have major costs in terms of modernization.

The 13th Party Congress: Mandate for a Third Wave

The immediate consequences of Hu Yaobang's fall were surprisingly limited. The need to reassure alarmed domestic and foreign audiences that China remained stable and would continue to pursue Deng's program set powerful limits on change. In an impressive display of political agility, Zhao, with Deng's backing, worked successfully to shut down the ideological campaign against bourgeois liberalization and to weaken the positions of its backers. Only a few senior officials linked to Hu lost their jobs, but through transfer rather than total dismissal from officialdom. At the party congress, Hu Qili and Qiao Shi were promoted to the Politburo standing committee along with Yao Yilin and Li Peng, thereby providing a balance of reformers and conservatives with Qiao holding the center. Zhao's political assets were greatly strengthened; he retained control of the party's finance and economic leading group and became first vice chairman of the military commission, both at Deng's insistence. As general secretary, Zhao also inherited oversight of party affairs. Nearly all the elders, including Deng, left the Politburo to leave room for younger technocrats; the elders then redivided other senior party and state positions among themselves. Experiments with more open voting procedures allowed indignant delegates to make certain that Deng Liqun was given no position at all, which overrode the elders' intent that he join the Politburo.[69]

The work report presented by Zhao at the congress contained concessions to concerns regarding the fighting of inflation, overall balances in the economy, and a continued role for state administrative intervention. The report also reflected Zhao's shift of priority in 1986 from price reform to enterprise reform. But overall, the work report provided a strong mandate for resumption of a third wave of radical reforms to create a new economic structure: a "socialist market system" that included capital goods, money, technology, labor services, land use rights, and stocks and bonds. Progress on these fronts would then promote price reform. The report legitimized the private economy for the first time and stated the necessity for further increases in income inequality. The report did not specify, however, whether such changes were to be implemented during the 7th FYP as originally intended. In fact, the plan was barely mentioned, an indication of the damage done by the 1985–1986 economic crisis to Zhao's prestige. Zhao stressed instead the gains of the prior ten years under Deng Xiaoping's leadership, claimed early accomplishment of the growth and welfare goals of the 1980s, and implied that the party congress was a new starting point for the 1990s.

All of the marketing measures Zhao announced were undergirded by a new conception of the plan-market relationship—the state regulated the market and the market guided the enterprises—and by a new conception of China's task of building socialism. Zhao redefined and endorsed the idea that China was only in the initial stage of socialism and would remain so into the middle of the next century (until the year 2049, the hundredth anniversary of the founding of the PRC). The primary task in this early stage was economic development, not collectivization of political and social life and preaching of communism.

Later media commentary on Zhao's conception of the initial stage
suggested that it was also a timetable for reforming the Chinese system.
During the 1990s, China would continue reform experiments, create
markets and supporting legislation, and strengthen government regulatory institutions; in the following ten years, ownership reform would
change state economic enterprises into modern corporate legal entities;
for the remaining forty years of the initial stage, China would univer-
salize reforms and create a fully modern economy and society.

In a bald restatement of Deng's more pragmatic views, Zhao
declared that "whether or not something is advantageous to the development of productive forces ought to become the point of departure
for our consideration of all problems and the fundamental standard for
judging all our work."[70] Specifically, Zhao explained, this meant that
the organization of production and distribution should be flexible to
allow more nonstate ownership and separation of ownership and management and sources of income other than wages, including rent, interest, and stock dividends. Zhao's statement also meant that forms of
political and social organization could and should be changed to suit
the needs of development.

The work report included a section pointing the way to political
and social reforms that would limit the power of the party, specifically
the introduction of a civil service in the government and more autonomy for the existing democratic parties and social organizations. These
issues had been highly controversial throughout the year, as reflected
in constant changes in the form, personnel, and mandate given the
political reform leading group responsible for drafting a programmatic
statement. The final draft had been hotly debated at the plenum preceding the congress; it received only general and lukewarm endorsement
and only parts of it were approved for inclusion in the work report.[71]
Timing on political reform was quite vague; some (unspecified) measures would be introduced immediately, and others would be gradually
introduced during a ten-year period, at least.

The direction of the approved political reform was for the party
to limit its direct involvement to strategic policymaking and personnel
appointments essential to maintain its continued political dominance,
but to delegate even more concrete policymaking and executive power
to the government, legislative power to the congress, and judicial authority to the courts. Responsibilities would be clarified and internal
supervision systems introduced. The former independence of the military bureaucracy would be limited by its inclusion in this more efficient
and stronger state system. The primary motive of such reforms seemed
to be improving bureaucratic accountability and efficiency within the
regime rather than introducing external democratic checks on power.[72]

Public supervision of the state was viewed as a necessary but distinctly secondary aim to be achieved indirectly, through public opinion surveys, letters to the press or administrative offices, and appointed or indirectly elected representatives to the legislature or people's consultative conference (composed of noncommunist and communist party representatives).

Overall, Zhao seemed to adopt a centrist stance on political issues so as to protect and advance his economic reforms. This was typified by his definition of the party line as one center (economic development) with two points (one being the principles of reform and opening up and the other being the four cardinal principles—socialism, party leadership, Marxism-Leninism–Mao Zedong Thought, and people's dictatorship). In other words, China needed both reform and stability for the sake of development. Zhao depicted himself as a gradualist and a pragmatist situated between two political extremes—ideological conservatives and reform radicals. In his work report, he specifically ruled out the adoption of the Western system of competitive party politics, contrasting it with China's sytem of cooperative party politics under Communist party leadership. Similarly, separation of powers was ruled out in favor of separation of functions within the party-led system. Nevertheless, Zhao criticized the major defects of China's overcentralized and bureaucratized political system and endorsed the goal of socialist democratic politics as a regime goal equal to and complementary to that of a socialist commodity economy.

Struggle Continues

Zhao's strategy, as it emerged from the party congress, appeared to comprise (1) continued efforts to stabilize the economy but acceptance of some inflation as inevitable; (2) enterprise management and ownership reforms supported by a reshuffling in the propaganda apparatus to reduce ideological constraints on economic policy research; (3) use of the spring people's congress session to showcase an increased "transparency" (press coverage) of government operations and increased openness to discussion of policy issues by official representatives of the public; and (4) comprehensive reform experiments in the coastal region in lieu of consensus on nationwide implementation. Research and discussion of reforms centered on the drafting of a new eight-year economic plan (1988–1995).[73]

In early 1987, Zhao visited the coast and publicized a new concept for development of its export economy known as extending both ends of the economy outside—that is, large-scale imports of materials and finances for rapid expansion of exports. Zhao stopped by rural factories and encouraged them to set up foreign ties for financing and markets. Guangdong and Fujian were given new leeway to experiment with political and social reforms, while the newly formed leadership for Hainan Island, now a separate province, heavily publicized its intentions to experiment freely with capitalist development methods. Shenzhen explicitly announced its intent to learn from Hong Kong's experience. The coast was implicitly exempt from efforts to cut inflation and growth rates. Despite tremendous controversy, which persisted through the year, the Politburo accepted Zhao's defense of a high-growth policy for the coast and endorsed Zhao's idea in February.[74]

These efforts were explicitly intended to integrate China's coast with the international economy; the resulting resources and added competition were to spur an economic takeoff on the coast that would inspire and draw in the interior. China under Zhao Ziyang appeared to be following the East Asian development model pioneered by Hong Kong, Singapore, South Korea, and Taiwan.

The coastal strategy was more than an economic program, however; it was closely linked to China's aspirations for political reunification with Hong Kong and Taiwan through a gradual and natural economic convergence. Just as Chinese leaders had been encouraging Hong Kong to invest in Guangdong, they now encouraged the Taiwan leadership to expand trade, investment, and visits. Hainan was designated as an experimental zone for the reunification policy and directed its appeals especially to Taiwan investors. Throughout the year, media articles in Taiwan and Hong Kong as well as on the mainland discussed the potential in the 1990s to develop a Chinese economic ring that would use Taiwan's funds, technology, and management expertise to help develop production sites on the mainland, with Hong Kong acting as an intermediary and outlet for market research and sales. The explicit assumption was that only through such cooperation could any of the three parties compete in the future as the regional economies of North America (the United States and Canada), Japan cooperating with Southeast Asia, and a unified Europe grew stronger but also more protectionist.[75]

Zhao's ambitions quickly ran aground as another economic crisis emerged in 1988, and leadership infighting was fueled by disagreement over economic and social policy.[76] Although details of key events and rivalries in 1988 remain unclear, it seems that complaints in the spring by congress delegates regarding continuing urban inflation rates close to 20 percent, rampant official corruption, and continuing lack of investment in agriculture, education, and social services prompted Deng Xiaoping and Zhao Ziyang to bite the bullet and shift again to bolder comprehensive measures centering on price reform. In statements to visitors in late May, around the time of a Politburo meeting in which Zhao called for building a new economic order, Deng spoke of the need for bravery in the face of risks, claiming it was better to bear short-term sufferings than long-term ones.[77] This decision, in which Deng appeared to lead and Zhao to follow with some reluctance, seemed a rather desperate move to get rid of the dual-track price system in order to shore up the reputation of the reform program. Neither corruption nor inflation seemed to respond to older solutions.

Zhao was forced to take the old comprehensive market reform plans off the shelf, repackage them to incorporate enterprise reform, and sell them to the rest of the leadership and the populace. Again, Zhao proceeded by asking eight groups to draw up proposals for conceptual approaches to reform; Yao Yilin supervised a State Council effort to draft concrete policies. Leadership discussions that stretched through the summer were quite stormy, and Zhao prevailed only with great difficulty and at cost to his own reputation. According to the Hong Kong press, Zhao came under criticism for mismanaging the economy by elders such as Bo Yibo who shared the skepticism evident in pronouncements by Yao Yilin and Li Peng regarding the wisdom of proceeding in an inflationary environment.[78] The Politburo in mid-August nevertheless endorsed a midterm plan that called for decontrolling the prices of the majority of commodities and subjecting them to market regulation; the plan also called for continuing political reform, especially separating the government from enterprise management. The Politburo concluded that the economy was in sufficiently good shape to begin the new effort in 1989, following a few more months of stabilization.

Within two weeks of the decision, however, the theme of reform was made secondary to that of inflation-fighting for 1989; a State Council meeting stressed that the price reform was only a long term goal for the next five or more years. A lengthy party work conference and plenum in September instituted a major new retrenchment program for the rest of the 7th FYP period. Zhao was forced to admit that policy mistakes had been made going back several years and to concede more control of economic affairs to Yao Yilin and Li Peng.[79] This abrupt turnaround was a direct result of a wave of panic-buying and runs of bank withdrawals in China's major cities in August. Fearing rapid price increases, people withdrew their money from the banks and purchased durable consumer goods. This demonstration of lack of confidence in the government quickly dissipated the fragile leadership consensus behind accelerated reform.

Although the immediate problem was rapidly ended with some quick fixes on interest rates and reassurances in the press, the political damage to the reputation of the reformers, including Deng Xiaoping himself, was done. Meetings held to commemorate the tenth anniversary of his reform program in December were marked by a lack of the self-congratulation so evident at the 13th Party Congress one year earlier. Into 1989, as Yao and Li fought with limited success to implement administrative controls on corruption as well as on prices, wages, credit, and investment, public confidence in the government remained at a low ebb. Attempts to reassure foreign investors were undermined by resource and credit constraints on the growth of coastal industry. Attempts to silence intellectuals who sought to question both the leadership's assessment of the economic problems and their policies fed tensions and political competition within both intellectual and leadership circles. Reform intellectuals offered increasingly radical critiques of the cultural and political roots of the interlinked problems of corruption and inflation. They discarded the Chinese literary tradition of moral remonstrance and began to organize a modern civil rights movement based on petitions and nonviolent demonstrations. Despite forewarning and other intentions, China was being sucked into the morass of inflationary-deflationary economic cycles, intellectual alienation, social unrest, and political stalemate that had come to characterize the Eastern European reform experience.

Notes

1. Bruce Reynolds, ed., *Reform in China, Challenges and Choices: A Summary and Analysis of the CESRRI Survey* (Armonk, N.Y.: M. E. Sharpe, 1987), p. 14.

2. Barry Naughton, "Industrial Planning and Prospects in China," in Eugene K. Lawson, ed., *U.S.-China Trade: Problems and Prospects* (New York: Praeger, 1988), pp. 185–186.

3. Zhao and Deng are cited in Wu Peilun, a member of the reform commission, "The Process of China's Urban Reforms," *Liaowang* [Outlook] 50 (16 December 1985), pp. 19–21, and 51 (23 December 1985), pp. 22–24, in Foreign Broadcast Information Service China Daily Report [FBIS], 15 January 1986, pp. K14–25; and Zhang Zhichu and Lin Chen, "Report from Zhongnanhai: 'Concept of the 7th Five Year Plan' of the Chinese Communists," *Liaowang* 39 (30 September 1985), pp. 9–12, in FBIS, 21 October 1985, pp. K9–14. Deng said, for example, "The strategic goal of economic development that we have set will not possibly be fulfilled if we do not introduce the reform and adhere to the opening up policy."

4. *Ching Pao* [Mirror] 126 (10 January 1988), pp. 18–22, in FBIS-CHI-88–009, 14 January 1988, p. 11.

5. Zhang and Lin, "Report from Zhongnanhai"; confirmed by interview with a senior economist, Beijing, May 1986.

6. Interviews with Liu Guoguang and others, Beijing, May 1986 and May 1987.

7. The following information is from Reynolds, ed., *Reform in China, Challenges and Choices.*

8. Zhang and Lin, "Report from Zhongnanhai," cited Hu Yaobang at a meeting held to discuss the draft party plan proposal; "The correct evaluation of the situation is our footing in drawing up the 7th 5YP." The report specifically mentioned domestic trips by Hu, Zhao, Wan Li, Hu Qili, Li Peng, and Tian Jiyun, along with Hu Yaobang's visit to the South Pacific, Peng Zhen's to Japan, and Zhao's to Western Europe. The report even claimed that a major purpose of these visits abroad was to assess the international situation. Inexplicably, Li Xiannian's July 1985 visit to the United States, in which Li Peng was included, was not mentioned.

9. *Wen Wei Po* (Hong Kong) [Literary Gazette], 21 July 1986, pp. 2, in FBIS, 24 July 1986, p. W1–3.

10. Yao Yilin, interview with a Japanese economic delegation, *Liaowang* 16 (21 April 1986), pp. 4–5, in FBIS, 29 April 1986, pp. W1–4.

According to Yuan Mu, *Lilun yuekan* [Theoretical Monthly] 1 (25 January 1986), pp. 1–9, in FBIS, 18 March 1986, pp. K1–12, in the spring the plan proposal had been kept within a small circle, going through four drafts before being released for review at higher and lower levels in June. Hu Yaobang convened two sessions of the Secretariat in early July during which the members went over the draft plan proposal "word for word," offered "many important opinions on amending it," and created a fifth draft for widespread distribution. It is not clear whether the Politburo members had been consulted as a body prior to this. More than two hundred central and local officials, scholars, and enterprise managers reviewed it in a ten-day meeting convened by the Secretariat and State Council in mid-July. The same draft was also circulated to local party committee members responsible for economic work nationwide and to all members of the Central Committee, advisory commission, and discipline inspection commission. Altogether, more than one thousand people were involved in the July review, which produced a sixth draft. A seventh draft was created after an expanded Politburo meeting on 20 August approved it in principle but made further suggestions. Then after "heated discussions" at preparatory meetings, this draft was approved in principle by the 4th Plenum on 16 September. Yet another and final draft was considered by the party conference and approved on 23 September.

11. A 5 percent increase in financial receipts required a 10 percent increase in GVIAO, according to Shen Liren, "Transformation of Economic Development Strategy," *Jingji guanli* [Economic Management] 9 (5 September 1986), pp. 3–5, in FBIS, 31 October 1986, pp. K6–12. According to Wu Jinglian, Li Jiange, and Ding Ningning, "Hold Down the Growth Rate of the National Economy Within an Appropriate Range," *Renmin ribao* [People's Daily], 17 May 1985, p. 5, in *Chinese Economic Studies* (Fall 1985), p. 55, from 1981 to 1984, GVIAO grew 41.8 percent; freight transport, 19.4 percent; power output, 21.1 percent; processing (machine-building and electronics) industry, 63 to 97

percent; and raw and semifinished materials (metallurgical/chemical) industry 30 to 40 percent.

12. Pan Zhaozong, *Fujian ribao* [Fujian Daily], 2 February 1985, p. 1, in Joint Publications Research Service [JPRS] CPS–85–068, 9 July 1985. Central directive no. 1 of 1983, which was the second of five no. 1 annual directives pushing forward the rural reforms, put forth the slogan, which was a bald statement of the shift from ideological to material incentives.

13. Gao Hongbi and Liu Yunzhou, "Poverty, We Declare War Against You," *Renmin ribao,* 8 November 1987, pp. 1, 2, in FBIS-CHI–87–219, 13 November 1987, pp. 40–44. Also see *The Economist,* 31 October 1987, p. 36. The official poverty line of 200 yuan has not changed since the early 1980s (when it was worth $100), despite inflation. (With devaluation of the yuan, it was worth $67 in 1984–1985 and $54 after 1986.)

14. Deng Xiaoping, *Fundamental Issues in Present-day China* (Beijing: Foreign Languages Press, 1987), pp. 101–104, defended the reform program at a meeting of the advisory commission and called on prosperous areas to help the backward areas. In 1984, Deng had seemed more confident in stressing that tens of billions of foreign funds could be absorbed without affecting socialism and that there was no possibility of economic polarization. See Deng Xiaoping, *Build Socialism with Chinese Characteristics* (Beijing: Foreign Languages Press, 1985), pp. 38–39.

15. For example, in 1982, following a visit by Zhao Ziyang to Gansu during a severe drought/famine, the party's finance and economics leading group decided to allocate 200 million yuan annually to a work relief program in central desert regions. World Bank development projects were directed to the interior. In September 1984, a central directive required government departments to make available special funds or cheap loans totaling 2 billion yuan per year to old liberated base areas, ethnic minority areas, border areas, poor areas, and underdeveloped areas. Part of this new assistance program involved requiring coastal areas to develop economic ties with the interior, to make use of their resources in place of imports and to transfer technology inland. For details of this background, see Chen Junsheng, "Sum Up New Experiences, Reform the Work of Helping Poor Areas," *Renmin ribao,* 24 November 1987, p. 5, in FBIS-CHI-87-224, 20 November 1987, pp. 26–32. Also see a report in *Renmin ribao,* 23 May 1988, p. 1, in FBIS-CHI-88-106, 2 June 1988, pp. 57–58, on a forum convened to discuss how the eastern and western parts of the country could make joint efforts to develop the poor areas.

16. The following background is from an interview with a science official who accompanied Wu to Sweden, Beijing, November 1985.

17. Interview with Wu Mingyu, initiator of the Spark Plan, interview, Beijing, May 1986. My thanks to Barry Naughton for pointing out the shift in the focus of the program.

18. Wu Mingyu, "A Fundamental Policy for Promoting the Technological Progress of Township Enterprises—A Few Points of Understanding on the 'Spark Plan,'" *Renmin ribao,* 27 January 1986, p. 5; and Song Jian, "The Origin and Prospects of the 'Spark Plan,'" *Liaowang* 45 (9 November 1987), p. 15, in FBIS-CHI–87–222, 18 November 1987, pp. 25–26.

19. Yi Yao, "Some Facts About the 'Spark Plan,'" *Liaowang* (overseas edition) 10 (10 March 1986), pp. 8–10, in FBIS, 19 March 1986, pp. K5–8. The World Bank report probably shaped Zhao's response as well. He had been particularly impressed by the report's emphasis on the importance of wider diffusion of already available production technology. This message, in turn, had been reinforced by the writings of science reformers who argued that China should not view high tech as a panacea for underdevelopment but should focus on "appropriate technology."

20. Ibid., p. K7.

21. Interview with Lin Zixin, secretary-general of the science and technology commission, Beijing, May 1986. Also see the *South China Morning Post,* 20 January 1988, p. 10, in FBIS-CHI-88-013, 21 January 1988, p. 38.

22. Wu, "A Fundamental Policy." Later reports on the commission's effort pointed out considerable difficulties. These were due in part to price rigidities for rural inputs and outputs but also due to the tendency of officials to start grandiose projects and use advanced, imported technology unsuited to local resources and needs. See Xue Tao, research work report, *Nongmin ribao* [Peasant Daily], 5 May 1987, p. 2, in JPRS-CAR-87-013, 1 July 1987, pp. 83–84; and *Banyuetan* [Fortnightly Talks] 18 (25 September 1987), pp. 20–23, in FBIS-CHI-87-203, 21 October 1987, pp. 21–23.

That the program was self-funding, even profitable, was perhaps even more important to the state than the success rate. According to science commissioner Song, "The Origin and Prospects," in only one year, the original five-year project was completed in terms of numbers of enterprises set up, and the money invested was recovered. With an investment of 2.3 billion yuan, 10 billion yuan were earned. According to Ke Xing, "International Cooperation in Carrying out the Spark Plan," *Liaowang* 45 (9 November 1987), p. 15, in FBIS-CHI-87-222, 18 November 1987, pp. 15–16, 25–26, Third World countries and the United Nations were trying to determine whether the project could be duplicated elsewhere as a means of developing the countryside and damping rural-urban migration. The science commission was discussing with the World Bank and a number of developed countries cooperative projects they might do under the Spark Plan umbrella.

23. Xinhua, 18 March 1987, in FBIS, 26 March 1987, p. K48.

24. Report from the planning commission, Xinhua, 10 February 1987, in FBIS, 22 February 1987, pp. K14–17. For an excellent article on the worsening conflict between regions after 1985–1986, see Yang Jisheng, "'East-West Dialogue' in China," *Liaowang* (overseas edition) 9 (27 February 1989), pp. 5–7, in FBIS-CHI-89-067, 10 April 1989, pp. 37–44.

25. See, for example, Liang Xiang, "The Policy of Developing Special Economic Zones Is Entirely Correct," *Renmin ribao,* 29 March 1984, in FBIS, 6 April 1984, pp. 1–5.

26. Bo Tao, "On 'Northward' and 'Southward' Strategy: Initial Probing on Developing China's Capital Cooperation with Foreign Countries," *Guangzhou yanjiu* [Guangzhou Research] 1 (1985), pp. 34–38, in FBIS, 17 April 1985, pp. K8–14.

27. See two articles in *Jingji ribao* [Economic Daily], 3 June 1985, p. 3, in FBIS, 12 June 1985, pp. K5–6 and FBIS, 14 June 1985, pp. K14–15; and one in *Renmin ribao,* 9 December 1985, p. 5, in FBIS, 16 December 1985, pp. K8–12. Gu Mu's trip was reported in the *South China Morning Post,* 20 January 1988, p. 10, in FBIS-CHI-88–013, 21 January 1988, p. 38.

28. Gu Mu, "Opening Up to the World—A Strategic Decision to Make China Strong and Prosperous," *Kaifang* [Opening] 9 (8 September 1985), pp. 2–8; in FBIS, 10 October 1985, pp. K1–10, referred to the five-year limit ending in "late 1984" and implied that the decision in April 1984 to renew for 1985–1989 had just been renegotiated with "new content and new plans."

29. See note 12. This and other evidence suggests that Hu Qiaomu was voicing the conclusions of a special study of the open policy done in the Secretariat's policy research center under Deng Liqun, perhaps in preparation for a central meeting convened in the fall of 1984 to evaluate the current state of the open policy. Speaking at that session, Gu Mu defended the policy against unnamed critics who charged that there were no socialist precedents for SEZs, that studying and applying capitalist production methods was heterodox, and that the zones and open cities were little different from the old treaty ports. See *Ming Pao* (Hong Kong) [Enlightenment Daily], 22 June 1985, in FBIS, 24 June 1985, p. W8; Luo Ping, "Notes on a Northern Journey," *Cheng Ming* (Hong Kong) [Contending] 94 (1 August 1985), pp. 9–13, in FBIS, 7 August 1985, pp. W1–8; and Zhu Bing, report on Gu Mu's speech, *Shijie jingji daobao* [World Economic Herald], 5 November 1984, pp. 1, 3, in FBIS, 6 December 1984, pp. A1–5. For excellent detailed treatments of debate over the SEZs, see George T. Crane, "China's Special Economic Zones: The Political Foundations of Economic Performance" (Ph.D. diss., University of Wisconsin, Madison, 1987); and Joseph Fewsmith, "Note: Special Economic Zones in the PRC," *Problems of Communism* (November-December 1986), pp. 78–85.

30. Luo, ibid.; and Luo Ping, "Notes on a Northern Journey," *Cheng Ming* 99 (1 January 1986), pp. 10–11, in FBIS, 7 January 1986, pp. W5–8. Crane, ibid., p. 45, said that Hu Yaobang encouraged Shekou to experiment with the election of factory leaders by workers and other political innovations.

31. *Hsin Wan Pao* (Hong Kong) [New Evening News], 31 March 1985, and Zhongguo xinwen she, 6 July 1985, cited in Fewsmith, "Note," pp. 6, 28.

32. My description of criticism of the zones is taken from Crane, "China's Special Economic Zones," pp. 53–58. He cited estimates of $1.5 billion loss in foreign exchange, which only emerged in the year-end accounts for 1984. Hainan Island's leadership, with the help of the navy, imported 10,000 vehicles and 2 million TV sets for profitable resale to the interior.

33. Ibid., p. 74.

34. Liu Guoguang et al., eds., *Zhongguo shehuizhuyi jingji de gaige, yanjiu he fazhan* [The Reform, Opening and Development of China's Socialist Economy] (Beijing: Jingjiguanli chubanshe [Economic Management Publishers], 1986), pp. 78–106. Fewsmith, "Note," pp. 19, 34, contrasted Liu's views with Zhao's "fan" approach, but there is less difference if Liu's idea of three stages is taken into account.

35. Ling He, report on the April seminar, *Renmin ribao,* 17 May 1985, p. 5, in FBIS, 24 May 1985, pp. K5–7. The forum and central directive were cited in *Wen Wei Po,* 15 April 1985, p. 2, in FBIS, 16 April 1985, pp. W1–2.

36. Xinhua, 29 June 1985, in FBIS, 2 June 1985, p. I1.

37. Gu Mu, Xinhua, 15 July 1985. Also see *Wen Wei Po,* 7 July 1985, p. 1, in FBIS, 9 July 1985, pp. W7–8. Shenzhen mayor Liang Xiang was replaced by Li Hao, formerly Gu Mu's secretary, vice minister of the economic commission and deputy secretary-general of the State Council (probably in charge of SEZ work). Throughout the rest of 1985 and into 1986, the Chinese press reflected continuing and heated debate about how to proceed with the zones, as a series of national symposiums discussed their appropriate development strategy in relation to overall national requirements. Historical allegories appeared that seemed to attack or defend Hu Qiaomu's implicit accusation that supporters of the zones were traitors selling out the national interest. See Fewsmith, "Note," p. 82.

38. See Fewsmith, ibid., pp. 82, 84. A remarkable commentator article in the youth newspaper *Zhongguo qingnianbao* [China Youth Daily], 26 October 1985, p. 1, in FBIS, 12 November 1985, pp. K8–14, revealed the sensitivity of this whole subject with a lengthy and elaborate historical treatment on patriotism and opening to the outside world. Harking back to nineteenth-century reformers, the article stressed the courage of those who were willing to learn from advanced foreign culture and pursue reform at home. When explaining all the ways in which current policy differed from past semicolonialism, the article insisted that "putting forward the policy of opening up to the outside world and adhering to that policy requires extremely great courage and resourcefulness." This seemed a direct defense of Deng Xiaoping.

39. Gu Mu, *Kaifang* 9 (8 September 1985), pp. 2–8, in FBIS, 10 October 1985, pp. K1–10; and interview with *Liaowang* 38 (23 September 1985), pp. 9–11, in FBIS, 17 October 1985, pp. K1–5.

Zhao continued to encourage large enterprises in the interior, including defense factories, but admonished these enterprises to "stretch their feelers to the coastal areas, open up windows and establish bases there." Cited in Wu Peilun, "The Process of China's Urban Reforms," *Liaowang* 50 (16 December 1985), pp. 19–21, in FBIS, 15 January 1986, pp. K14–26.

After the plan proposal was adopted in September, and before the full plan was finalized in early 1986 for the people's congress, a major convocation of officials and scholars in Shenzhen discussed zone policy for more than two weeks. The State Council circular approving and transmitting the summary of the meeting for implementation was reported in Xinhua, 27 February 1986, in FBIS, 28 February 1986, pp. K2–3.

40. Plan proposal, in FBIS, 26 September 1985, pp. K1–24.

41. Zhao Ziyang, speech to the party conference presenting the 7th FYP proposal, 18 September 1985, in FBIS, 26 September 1985, p. K25ff; Zhao Ziyang, report to the National People's Congress, 25 March 1986, in FBIS, 28 March 1986, p. K1ff.

42. Ibid.; Hu Qili, *Hongqi* [Red Flag], 16 April 1986.

43. Deng Xiaoping and Chen Yun, speeches at the national party conference of 23 September 1985, in FBIS, 23 September 1985, p. K16ff. For an excellent study of conservative complaints about the reform program, see Lawrence R. Sullivan, "Assault on the Reforms: Conservative Criticism of Political and Economic Liberalization in China, 1985–86," *China Quarterly* 114 (June 1988), pp. 198–222.

44. Articles defending the reform included those by Xue Muqiao, *Jingji ribao,* 25 January 1986, and Yuan Mu, in *Guangming ribao* [Enlightenment Daily], 25 January 1986, and in *Lilun yuekan* 1 (25 January 1986), all in FBIS, 18 March 1986, p. K1ff. For the main themes from Liu's report see Liu Guoguang, *Renmin ribao,* 28 March 1986, p. 5, in FBIS, 10 April 1986, pp. K1–6.

45. Xinhua, 4 March 1986, in FBIS, 5 March 1986, pp. K11–12.

46. Early January announcement, Zhongguo xinwen she, 3 January 1986, in FBIS, 7 January 1986, p. K13. Zhao Ziyang, speech at the national planning and economic work conference on 13 January 1986, Xinhua, 17 January 1986, in FBIS, 22 January 1986, pp. K1–3.

47. Interviews with Hungarian planners and researchers, Budapest, May 1986.

48. Plan proposal. The first passage said that the "key element" in the reform program for the next five years was invigorating enterprises; this required separation of governments from enterprise decisionmaking and subjection of enterprises to market competition. The passage further stated that effective enterprise management would be impossible without expansion of markets, including those for funds, technology, and labor. "The key to the gradual establishment and perfection of the market system is reform of the pricing and price control systems." As the market network steadily improved, the (always limited) scope of mandatory planning would be further reduced in favor of guidance planning, and the emphasis of planning would be shifted to comprehensive policy planning.

The second passage, however, discussed three stages for implementation that did not seem to conform to the same logic: (1) reinforce indirect macroeconomic controls while revitalizing enterprises, and follow these up with the use of economic levers, better economic legislation and supervision, and the establishment of information networks; (2) gradually reduce the scope of mandatory planning, reform the price structure and control system, and further improve the taxation and financial systems; and (3) gradually set up organizational structures that conform to these new systems, "with a view to the eventual separation" of government and enterprises.

49. Xiao Jie, "Diversified Views on the Focus of Economic Reform in the 7th Five Year Plan Period," *Shijie jingji daobao,* 6 January 1986, p. 3, in FBIS, 12 January 1986, pp. K11–14. The author also mentioned a third, less cohesive, group that pointed out the even greater complexities that were not being addressed, including vast geographic differences in economic development; the issue of the economic role of local governments; and the importance to enterprise vitality of reforms in wages and employment mobility.

The identification of individuals and institutions with these schools of thought, in the following, has been added by me. I have benefited greatly in my understanding of these positions from the work of Joseph Fewsmith. See his paper, "Price Reform: Intellectual Approaches and Policy Conflict" (Presented at the Forty-first Annual Meeting of the Association for Asian Studies, Washington, D.C., 17–19 March 1989).

Li Yining, "Why It Is Inadvisable to Turn State-Owned Large and Medium Sized Enterprises into Privately Owned Ones," *Ta Kung Pao* (Hong Kong) [Selfless Daily], 30 January 1989, p. 2, in FBIS-CHI–89–022, 3 February 1989, p. 43, mentioned that he first proposed the implementation of the stock ownership system in May 1980 and the establishment of stock exchanges in May 1984.

50. Interview, Washington, D.C., 1988; and Pei Ni, "CCP Planning Major Reform Measures," *Chiu Shih Nien Tai* (Hong Kong) [The Nineties] 200 (1 September 1986), pp. 42–44, in JPRS-CEA–86–109, 10 October 1986, pp. 41–47. I want to thank Barry Naughton for information about the drafting group and their proposal. Fewsmith, ibid., p. 7, cited Tian Yuan, chief of the State Council's price reform research group, on reasons for Zhao's change of mind.

51. Beginning in 1981, all annual and midterm plans included budgetary allocations for education, recreation, and so on, but both the monies and the guidelines for development were minimal. In 1985, some key localities (including Shanghai, Guangzhou, Sichuan, and Beijing) began drafting cultural development plans. In December 1985, the policy study office of the ministry of culture and the editorial department of *Guangming ribao* convened a forum on cultural development strategy. A central figure in this and subsequent local meetings on cultural development was Yu Guangyuan. See a report on the forum in *Guangming ribao*, 31 December 1985, p. 1, in FBIS, 10 January 1986, pp. K19–20.

According to a U.S. academic who interviewed some members of the drafting group for the national ideology and reform decision, 140 drafts were written in the nine months from January to September 1986. It is not clear whether the document originally was to include guidelines for political reform, but I believe it was, judging from leadership statements and academic writings throughout the year addressing problems in the political system and the need to include political reform with reforms in other arenas.

52. Hu Yaobang, speech at meeting of cadres of central organs on 9 January 1986, Xinhua, 10 January 1986; Tian Jiyun, Xinhua, 11 January 1986, both in FBIS, 13 January 1986, pp. K1–22. Hu's speech in April, which addressed the problem of "contradictions" within the party, was not published until July, *Renmin ribao*, 1 July 1986, p. 1, in FBIS, 2 July 1986, pp. K1–7, which indicated how controversial it was.

53. On 17 January, at a meeting of the Politburo standing committee, Deng authorized the investigation of illegal activities by children of senior cadre. See Deng, *Fundamental Issues*, p. 136. Benedict Stavis, ed. and trans., "Reform of China's Political System," *Chinese Law and Government* 20:1 (Spring 1987), pp. 5–6, cited the Hong Kong Communist press on these

interventions. At an April governors conference convened by Zhao Ziyang, Deng spoke on the political reform themes from his August 1980 speech. On 20 May, he criticized feudalism. On 20 June, he declared, "Unconditional power is the source of all unhealthy tendencies." Hu Qili spoke in April on the theme of feudalism, and Wan Li spoke that same month on freedom of thought and research.

The statements by Deng that fueled the liberalization of 1986 were not included in the collection of Deng's post-1982 statements compiled in the more conservative atmosphere of 1987. The announcement regarding urban experiments was made public later by Xinhua, 22 August 1987, in FBIS-CHI–87–163, 24 August 1987, p. 11.

54. *China Daily,* 21 May 1986, p. 1. The real post-2000 target dates have symbolic meaning; 2021 will be the centennial of the founding of the Chinese Communist Party, and 2049 will be the centennial of the founding of the PRC. I use 2050 as shorthand because the connection is not immediately obvious.

55. Interviews with scholars at the social science academy, Beijing, May 1986. The Hong Kong press at the time spelled out details of the Ma Ding affair.

56. See Stavis, ed. and trans., "Reform of China's Political System," p. 5, on several of the conferences. On the Shanghai meeting, see Xinhua, 10 May 1986, in FBIS, 13 May 1986, pp. K13–14; *Jiefang ribao* [Liberation Daily], 14 May 1986, p. 1, in FBIS, 20 May 1986, pp. K5–6; Xinhua, 14 May 1986, in FBIS, 23 May 1986, pp. K17–18; and *Ming Pao,* 31 May 1986, p. 5, in FBIS, 3 June 1986, pp. W1–2. The Shanghai meeting was attended by the new propaganda department director Zhu Houze; the mayor and party secretary of Shanghai; Hu Yaobang's son, who was deputy director of the united front work department; a vice minister of culture; Yu Guangyuan; and well-known theorists and writers such as Xia Yan, Li Zihou, and Liu Zaifu. The meeting discussed Shanghai's very rough draft five-year plan for cultural development, but exploration expanded far beyond this into the issues of modern and traditional culture, Westernization, the role of the press, and the relationship among culture, politics, and economic development.

According to Zhongguo xinwen she, 10 September 1986, in FBIS, 15 September 1986, pp. P2–4, Guangzhou held a similar meeting in September to discuss its year 2000 plan for cultural development, again attended by Zhu Houze and Yu Guangyuan as well as Huan Xiang and political science institute director Yan Jiaqi.

57. Wan Li, "Making Decisions with a Democratic and Scientific Approach Is an Important Aspect in Restructuring the Political System," Xinhua, 14 August 1986, in FBIS, 19 August 1986, pp. K22–33. Also see Song Jian, Qian Xuesen, and Hu Ping, "Reflections on Making Policies Democratically and Scientifically," *Renmin ribao,* 8 December 1986, p. 5, in FBIS, 17 December 1986, pp. K1–7. A U.S. academic was told by Hu Ping that originally the speech was drafted for Zhao Ziyang to give; it is not known why Wan Li delivered it instead.

58. Stavis, "Reform of China's Political System," p. 6, mentioned the leading group. Postponement was announced by Deng, *Fundamental Issues,* p.

149. For the text of the ideology and cultural resolution, see Xinhua, 28 September 1986, in FBIS, 29 September 1986, pp. K2–13.

59. Xinhua, 4 November 1986, in FBIS, 5 November 1986, pp. K4–5.

60. According to *Ta Kung Pao,* 7 April 1988, p. 2, in FBIS-CHI-88-070, 12 April 1988, pp. 30–31, the new political reform study (read, leading) group was still led by Hu Qili, but the other current leading members were Tian Jiyun, Bo Yibo and Peng Chong. The addition of Bo and Peng represented a decidedly conservative shift. The staff office, run by Zhao's secretary Bao Tong, included the deputy director of the party's general office, reform commission vice minister He Guanghui (formerly secretary to Bo Yibo), and Yan Jiaqi, the young reformist director of the political science institute. They set up seven special topic research groups in November.

See Stavis, ed. and trans., "Reform of China's Political System."

61. The three intellectuals were world-class astrophysicist Fang Lizhi, muckraking *Renmin ribao* journalist Liu Binyan, and writer and social critic Wang Ruowang of Shanghai, all former rightists and all of them criticized by Deng and defended by Hu for several years before. See James Tong, ed., "Between Party and Principle: The Exit and Voice of Fang Lizhi, Liu Binyan, and Wang Ruowang," *Chinese Law and Government* (Summer 1988).

62. Examples of former rightists include Zhu Rongji, the mayor of Shanghai; Ruan Chongwu, the minister of public security; Wang Meng, the minister of culture; and Zhu Houze, the director of the propaganda department. Ding Xueliang, "The Disparity Between Idealistic and Instrumental Chinese Reformers," *Asian Survey* 28:11 (November 1988), pp. 1117–1139, skillfully analyzed the differences between two approaches to ideological and political reform that are quite similar to what I call humanistic and technocratic.

63. Chen and Yao seemed more accepting of Zhao's leadership in the early 1980s and probably blamed him for the crisis of 1985; they would have had a strong voice in the March 1980 decision to turn over party control of the finance and economics sector to Zhao since Deng at that time acquiesced to Chen's leadership in this sphere.

64. See, for example, Hu's comments cited in Commentator, Xinhua, 18 February 1985, in FBIS, 25 February 1985, pp. K20–21. After Hu's visit in early 1984 to the Shengli oil field, the workers promised to quintuple output by the year 2000; a visit by Zhao a few months later toned down commentary considerably with his emphasis on efficiency and quality.

65. According to the rumor mill, in early 1983 Zhao was upset with Hu Yaobang for pressing ahead on reforms while Zhao was in Eastern Europe. When Hu made some pronouncement about the economic reforms, Zhao sent a note to Deng asking, "Is it 'I' or 'we' in charge of the economy?" Deng circled "I." According to researchers close to Zhao, Deng first asked Zhao to become general secretary around that time.

Party historian Hu Hua, on a visit to the United States in May 1987, mentioned the long hours Hu Yaobang spent with him in the early 1970s reading and discussing writings from Eurocommunist and Eastern European sources and rethinking socialism. Comparing public statements regarding the superpowers by Zhao and Hu in the early 1980s, I concluded that Hu was consistently "softer" on Moscow and "tougher" on the United States than Zhao was. The difference is only partially explainable by their respective responsibilities.

66. Interview with a foreign affairs official, Beijing, May 1987.

67. For an excellent review of the context and issues involved in Hu Yaobang's fall, including the military commission meeting, see James Tong, ed., "Party Documents on Anti-bourgeois Liberalization and Hu Yaobang's Resignation, 1987," *Chinese Law and Government* 21:1 (Spring 1988), Introduction; also see the report prepared by Bo Yibo accusing Hu of ideological liberalism, advocacy of development by means of a consumer-oriented economy, intervention in the legislative process, and unauthorized statements on major issues. The Hong Kong press also speculated that advocacy for Deng's retirement in the fall of 1986, such as that by the youth paper in Shenzhen, was viewed by Deng as an unseemly effort to hurry his decision.

68. Interviews with younger researchers involved in the drafting of the report, Washington, D.C., 1987–1988. The *South China Morning Post,* 19 June 1987, p. 10, in FBIS, 19 June 1987, p. K6, stated that Bo Yibo and Yang Shangkun were heads of a leading group overseeing preparations for the congress, with respective responsibilities for civilian and military arrangements. Input for civilian affairs came from Peng Zhen, Xi Zhongxun, Song Renqiong, Yao Yilin, Wan Li, and Gao Yang, the director of the central party school; for military matters, ideas came from Wang Zhen, Yu Qiuli, and Wu Xiuquan. *Cheng Ming* 122 (1 December 1987), pp. 6–9, in FBIS, 87–230, 1 December 1987, p. 13, mentioned a personnel nominating group with many of the same figures that was to recommend members of the Central Committee, discipline inspection commission, and advisory commission. Hu Qiaomu, Deng Liqun, and Gao Yang joined the political reform group as "visiting members."

69. For this and the following background on the congress, see Joseph Fewsmith, "China's 13th Party Congress: Explicating the Theoretical Bases of Reform," *Journal of Northeast Asian Studies* (Summer 1988), pp. 41–63.

70. Zhao Ziyang, report to the 13th Party Congress, Xinhua, 25 October 1987, in FBIS-CHI-87-206S (supplement), 26 October 1987, pp. 10–33. The "productive forces criterion" had a long political history. It was attributed to Liu Shaoqi and Deng Xiaoping by Maoists during the Cultural Revolution and cited as evidence that they were taking the capitalist road. The communiqué of the 3rd Plenum in 1978 resurrected the criterion indirectly when insisting that development of productive forces, not class struggle, would be China's priority. The "one center, two points" formula first appeared in the economic reform decision of 1984.

The Chinese press released a number of reports on the lengthy process of drafting the work report, whose intent seemed to be to show that Deng fully supported Zhao's efforts and that regularity had returned to party affairs. See Xinhua, 2 September 1987, in FBIS-CHI-87-170, 2 September 1987, p. 9, and 6 November 1987, in FBIS-CHI-87-215, 6 November 1987, p. 11; two reports in Zhongguo xinwen she, 4 November 1987, in FBIS-CHI-87-213, 4

November 1987, p. 8, and FBIS-CHI-87-215, 6 November 1987, p. 11; and *Liaowang* (overseas edition) 35 (31 August 1987), pp. 3-5.

71. Fewsmith, "China's 13th Party Congress," p. 57.

72. See Carol Lee Hamrin, "The Party Leadership System," in M. David Lampton and Kenneth G. Lieberthal, eds., *The Structure of Authority and Bureaucratic Behavior in China* (forthcoming).

73. *Ta Kung Pao,* 17 November 1987, p. 1, in FBIS-CHI-87-222, 18 November 1987, reported on a meeting convened by the reform commission to "study the formulation of the 1988-95 medium term program for reform of the economic structure." Again, Zhao was requesting several organizations to put forth their own comprehensive designs, including the social science academy, the development center, and the planning commission. Three stages of reform plans were envisaged: one to cover the period to 1990, one through 1992, and the whole plan for 1995, by which time China was to finish setting up a new economic structure. Meanwhile, the regular drafting process for the 8th FYP was begun, according to a researcher at the development center, interview, Washington, D.C., summer 1988.

74. For reports on Zhao Ziyang's visits in December-January to Fujian, Guangdong, and Hainan, during which he promoted his ideas, see *Ta Kung Pao,* 20 February 1988, p. 2, in FBIS-CHI-88-034, 22 February 1988, pp. 8-10; *Shijie jingji daobao,* 29 February 1988, p. 1, in FBIS-CHI-88-049, 14 March 1988, pp. 22-23; and *Beijing Review* 1-7, 8-14, and 15-28 February 1988. Xinhua, 6 February 1988, reported the Politburo's approval and on 4 March 1988, reported a work meeting of the State Council convened by Tian Jiyun and Gu Mu to work out specific policies.

The work of several young theorists lay behind the new policy; all of them argued that China must seize every opportunity to join the developed world before a conjunction of negative developments occurred early in the next century. These included a population bulge of aging dependents and a debt crisis. See *Ching Pao* 127 (20 February 1988), pp. 13-17, in FBIS-CHI-88-030, 16 February 1988, pp. 11-16.

75. See *South China Morning Post,* 4 March 1989, p. 8, in FBIS-CHI-89-043, 7 March 1989, pp. 58-59; Ding Xinghao, "China's Policy on a Multipolar World," *Beijing Review,* 3-9 April 1989, p. 10, in FBIS-CHI-89-064, 5 April 1989, p. 1; and Shi Min, "The World Trend of Regional Economic Blocs," *Liaowang* (overseas edition) 4 (23 January 1989), pp. 26-27, in JPRS-CAR-89-029, 4 April 1989, p. 1.

76. Fewsmith, "Price Reform."

77. Deng Xiaoping, comments to visitors, Xinhua, 19 May 1988, in FBIS, 19 May 1988, p. 8; 24 May 1988, in FBIS, 26 May 1988, p. 2; and 3 June 1988, in FBIS, 3 June 1988, p. 17.

78. Fewsmith, "Price Reform," pp. 22-25.

79. Zhao Ziyang, report to the 3rd Plenum of the 13th Central Committee, 26 September 1988, in FBIS, 28 October 1988, pp. 13-20. The only reporting on the work conference appeared in the Hong Kong Communist press; see reports in FBIS, 19 September 1988, pp. 19-20, and 26 September 1988, pp. 22-24.

7
Conclusion

The decade of rapid economic reform from 1979 to 1989 under the leadership of Deng Xiaoping was a time of transition from rule by a tiny oligarchy of revolutionaries toward a new, more open, and inclusive type of politics. As the leadership sought to revitalize the economy, they opened up channels for the commercialization, privatization, and internationalization of the economy. Economic development along these lines then fostered structural differentiation, cultural pluralization, and subsystem autonomy. The decade witnessed some changes in political patterns necessary to accommodate these trends. These included a more collegial approach to decisionmaking at the very top; retirements and the incorporation of younger and better-educated officials into senior decisionmaking circles; a decrease in the political influence of military and security forces and an increase in the influence of government (economic and technological) officials, the people's congress, and people's political consultative conference; the regularization and improvement of bureaucratic policy data gathering, analysis, and implementation; the incorporation of the intellectual elite into public policy discourse and the lowering of secrecy barriers required to do this; the explosion of foreign contacts and the growing impact of foreign opinion, intellectual concepts, values, and methodologies on Chinese policy choices; the transformation of the content of the media to include much rich and objective information about conditions in China and elsewhere; the extension of television as well as the cinema and print media to create a truly national awareness of events and issues for the first time; and the first steps toward recognizing and allowing the articulation of pluralistic social interests.

Limits to Reform Under Deng Xiaoping

The process of transition to a more open politics had only just begun, however, after ten years of reform. Strategic decisionmaking about China's future remained dominated by the party elite and constrained by the ideological and institutional imperatives necessary to retain that dominance. Although the climate in China had greatly improved in comparison with the economic stagnation and political stalemate of 1976, many basic political patterns were linked to the Leninist political structure; thus, they had roots in the Mao era and would remain to shape Chinese politics after Deng and his revolutionary colleagues were gone.

Ad Hoc Reformism

The most obvious pattern was ad hoc reformism marked by sharp swings in policy that reflected reaction to the economic cycles inherent in a semiplanned economy. As the planned portion of the economy shrank, the five-year cycles had less effect in shaping politics, and the more unpredictable fluctuations of a mixed economy made the regularization of the policy process more difficult. This tendency was enhanced as the succession to Deng Xiaoping began because of the prolongation of the dual-price economy and heightened political competition.

Reactive rather than anticipatory reform also derived from the experiential mode of thinking that prevailed. Traditional ways of thinking and ideological blinders inhibited the development of economic theory that might have allowed more anticipatory policies. The unanticipated consequences of economic policies in recent years reflected a continued lack of understanding among China's leaders about how the economy really functioned as distinct from dogma about how it was supposed to function. Chinese leaders often found themselves "riding the tiger," seemingly in the driver's seat but actually hanging on for the ride. Innovative leadership reforms often turned out upon closer examination to be ex post facto approval for developments well underway, such as the earliest decollectivization actions by starving peasants in Anhui, the development of labor service markets in Jiangsu, and the emergence of stock exchanges in coastal cities. Under political liberalization, more individuals and social groups were willing to take the risk of ignoring official policy and doing what suited their interests. As China's economy became more bound to the international economy, international developments largely beyond China's control loomed larger on the political agenda at home.

Politicized Institution Building

The political use of the policymaking structure and process to build power continued through the 1980s. The wide discretion given individual leaders to set up new institutions and staff them with loyalists and to use resources within institutions under their control ensured this. As part of a bid for power, Li Peng reorganized the State Council setup in 1988–1989 just as Zhao Ziyang had done in 1980–1982. Meanwhile, the symbolic use of policy programs to display power and status meant that problems of policy implementation and evaluation got short shrift.

Focus on Short-Term Gains

A focus on short-term gains characterized the reformers' approach as they sought to build political support for the reform. Between 1979 and 1989, real incomes rose by 180 percent in the countryside and 85 percent in the cities, but consumption gains came at the expense of addressing long-term problems. Under Deng Xiaoping, desert lands grew and farmlands shrank; the problem of pollution grew exponentially; the quality of education did not improve substantially; the water table in north China continued to drop; and the infrastructure for farming, especially irrigation projects, and the infrastructure for transportation and production all deteriorated.[1]

Specialists doing projections beyond the year 2000 began talking about a set of related yet conflicting trends: Farmland and agricultural investment is declining while the population and grain consumption per capita are increasing. The population problem will be an especially serious constraint. Because of policy inconstancy with regard to this highly critical factor, another baby boom from now into the early part of the century will produce a population of 1.3 billion by 2000 and 1.5 billion in 2020; this threatens all the carefully crafted development goals pegged to population stability closer to 1.2 billion.[2] This, advisers suggest, will require another readjustment of modernization plans to require low consumption of resources and moderate expenditures. Yet younger leaders, lacking either revolutionary credentials or personal charisma, will be even more inclined to seek quick payoffs to attract the support of powerful bureaucratic actors, including provincial and military leaders.

The compulsion for quick gain has infused the popular culture as well as the bureaucratic culture; some have called China a "nation of scavengers" who seek immediate material gain before the opportunity passes, never to return. One Chinese sociologist has attributed this behavior to the mass uncertainty that stems from the fragility of a reform program based on policy pronouncements rather than on law. Knowing leaders have changed and will change policy overnight; managers, workers, and merchants all use their new autonomy to exhaust state assets rather than to invest for the long term; and consumers hide or consume their wealth.[3] The contradiction between high expectations for growing immediate prosperity and the constraints imposed by resource realities will grow during the next decade and is likely to produce severe economic, social, and political strains.

Search for Shortcuts

Overly ambitious goals and a search for panaceas persist. The belief that science and technology can be easily adapted to help China catch up with the developed world has a long history and is one that dies hard. In fact, remembering Lenin's obsession with electrification, Stalin's with the tractor, and Mao's with the atom bomb makes Deng's vision for a computerized China appear less innovative. Most recently, in the midst of the severe economic crisis of 1988, Zhao Ziyang met in Beijing with Alvin and Heidi Toffler and during the conversation said, "The new technological revolution or information revolution . . . may help China skip over some of the stages which have been experienced by other developing countries."[4]

Overreliance on Technocratic Solutions

The tendency to turn to technocratic solutions for socioeconomic problems has increased with the emergence of a new generation of leaders and officials trained largely as engineers. The values and vocabulary of centralized social engineering pervade the intellectual and political discourse. In 1988–1989, for example, there was less talk of ownership reform to create a decentralized, pluralistic market structure; the development center and the World Bank were drafting a national industrial restructuring policy to guide the economy through the next FYP period.[5] Younger leaders are likely to use technocratic symbols and rhetoric, in combination with seniority status, as the source of individual and regime legitimacy and authority.[6]

Yet this bent of mind ensures that democratic reforms lag behind both the public demand for them and the requirements of continued scientific progress. Deng's legacy of centrally initiated and controlled reformism, combined with the social engineering mentality and strong fears of social instability in the rising leadership generations that suffered from the Cultural Revolution, has fostered a decided lean toward policies of social and economic order. Symbolic of this were early 1989 rumors that the leadership wanted the celebrations of the seventieth anniversary of the May Fourth student movement of 1919 to focus on the theme of science rather than democracy. Popular demands for political expression and desires for personal freedom in developing spiritual values weigh lightly according to highly instrumentalist criteria.

Bureaucratic Entrenchment

Politics as the elders gradually began to leave the scene were still colored by personal factionalism, but the elements of intrabureaucratic and geographic competition were growing. So much control over resources had devolved to local officials that their power in the system grew in comparison with the central bureaucracies. Demands from the localities to readjust the severe inequities between regions caused by inherent advantages of the coast but exacerbated by biases in policy and in the pricing system continued to escalate. In 1988, leaders were forced to back off from the East to West development strategy and were talking about a more equitable "coordinated regional strategy."[7] Yet younger leaders without the strong affiliation with the military or localities of the revolutionaries will find it hard to impose tough decisions because they must compete for support from key bureaucratic and geographic actors. Reluctance to force unpopular retrenchment policies on local officials was one reason for the serious weakness of central authority by 1988.

Neglect or Repression of Nonbureaucratic Groups

The Leninist system is ineffective in promoting economic development precisely because it is highly effective in weakening socioeconomic institutions that would compete for resources and decisionmaking power. There are no autonomous organizational networks that can mediate competing interests outside the state structure; the values, concerns, and processes of regime politics dominate everything. In a vicious circle, the regime structure reinforces social atomization (and anomie), which provides the seedbed for either anarchy or fascism; fear of such development is used to rationalize the regime monopoly.

During the 1980s, the relationship between officialdom and the intelligentsia became more and more central to Chinese politics precisely because the interests of nonbureaucratic groups were being articulated indirectly through the intellectuals. Examples include the voicing of the interests of young, high-tech entrepreneurs by Cao Siyuan of the Sitong research institute; those of rural enterprise managers by Du Runsheng and other officials of the rural development center; and those of religious believers by prestigious scholar-officials such as Zhao Puchu (head of the Buddhist patriotic association and a vice chairman of the people's political consultative conference), Ding Guangxun (president of the

Nanjing theological seminary), and Zhao Fusan (vice president of the social science academy).

The leadership under Deng Xiaoping oscillated between attempts to include intellectuals in the political process through consultative arrangements and recruitment and promotion in the party (the hallmark of Hu Yaobang's leadership) and efforts to exclude them from politics through expulsion from the party and prohibition of publication and travel (as in early 1987 and again in late 1988). The dismissal of Hu and purge from the party of scientist Fang Lizhi, social critic Wang Ruowang, and journalist Liu Binyan, all of them former rightists from 1957, symbolized a retrogression toward a confrontational relationship between the state and society and all but guaranteed the emergence of the civil rights movement in early 1989, led by intellectuals who feared the loss of reform momentum.

The Challenge of the Future

In late 1988, on the tenth anniversary of the 3rd Plenum that made Deng Xiaoping China's paramount leader, the leadership faced daunting economic and political difficulties. Defensively, they pointed to the tremendous gains of the previous decade as proof that the direction for China set by Deng Xiaoping and his protégés was the only correct program for the future.[8] This tactic was reminiscent of most post-1949 Chinese politics—using comparisons with China's dismal past to highlight the benefits of current policy and thereby buttress the authority of the current regime. Leaders have also typically used visions of a bright future to spur on the Chinese people to greater efforts and sacrifices.

China's future progress will not be judged, however, according to a utopian fantasy in which inevitable historical progress or class struggle finally yield a society based on equality and harmony. Rather, China will have to judge itself against the probable breakthrough of the nonsocialist, technologically advanced nations to an entirely new level of development that will leave China even further behind if it does not adapt quickly, smoothly, and continually to the onrushing global technological revolution. As China faces the future, there are four main obstacles to achieving its dream of restoring its historical greatness: the accelerating development gap caused by international economic trends; China's resource/population pinch and highly uneven regional and sectoral development; the rigid, highly authoritarian Leninist structure and political culture of dependency; and a severe moral-cultural depression characterized by friction between generations and among social groups and alienation from the regime.[9]

Although China's GNP grew in absolute terms during the 1979–1989 period, it shrank in relation to Japan's, and neighboring countries such as Malaysia and Thailand appeared poised to follow first in the development wake of Japan and the NIEs. The prospects for cutthroat regional economic bloc competition among friends—North America (the United States and Canada and perhaps Mexico and the Caribbean) against a more integrated European Economic Community, against a Japan-dominated Asia-Pacific economic cooperation group, against China—were perhaps more plausible than Chinese hopes for mutual and equal economic cooperation among all. These trends could pose a challenge to China's goals of reunification as well as development, particularly if regional tensions lead to military conflict and once more divert China's scarce resources from civilian development. By late 1988, military planners were thinking through potential threats from India and Vietnam and new requirements for power projection capability to protect China's maritime rights and international trade line.[10]

To compete in this brave new world China needs at a minimum even more accurate strategic research and decisionmaking; realistic and anticipatory planning rather than manipulation of future goals as political promises and symbols of power; flexible and innovative decentralized economic entities that can respond quickly to the rapid changes in demand characteristic of computerized economies; a means of increasing productivity not just in production but in the integrated process of production and services; a capable economic elite constantly upgrading managerial methods; a strong central financial control system that can fine-tune the economy to avoid serious fluctuations between inflation and recession; and a free intellectual environment conducive to scientific advancement. In this competition, cheap labor and raw materials are worth less and less. Knowledge is the resource of greatest value, and flexibility and creativity are required to manage industries that must conduct high-speed operations with precision scheduling and smaller and more complex work operations. From this perspective, China's giant smokestack state industries are the most backward sector, and the farmers running coastal processing industries may be in the vanguard.[11] Chinese leaders have become aware of these economic and managerial requirements and since 1984 have geared the reform program to try meeting them.

But Chinese leaders and the broader elite have been slower to give equal attention to the political and cultural requirements of this technological competition, in large part because they are more difficult to address and problems take much longer to remedy. To handle the social conflicts that emerge with middle-level development and to create a new society rich in information and creativity will require both a radical increase in freedom of expression in all arenas and the growth of a new public morality that allows individual choice and expression while still encouraging social cooperation. So far, although Chinese leaders now see a connection between development and democracy, the majority views it through the lens of materialism and concludes that some form of democratic politics can only follow development, step by step. But the problem is that the Leninist system inhibits the information feedback, policy flexibility, and public confidence required to fuel steady development.

The Chinese order, only partly disguised by the thin veneer of a unitary state, seems to be a semifeudal and semi-Stalinist decentralized despotism; this is the social order that had reemerged by the end of the Cultural Revolution. The Leninist bureaucratic system is one means of countering this tendency and creating a national economy and culture, but this system is especially ill-suited for the task of modernizing in a postindustrial era. China's best hope for moving to a new dynamic socialist order lies in creative reforms of the state structure to more rapidly create channels for the open competition of ideas, values, and power. Open societies, despite their complexities, achieve relative stability through competitive self-regulation and independence through interdependence. A nation cannot keep up in the postindustrial era without such political processes. Yet the prospects for reforms to create these processes have dimmed steadily since 1986 with the heightening of political struggle. Deng's failure to institutionalize a more democratic succession process for the political leadership at all levels proved to be the undoing of his reform program. With the need to deflate consumption expectations and address resource crises, it was almost inevitable that Deng's program would be repackaged to introduce an austerity version premised on recentralized authoritarian bureaucratic control. The Leninist imperative of maintaining central party domination meant that political and cultural reform lagged far enough behind to fuel continual political and social instability and thus hinder progress. Ironically, such regimes aimed at stabilization are still relatively unstable; they are a kind of half-way house, fluctuating between open and closed politics. The slow, uneven progress they are able to achieve risks international weakness and dependence.

Postscript: Reaction and Bloodshed

The year 1988 was a watershed for China. The new 13th congress leadership headed by Zhao Ziyang was faced with decisions on reform that both the leaders and their critics, including semiretired elders, knew represented a crossing of the systemic rubicon between plan and market. For the newly established market relations to perform their efficiency-promoting functions, new market institutions in the economy and new pluralistic institutions in the polity would have to be established along the lines of reforms underway at the time in Eastern Europe. The alternative was continued tinkering with the system through use of more scientific planning as a functional substitute for the market and liberalization of existing social and political institutions as a substitute for democracy, along the lines the Soviet Union was pursuing.[12]

In pursuit of Deng Xiaoping's dual strategy (bold economic reform combined with cautious political change), Zhao Ziyang attempted to combine bold marketization, through ownership reform, with cautious political "transparency," through press liberalization, public opinion polling, and enhanced consultative roles for the people's congress and noncommunist party members. Zhao's young advisers explored ways to create the conditions in China to repeat the "miracle" of the east Asian NIEs—a market economy relatively independent from but regulated by an authoritarian leader advised by intellectuals in government think tanks. These efforts only aroused suspicion—conservatives believed Zhao was anxious to seize the reins of power, and idealistic intellectuals suspected it was a ruse to postpone democratic reform indefinitely.[13]

Zhao had a strong policy mandate for a third wave of reform in the work report approved by the 13th Party Congress, but his power base was fragile and steadily weakening with the systemic crisis. Throughout 1988, China was caught in a downward spiral into a confusing and damaging policy cycle of reform and counterreform, despite foreknowledge and the best of intentions. Political divisions led to halfhearted half-measures set forth in alternating policy spurts that took advantage of momentary opportunity but were poorly planned and implemented. This in turn encouraged noncompliance with regime directives among lower-level officials and undermined public confidence in the regime. The depth of the crisis was reflected in debates within the intellectual elite regarding fundamental issues such as the cultural origins of China's modern failure and the proper source of state authority. The crisis of authority and continuing economic imbalances further polarized the leadership.

The reputations and influence of Deng Xiaoping and Zhao Ziyang and all that they stood for suffered as they took the brunt of the blame for the regime's loss of prestige. But the opposition had no strong support for their austerity program either. By early 1989, even politically moderate delegates to the people's congress and consultative conference seemed fed up with the leadership as a whole and demanded a strengthening of procedures that would place checks on sudden, destabilizing shifts in policy and personnel. Draft legislation intended to protect the constitutional freedoms of the press, assembly, and religious belief were brought closer to fruition. Indirectly, delegates aired the growing conviction in the elite that the days when the people looked passively to a strong man or to a tiny group of party elders to solve China's problems and determine its future were over.

Showdown

Leading party and nonparty intellectuals, increasingly radicalized by the deteriorating situation, chose this moment to launch an unprecedented challenge to the leadership by starting a petition campaign in which hundreds of well-known intellectuals, joined by thousands of overseas Chinese and students at home and abroad, requested an amnesty for China's political prisoners to celebrate the seventieth anniversary of the May Fourth Movement and the fortieth anniversary of the founding of the PRC. Petitions gave way to nonviolent mass demonstrations modeled on the civil disobedience movements led in India by Mohandas Gandhi and in the United States by Martin Luther King, Jr.[14]

Originally planned for May by intellectuals inside and outside the government and by student leaders, the demonstrations were launched early when Hu Yaobang died suddenly of heart failure and his memorial service on 22 April provided a safe forum to express popular outrage over official corruption and abuse of power. Public security forces were morally disarmed and by late April were also overwhelmed in numbers by the demonstrators. The response by Chinese leaders to the escalating demonstrations and demands during the next month was too little and too late at each crucial moment. Their personal relationships were already poisoned by succession infighting. Zhao Ziyang perceived an opportunity to use popular demands for democratic reform to shore up his weak position while his critics sought to blame him for letting dissent get out of hand. Normal decisionmaking procedures were disrupted by Zhao Ziyang's week-long absence in North Korea beginning 21 April and then by leadership preoccupation with the visits to Beijing of important foreign dignitaries. Most noteworthy, of course, was the arrival of Gorbachev on 15 May for the first Sino-Soviet summit in thirty years, but nearly as important were senior officials of the Asian Development Bank, including the first official to visit the mainland from Taiwan since 1949. The use of force against demonstrators with the whole world watching was not an easy option.

Pressures from conflicting interests in the tense atmosphere finally ruptured the relationship between Deng and Zhao. When Zhao signaled support for the students by calling them patriotic before the Asian Development Bank audience on 4 May, indirectly repudiating a *Renmin ribao* editorial reflecting Deng's hard-line stance, Zhao challenged Deng's authority. During this time, the leadership reluctantly followed Zhao's lead by attempting dialogue without concession, but divisions widened when this approach failed to send students back to class. The decision by demonstrators to initiate a hunger strike, which within a few short days threatened the lives of several thousand students, galvanized mass popular support and aroused emotions to a peak. The domestic crisis overshadowed Gorbachev's meetings, thereby destroying the intended impression that Deng Xiaoping would enter retirement having reversed Mao's mistakes and having restored China to its proper place as a powerful global actor.

Demonstrators took advantage of leadership wavering and the massive foreign press contingent in Beijing for the summit to gain domestic and foreign sympathy. The sophistication of the demonstrators probably reflected behind-the-scenes advice from mentors among the university staff and party and government researchers, many of them Red Guard veterans and/or returned students from the West. Their successful tactics included proclamation of support for the one-party system, disciplined nonviolence, and moderate public demands (recognition for their movement and organizations, opposition to corruption, and protection of civil rights beginning with free press and assembly). Chinese reporters chafed at constraints on their own coverage of these remarkable events, while foreign television and radio broadcasts were beamed back into the country. Encouraged by Zhao's apparent willingness to consider concessions and his approval of freer press coverage, on 18 and 19 May 1 million Beijing citizens went to the streets, including organized contingents from many of China's government and press units. The depth of dissatisfaction with the regime was reflected not only in the increasingly radical slogans and manifestos but in the involvement by some party, security, and military units (primarily students or trainees).

A Polish Solution

The beleaguered and divided leadership, following the logic of a siege mentality in the face of popular revolt, declared martial law on 20 May in a desperate attempt to restore order and the status quo ante. The decision reflected the revolutionary experience and traditional mindset of party and military elders whom Deng brought back into the decisionmaking process in the midst of the crisis. All other considerations, including popular opinion, bureaucratic interests, and foreign reaction, gave way to the felt necessity to reassert the appearance of uncontestable power.

Although the use of martial law was unprecedented in the capital city—and proved to be both alarming and unacceptable to its citizenry—the thought was not new to the leadership. According to the Hong Kong press during the earlier 1986–1987 leadership crisis, Deng Xiaoping said then that "if the student unrest spreads wider, martial law as in Poland must be enforced."[15] In early 1989, martial law was imposed in Tibet to prevent an escalation of conflict there. Presumably, based on these precedents, the leaders expected through a show of military force to reassert control with a minimum of violence. They were probably stunned at the unfolding of events under martial law—Beijing citizens stopped the troops from advancing into the city by using physical and verbal barricades, many officials and scholars refused to cooperate and even continued to join in demonstrations, and official media organs continued to report events in ways that clearly showed and encouraged opposition to martial law.

This defiance reflected awareness (achieved through official leaks to the grapevine) that the party leadership and even the elders and the military were split over the martial law decision and that Zhao Ziyang refused either to endorse martial law or to resign under pressure. It took Deng Xiaoping and his backers nearly two weeks to jawbone key leaders into supporting the removal of Zhao from office, reduce foreign press access, and position military troops around the city before the final bloody assault on Beijing in the early morning of 4 June. In the process, all regular procedures were abandoned. In what can only be called a coup by the elders, Deng and Yang Shangkun ignored the Politburo and the Central Committee, convened ad hoc meetings of the elders and select members of the military commission, and gave orders to the remaining members of the Politburo standing committee.

Throughout 4 June and into the week following, ill-disciplined troops fired indiscriminately into crowds of hostile residents and on 8 June deliberately fired on a housing compound for foreign diplomats, all in an attempt to cow the city (and foreign observers) into submission. Eyewitness accounts are contradictory regarding who initiated the violence and when and where, and different tallies of dead and wounded range from several hundred to several thousand, but the ultimate responsibility for the carnage must rest with Deng Xiaoping and other senior leaders who made the decision and with those who failed to oppose it. The decision to use lethal force against citizens who were not threatening a violent overthrow of the government is not justifiable by either the PRC constitution or international norms to which the PRC ascribes. The regime's own implicit recognition of this is evident from its subsequent distortion of facts to "prove" that the demonstrations were violent and antiregime in nature.

In the weeks immediately following the Beijing massacre, there was overwhelming evidence of massive confusion and recrimination within the elite, even as a new leadership lineup was approved by the 4th Plenum and carried out Deng Xiaoping's instructions to round up, detain, and severely punish all those who inspired, organized, and implemented the "counterrevolutionary rebellion." Thousands of arrests and dozens of death sentences (mainly of those who had committed violence) testified to the extraordinary depth of hostility on the part of the regime toward its critics and its intent not only to intimidate critics and skeptics, but to destroy the roots of any potential opposition for at least another generation. The response from those who survived was equally hostile and increasingly radical. Activists at home sought to go underground; sporadic violence probably included acts of personal revenge. Democracy Movement leaders who escaped to the West announced plans to organize in exile to defeat the martial law regime and create a democratic system in China.

As the "big lie" churned out by the propaganda machine now controlled by martial law authorities was met by profound disbelief at home and outrage overseas, and attempts to purge the bureaucracy met with passive resistance, the regime turned to scapegoating. Unwilling and unable to admit to massive popular hatred for the regime, Chinese leaders were forced to manufacture evidence of a sinister conspiracy by anti-China enemies at home and abroad. Typically, the regime sought to undermine sympathy for the students and intellectuals and silence their peers by revealing them to be traitors, not merely dissidents. Anger at Western reporting and commentary on the crisis, diplomatic and economic sanctions, and help for activists in escaping punishment was reflected in media accusations that Western powers were pursuing a decades-long campaign to subvert China. Using Cultural Revolution language that suggested they had fallen into a time warp, the leadership praised the elderly revolutionaries for once more saving China; required all functionaries to spend hours in political meetings confessing any activism and studying speeches by the wise helmsman, Deng Xiaoping; and launched a campaign against bourgeois liberalism that quickly took on an antireform and anti-foreign cast.

Prospects

The events of 4 June 1989 probably guaranteed what before was only a possibility—the eventual end of Leninist rule in China. They also guaranteed that China's road to modernization will be much slower and much rockier than was the case at middecade. Deng Xiaoping's choice of military repression destroyed what he had worked a decade to gain—a revitalization and modernization of party rule and his own place in history as China's modernizer and reunifier. It will take at least a decade to refill the reservoir of confidence among China's urban citizens, residents of Hong Kong and Taiwan, and government and business partners worldwide.

It is now a matter of time and timing, as the elders leave the stage one by one, when martial law will be rescinded, its implementors will be removed from office, and the third wave of reform will finally emerge. The advanced age of the elders, the breadth and depth of opposition to current leaders within the elite, and the potential for economic collapse all point to a reversal of trends sooner rather than later. Global and regional trends will be important factors in this outcome. Few socialist nations in the midst of their own delicate reforms welcome China's reversion to Stalinism. The crisis of June has unified overseas Chinese minds and hearts in ways that may profoundly affect China's future. The Democracy Movement in exile may become the focal point of loyalty for a new global "China lobby." Few in China want to return to isolation, knowing the tremendous potential cost in terms of loss of resources, prestige, and security.

Given the depth of the legitimacy crisis that now exists, the overwhelming odds are that the younger members of the current leadership, struggling in the shadows of the elders and chosen for their lack of vision and principle, will not prove to be agents for the constructive change China needs. Continuing episodes of official repression, corruption, and factionalism will spawn chronic social alienation and lack of cooperation. The potential for serious economic and social crisis and systemic collapse before the next century dawns is now far greater than the prospects for an economic and social miracle, and the difference will be of enormous importance to the rest of the world.

China's chance in the world may have to await the eventual rise of a stronger middle class based on the reconsolidation of economic reform along the south China coast and the reconstruction of an educated and prosperous socio-political stratum—largely in Beijing and other urban centers—made up of modern civil service officials, intellectuals, and economic managers. Even these economic and social changes alone would not ensure China's full positive contribution to humankind. That can come only with a deeper spiritual revival and cultural renaissance.

Notes

1. Xinhua, 31 December 1988, in FBIS–88-002, 4 January 1989, p. 50.
2. Xinhua, 6 January 1989, in FBIS-CHI–89-005, 9 January 1989, p. 34.
3. Ding Xueliang, "The Disparity Between Idealistic and Instrumental Chinese Reformers," *Asian Survey* 28:22 (November 1988), pp. 1132–1136.
4. Alvin and Heidi Toffler, "Socialism in Crisis: China Maps a Way Out of Communism's Rut," *World Monitor* 2:1 (January 1989), pp. 34–43.
5. Interviews with staff members of the development center, Washington, D.C., summer 1988 and summer 1989.
6. Frederick C. Teiwes, *Leadership, Legitimacy, and Conflict in China: From a Charismatic Mao to the Politics of Succession* (Armonk, N.Y.: M. E. Sharpe, 1984), pp. 76–92, 118–132.
7. Yang Jisheng, "'East-West Dialogue' in China," *Liaowang* [Outlook], 27 February 1989, pp. 5–7, in Foreign Broadcast Information Service [FBIS] CHI–89-067, 10 April 1989, pp. 37–44. Guo Fansheng, head of the reform institute's western China center, interview, *China Daily,* 5 January 1989, p. 4, in FBIS-CHI–89-004, 6 January 1989, pp. 33–35, discussed the price inequities that for decades have paid low return to the interior for energy, raw materials, and primary products, while it must purchase high-priced machinery and light and textile industrial products from the east.
8. A good example was the *Renmin ribao* [People's Daily] editorial, March 1989, p. 1, calling for unity and stability in the wake of the imposition of martial law in Tibet.
9. For a rare discussion of the importance of cultural strength in international competition and admission of China's cultural depression, see Zi Zhongyun, "The Confluence of Interests: The Basis of State Relations," *Renmin ribao,* 30 December 1988, p. 7, in FBIS-CHI–89-006, 10 January 1989, pp. 6–12.
10. See, for example, Liu Zhonglai, "Plain Talk on the Status of the Armed Forces in Peacetime," *Jiefang junbao* [Liberation Army Daily], 12 January 1989, p. 3, in FBIS-CHI–89-016, 26 January 1989, pp. 36–38.
11. Toffler, "Socialism in Crisis," p. 40, made this point.
12. Jan S. Prybyla, "China's Economic Experiment: Back from the Market?" *Problems of Communism* (January-February 1989), p. 17, discussed the economic crossroads; Wang Yizhou, interview, *Jingjixue zhoubao* [Economics Weekly], 18 June 1989, p. 3, in FBIS-CHI–89-128, 6 July 1989, p. 3–4, posed the related economic and political alternatives.
13. Ding, "The Disparity," p. 1136, discussed Deng's dual strategy in the context of the East Asian model, pointing out why it could not work in China unless and until there is much greater autonomy from politics for the economy and society. Interviews with Chinese intellectuals, Washington, D.C., spring and summer 1989, revealed the different, but largely negative, reaction to the concept of neoauthoritarianism. For summaries of the debate on the concept, see Robert Delfs, "Little Dragon Model," *Far Eastern Economic Review,* 9 March 1989, p. 12; Zhang Weiguo, "Beijing Holds Successive Seminars on

Neoauthoritarianism," *Shijie jingji daobao* [World economic herald], 13 March 1989, p. 10, in FBIS-CHI–89–059, 29 March 1989, pp. 39–44.

14. The following account of the events of 1989 is my own analysis based on detailed, daily observation of a massive amount of media—official Chinese press, Hong Kong press, and foreign press.

15. Chuang Ming, "Zhao Ziyang Receives Instructions in Time of Danger to Save a Desperate Situation," *Ching Pao* [Mirror], 10 February 1987, pp. 26–29, in FBIS, 12 February 1987, p. K6.

Chronology

1953–1957	1st five-year plan (FYP)
September 1956	8th Party Congress
1956	100 Flowers Movement
1957	Antirightist Campaign
1958–1962	2nd FYP replaced by the Great Leap Forward
1961–1965	Readjustment program
1966–1970	3rd FYP drafted 1964–1965 but replaced by the third-front strategy; Cultural Revolution
1971–1975	4th FYP, "flying leap," replaced by a readjustment program
1976–1985	Ten-year plan in draft in 1975, adopted February 1978 as the "four modernizations program" and abandoned April 1979 for a three-year readjustment program
1976–1990	Fifteen-year plan in draft 1979–1980; abandoned December 1980
December 1978	3rd Plenum of the 11th Central Committee
1979–1980	First wave of reform; Democracy Wall Movement
1981–1982	Readjustment program continued
1981–1985	6th FYP adopted late in December 1982
1981–2000	Twenty-year plan, unpublished outline
September 1982	12th Party Congress
1983–1984	Second wave of reform begins
October 1983–April 1984	Antispiritual pollution and anticrime campaigns
1984–1987	Party rectification campaign
October 1984	3rd Plenum of the 12th Central Committee; economic reform decision

March 1985	Science and technology reform decision
May 1985	Education reform decision
September 1985	Party conference; party's plan proposal
1985–mid-1986	Readjustment program
February 1986	Anticorruption campaign
1986–1990	7th FYP adopted April 1986 by the National People's Congress
September 1986	6th Plenum of the 12th Central Committee; ideology and culture reform decision
December 1986	Student demonstrations
January 1987	Hu Yaobang's dismissal; start of antibourgeois liberalization campaign
October 1987	13th Party Congress; mandate for a third wave of reform
1988–1995	Eight-year reform plan, unpublished draft
September 1988	3rd Plenum of the 13th Central Committee; readjustment program introduced
January–May 1989	Democracy Movement
4 June 1989	Beijing massacre
23–24 June 1989	4th Plenum of the 13th Central Committee; Zhao Ziyang's official dismissal

Major Individuals
and Institutions

Advisory commission: Central [Committee] Advisory Commission, created by the 12th Party Congress in September 1982 as a means of honorary semiretirement for veterans of the revolution. Many were former members of the 8th Central Committee who were purged by Mao during the Cultural Revolution, returned to positions of influence by Deng and Hu Yaobang, but who then used the commission to press the conservative cause in the late 1980s.

Bao Tong: Middle-aged reformer who served as Zhao Ziyang's political secretary and after the 13th Party Congress in October 1987 became the secretary of the Politburo standing committee. Bao was the chief conduit to Zhao for younger officials promoting radical systemic reform, including those in the economic reform institute; he also headed the several party organizations created in 1987–1989 to research and experiment with political reform. After the 4 June 1989 Beijing massacre, Bao and the others were investigated and accused of counterrevolutionary activity in connection with the prodemocracy demonstrations.

Bo Yibo: Veteran revolutionary who worked with Deng Xiaoping and Yang Shangkun in the Shanxi regions under the control of Japanese forces after 1937 and with Chen Yun in industrial economic planning in the 1950s, 1960s, and 1980s. His economic and political views were closest to those of Chen. Never a member of the Politburo, Bo nonetheless had great influence through these close personal ties and as first deputy and chief executive on the advisory commission, under Deng (1982–1987) and then Chen Yun (after October 1987). Bo chafed under Hu Yaobang's reformism when he served as Hu's deputy on the rectification commission (1983–1987) and led the attack on Hu. In 1989, Bo was rumored to be quite ill and made few appearances.

Chen Junsheng: Reformist secretary-general of the State Council and head of the party committee for government organs under Zhao Ziyang in the mid-1980s, continuing under Li Peng into 1988. Chen also headed the State Council leading group responsible for the poverty program set up in 1986.

Chen Yizi: Middle-aged leader of an informal group of young radical reformers who had known each other as students and Red Guards at Beijing University and were sent down to the countryside together, where they studied classical western political thought. In the late 1970s and early 1980s, they helped formulate experimental rural reforms under the protection of Du Runsheng, head of the party's rural development center. In 1984, some were brought into the State Council to work on experiments in urban reform in the reform institute headed by Chen Yizi, some were in the State Council's rural development center (essentially the same as the party's center and also headed by Du), and some went to the social science academy's rural development institute. Chen also headed the Society of Young Economists, a professional organization used by this group to promote research and public education regarding radical reform. In 1989, Chen and some of the others were in exile after being branded counterrevolutionaries along with Bao Tong, their conduit to Zhao Ziyang.

Chen Yun: The most senior veteran of the revolution, having joined the select handful of top leaders in the 1930s and 1940s, when he served as a liaison with Moscow and was responsible for organization and personnel. China's leading economic official in the 1950s, early 1960s, and 1970s, with strong influence on economic and organization/personnel affairs through the 1980s despite age (born around 1900) and illness. A consistent advocate of a balanced sectoral development strategy and financial caution, Chen's views put him on the liberal end of the political spectrum in the Mao era and the conservative end of the spectrum by the late Deng era. By 1989, he was supporting Yao Yilin, Li Peng, and Song Ping.

Chinese People's Political Consultative Conference: Set up in the mid-1940s as a united front organization intended to explore the possibility of a coalition government between the Chinese Communist party, the Nationalist party, and several small democratic parties. Beginning in the 1950s, its authority and influence were severely circumscribed, and it was disbanded in the Cultural Revolution. Revived in the 1980s by Deng Xiaoping as its chairman for a brief time, the conference provided a platform for advice to the party from prominent noncommunist individuals, parties, and professional groups. The conference normally met concurrently with the annual National People's Congress (dominated by Communist party members) to discuss government policy. The leadership was ambivalent regarding recruitment, research, and discussion activities allowed the conference. The increasingly vocal and critical debates in the annual sessions after 1984 and the 1989 prodemocracy activism of the democratic parties and religious groups represented on the conference left these noncommunists quite vulnerable to repression when the Secretariat member responsible for united front work (Yan Mingfu) was demoted.

Deng Liqun: Veteran political theorist and propaganda official from the 1930s on, who in the 1980s helped build up the social science academy and funnel its resources into policy research, supervised the Secretariat policy research center, and served as propaganda department director. Deng became a chief critic of Hu Yaobang and Zhao Ziyang, and competed with Hu Qili for control of the Politburo's propaganda and ideology leading group. In revenge, Zhao—with the support of Deng Xiaoping—humiliated Deng Liqun at the 13th Party Congress, when delegates refused to promote him from the Secretariat to Hu Qiaomu's old position on the Politburo overseeing ideology, as had been planned by Chen Yun and other patrons.

Deng Xiaoping: Secretary General of the Communist party and member of the Politburo standing committee after the 1956 8th Party Congress and a chief victim of the Cultural Revolution. Deng was brought back to power by Mao in 1974 when it was learned that Premier Zhou Enlai was dying of cancer. Deng became paramount leader at the 1978 3rd Plenum after years of political struggle against Mao's close associates and Hua Guofeng. Deng chose to give the top formal posts of party chief and premier to his protégés, but like Mao he retained control of the Central Military Commission, thus ensuring his unassailable preeminence.

Development center: The State Council Research Center for Economic, Technological, and Social Development, evolved from the 1979 structural adjustment group, which in 1980 became the technical economic research center and then merged in 1985 with the economic reform and price reform research centers. Headed by Ma Hong, concurrently president of the social science academy, the development center served as one of Zhao Ziyang's most influential think tanks. Its leading officials and researchers, many of them recruited into policy research from the academy, helped shaped the development strategy and reform policies of both the 7th FYP adopted in 1986 and the draft 8th FYP circulating in 1988.

Discipline inspection commission: Central [Committee] Discipline Inspection Commission, established by the 12th Party Congress and headed by Chen Yun until Qiao Shi replaced him at the 13th Party Congress. Intended to enforce party regulations against corruption, abuse of power, heterodoxy, and disobedience of central committee directives, the organization was relatively ineffective because networks of personal patronage circumvented it.

Dong Fureng: Prominent reform economist, director of the prestigious economic research institute of the social science academy, and associate of Yu Guangyuan. Dong pioneered the ideas for ownership reform in 1979.

Du Runsheng: A key originator and promoter of the rural reforms of the 1980s, in close cooperation with Wan Li and Zhao Ziyang. Deputy to Wan Li, the minister of agriculture, in 1980 and director of the party's high-level rural development center and of its State Council counterpart. Close associate of reformers at the science and technology commission and a patron of Chen Yizi and young radical reformers.

Economic commission: State [Council] Economic Commission, which played an important role in promoting industrial and planning reforms in the 1980s, especially under Zhang Jingfu's leadership.

Economic policy research groups: Four main groups plus task forces set up by the State Council's finance and economics commission in early 1979 to rethink China's approach to economic development. The main four were the technical transfer group, the economic structural readjustment group, the economic theory group, and the economic system reform group. Headed by important officials and staffed by prominent economists, these groups were strengthened and reorganized as offices, commissions, and research centers during the 1980s. Officially run by the State Council, they were actually party organizations under Zhao Ziyang as head of the party's finance and economic leading group.

Economic reform drafting group: Set up in early 1986 by Zhao to create a set of comprehensive, concrete policies to carry out the general reform strategy adopted for the 7th FYP period.

Economic reform group/office/work group: See economic policy research groups.

Economic research institute: Prestigious institute under the social science academy, which under its director Dong Fureng and academy vice president Liu Guoguang provided important policy research functions as well as training and experience for new economists.

Economic theory group: See economic policy research groups.

Fang Lizhi: China's most famous and internationally recognized astrophysicist. Fang's professional efforts to defend the autonomy of research on cosmology from party interference led him to focus his thinking, writing, and speaking more and more on the relationship between state and society. By the mid-1980s, his administrative duties at China's premier science and technology university in Hefei, Anhui, included experiments (backed by Hu Yaobang) with independent professional control of tertiary education. Expulsion from the party in 1987 for promoting prodemocracy activism by intellectuals and students only made him bolder. Fang's petition to Deng Xiaoping in early 1989 on behalf of jailed dissident Wei Jingsheng sparked the civil rights movement that ended with the bloody crackdown on students demonstrators in June. Tensions between the United States and China due to conflicting values were symbolized by PRC prevention of Fang's attendance at a banquet hosted by President Bush in Beijing in February 1989 and by the offer to Fang and his family of protective refuge by the United States after the Beijing massacre.

Finance and economic commission/leading group: The Central Committee's policy-making body for economic matters, usually headed by the premier. Departing from custom, Zhao Ziyang retained control of this group when he became General Secretary at the 13th Party Congress. Premier Li Peng and Vice Premier Yao Yilin probably controlled the group after the 1988 3rd plenum, when Zhao's economic management record was criticized and readjustment policies were introduced.

Foreign affairs leading group: The Central Committee's policy-making body for foreign affairs, under the close supervision of the paramount leader. Both Mao and Deng always retained control over basic national security strategy. Normally headed by the premier, this group was headed in the late 1970s and early 1980s by Li Xiannian, then by Zhao Ziyang, and now by Li Peng. Although a member of the International Liaison Department of the party, as well as representatives from the military and security organs, sits on this body for coordinating purposes, these matters are controlled by other groups.

Foreign affairs office: The staff office for the foreign affairs leading group, located in the State Council.

Foreign expertise leading group: A State Council organ set up under State Councilor Zhang Jingfu in the mid-1980s to implement a new policy of adapting foreign management experience as well as technology.

Foreign investment leading group: A State Council organ headed by State Councilor Gu Mu to oversee not only foreign investment policy but also more general reform experiments being carried out in the special economic zones and the open coastal cities.

Hu Jiwei: Editor-in-chief of *Renmin ribao* [People's Daily], who lost his position in the 1983 antispiritual pollution campaign. Hu Jiwei continued to advocate press reform and for a time was responsible for drafting a new, liberal press law as a vice chairman of the Education, Science, Culture, and Public Health Committee of the National People's Congress and president of the China Federation of Journalism Societies. In 1989, Hu Jiwei spearheaded an effort to hold an extraordinary session of the congress's standing committee to address student demands and rescind martial law, thereby becoming a main target of the antibourgeois liberalization campaign that followed the crackdown.

Hu Qiaomu: Veteran revolutionary and political theorist, member of the Politburo responsible for propaganda and ideology until his retirement to the advisory commission in October 1987, and patron of Deng Liqun and other conservative officials in propaganda affairs, especially at the social science academy. Hu Qiaomu was founding president of the academy in 1978.

Hu Qili: Chief deputy to Hu Yaobang on the party Secretariat, member of the Politburo after September 1985 and of its standing committee after the 13th Party Congress, and head of the propaganda and ideology leading group from 1984 to 1989. With the fall of Zhao Ziyang in June 1989, Hu Qili was removed from all these offices but retained his central committee membership. Hu Qili was typical of the younger, better educated officials being promoted within the party by Hu Yaobang, especially from among his former associates at the Communist Youth League.

Hu Yaobang: Deng Xiaoping's chief lieutenant in the effort to demote Maoists and rehabilitate veteran officials in the late 1970s. Hu served variously as chief of the academy of science, the central party school, and the propaganda and organization departments in that period. He became the party's secretary-general in 1980 and after the fall of Hua Guofeng took on the top job of General Secretary after a reorganization of titles and organizations at the 12th Party Congress. As a result of attacks by party and military conservatives and a falling out in 1986 with Deng over the issue of Deng's retirement and Hu's promotion, Hu was dismissed from office after admitting to serious mistakes in January 1987. Zhao replaced him.

Huan Xiang: Former ambassador to Great Britain and senior national security adviser to Premier Zhou Enlai, Deng Xiaoping, and then Premier Zhao Ziyang. With training in economics as well as international affairs, Huan played a unique role in coordinating foreign economic and geopolitical strategy to support China's economic development program. Huan's death in 1988 left a vacuum hard to fill.

International studies center: With the support of Zhao Ziyang, Huan Xiang attempted to set up the international studies center under the State Council as a counterpart to the U.S. National Security Council to serve a coordinating function, but existing foreign affairs and national security organs fiercely guarded their prerogatives and defeated the effort. The organization became a ship without a rudder after Huan's death and Zhao's purge.

Jiang Zemin: Deputy secretary (1985) and then secretary (1987–1988) of Shanghai, Jiang was the compromise candidate chosen to succeed Zhao Ziyang as General Secretary in June 1989. Said to be favored by or even related to Li Xiannian, Jiang's appointment seemed a signal to the West of continuity in foreign policy, given his skill in western languages and his involvement in foreign investment affairs for much of the 1980s. Jiang was in a very weak position coming into office, however, with the elders setting policy direction under martial law, especially for military and foreign affairs, and other powerful officials sharing his responsibilities for propaganda, personnel and united front work.

Li Peng: One of a number of children of revolutionary martyrs looked after by Premier Zhou Enlai, Li had a privileged upbringing. He headed the party's student organization in Moscow while being educated as an engineer in the 1940s. His career was spent primarily in the energy sector, with promotion and special protection during the Cultural Revolution from Zhou's associates. Favored by Chen Yun and others once close to Zhou, Li became vice premier in 1983 and a member of the Politburo and Minister of the State Education Commission in 1985 and then formally succeeded Zhao as Premier in 1988. He was passed over by Deng in favor of Jiang Zemin as party chief in place of Zhao in June 1989, reflecting in part the unpopularity of the martial law regime he had come to symbolize.

Li Ruihuan: A former construction worker educated and promoted under Zhou Enlai's special program for workers in the 1950s. Li recently proved himself to top leaders, especially Deng Xiaoping, as the no-nonsense chief of Tianjin city, where student demonstrations were kept under control without violence. Although not a liberal in political-ideological matters, Li gained the acceptance of Tianjin citizens for solving their practical problems. He was promoted to the Politburo at the 13th Party Congress and then to its standing committee with responsibility for propaganda in the wake of Zhao's purge.

Li Tieying: Son of a revolutionary martyr and of Deng Xiaoping's former wife and thought to be a favorite of Deng's. Li became minister of electronics industry in 1985, replaced Zhao as head of the reform commission in 1987, and then was appointed minister of education in 1988. Li joined the Politburo in October 1987.

Li Xiannian: A veteran of the revolution, a key economic official after 1949; as a close associate of Zhou Enlai Li survived the Cultural Revolution as a member of the Politburo since 1956. In the 1980s, Li served as President of the PRC, traveling to the United States on a state visit in 1985. Since 1987, head of the Chinese People's Political Consultative Conference.

Lin Zixin: A reformer at the science and technology commission and organizer of the first China 2000 study, after which he was promoted to secretary-general of the commission. Li founded *Keji bao* [Science and Technology Daily], which was devoted to introducing new ideas about advanced development to China. The paper was criticized for promoting heterodoxy in 1987 and again after the crackdown of June 1989, when Lin was forced to retire.

Liu Guoguang: Senior economist and vice president of the social science academy, head of the 1979 task force on comparative economic models.

Ma Hong: An experienced economic planning official who was out of office from 1959 (when he opposed the Great Leap Forward) to 1979, when he began to take on growing responsibilities for economic policy research as president of the social science academy and director of the State Council's development center.

Marxism-Leninism research institute: Institute for Research on Marxism-Leninism–Mao Zedong Thought of the social science academy, established in 1979 over the opposition of some who argued that orthodoxy was to be taught as dogma (the traditional role of the Central Party School), not subjected to research and development. Yu Guangyuan was its founding director; he was succeeded by his close associate Su Shaozhi in 1983 when Yu retired to the advisory commission. Yu and Su sought to promote the updating of Marxist theory to absorb new accomplishments in western social science and European Marxism and to address theoretical problems posed by postwar developments in the global economy and politics. In 1983, 1987, and 1989 both were denounced as advocates of bourgeois liberalism.

Military commission: Central Military Commission, an organ of the central committee always headed by the paramount leader, Mao and then Deng. Its senior membership included the chiefs of the general staff, logistics, and political departments as well as of the air force and navy. At the 12th Party Congress, a counterpart organization with the same name and nearly identical membership was set up in the state structure. The apparent intent of reformers to gradually shift authority over the army from the party to the state never got off the ground. Deng reportedly sought to turn over his control of the commission to Hu Yaobang after 1981, but military opposition prevented it. Zhao became first deputy chairman in 1987, but was removed in 1989, again leaving Yang Shangkun second in command and thus kingmaker in the succession to Deng.

National defense science and technology and industry commission: Created in 1982 from a merger of the national defense industry office, national defense science and technology commission, and the military commission's office of science, technology, and armament commission. Ostensibly a state organization but in fact under the primary control of the party's military commission, cooperating closely with the science and technology commission. Responsible for military research, development, and industrial production.

National People's Congress: China's legislature, ostensibly independent but in fact subordinate to the Central Committee, which controls all appointments of its standing committee. The chairman is always a high-ranking party leader; policies are recommended and implemented through the Politburo's political and legal commission or leading group. Elections of delegates (every four years) are managed and approved by the party, although there have been experiments (especially in 1980 and 1988) with competitive electoral procedures at lower levels, greater involvement (with State Council offices) in drafting legislation by new functional standing committees, and freer discussion of legislation at annual sessions.

Organization department: One of the most powerful units in the party bureaucracy, responsible not only for personnel appointments, supervision, and dismissal but also for reorganizing, disbanding, or adding bureaucratic units, a key tool in political competition. The department works closely with the secret police and the general office of the party in managing the secret files that accompany cadre through life, covering everything from family background and school behavior to attitudes during political campaigns and accomplishments or errors in regular assignments.

Peng Zhen: Revolutionary elder, powerful member of the Politburo and Secretariat before the Cultural Revolution, with responsibility for Beijing city and political and legal affairs. He regained influence in both arenas in the 1980s, as head of the party's political and legal affairs commission (1980–1985) and chairman of the National People's Congress (1984–1988). A long-time competitor to Deng, Peng never regained a formal post on the Politburo and was retired in 1988 without retaining even an honorary post.

Planning commission: State [Council] Planning Commission, responsible for creating annual, medium- and long-term economic development plans for distribution of material commodities and human resources among nationally controlled organizations. Usually headed by a member of the Politburo or its standing committee. The portion of the economy under the commission's control diminished steadily in the 1980s, as more economic exchange was commercialized and controlled by fiscal-monetary mechanisms. In 1988, a powerful standing committee was created for the commission that included most senior economic officials. Headed alternately in the 1980s by Yao Yilin and Song Ping, close associates of Chen Yun.

Politburo: A group of twenty to twenty-five leading officials, with individual responsibility for the different main functional subsystems (e.g., security, or propaganda, or industry). Ostensibly the primary full-time policy-makers when the Central Committee was not in (annual or biannual) full session, in fact many key decisions are made by the Politburo's standing committee of five or six top leaders or by the paramount leader alone. In the mid-1980s, the aging members of the Politburo met irregularly, while Hu and Zhao ran the country through the Secretariat and the State Council. In the 1987–1989 period, Zhao held meetings of the now younger Politburo more regularly, in another attempt to sideline the elders.

Political and legal commission/leading group: Powerful functional leading group, usually headed by a member of the Politburo standing committee (elder Peng Zhen in the early 1980s and Qiao Shi thereafter, probably in cooperation with Wan Li). Supervises the National People's Congress, the Supreme Court, and the ministries of public security, state security, and justice as well as the armed police.

Political reform leading group/work group/research center: A leading group was first set up in early 1986 under Hu Yaobang and Hu Qili, to oversee the drafting of a central committee resolution on reform in ideology, culture, and the political system. In late 1986, due to opposition to Hu's approach and a shift toward more moderate political reform that did not so severely constrain the party's monopoly on power, a work group was set up under Zhao Ziyang and his secretary Bao Tong, which involved Chen Yizi and others from the reform institute and prominent intellectuals like Su Shaozhi and Yan Jiaqi. Work temporarily ceased during the campaign against Hu Yaobang in early 1987; Chen then took the lead in drafting a section of Zhao's work report to the 13th Party Congress calling for political reform. Owing to much controversy, only some of his draft was approved and only in general terms. After the Congress, Bao Tong created a formal Politburo-level policy research center to continue research and local experimentation with political reform. Those involved were among the key targets of conservative wrath when Zhao fell.

Political science research institute: Created in 1985 after much preparation and considerable skepticism by conservatives that Marxist political theory should be subjected to research and modification. Founded and headed by Yan Jiaqi.

Propaganda and ideology leading group: Powerful functional policy-making body, usually headed by a Politburo standing committee member (Hu Qiaomu in the early 1980s and Hu Qili until his demotion to central committee membership in 1989). Responsible for supervising the party propaganda department and State Council bodies responsible for culture, publishing, education, and the media and for coordinating with the political department of the army. Able not only to set guidelines for and censor the content of education curricula and the media but also to appoint personnel in this broad arena and to orchestrate political study sessions throughout the system. Control of this subsystem is a key prize in every power struggle; mass political campaigns such as those against bourgeois liberalization give its leadership extraordinary political power.

Qiao Shi: Politburo standing committee member after the 13th Party Congress, Qiao spent his early career in the party's International Liaison Department, responsible for China's relations with foreign communist or socialist political parties. Beginning in 1985, he rapidly rose to the heights of power with responsibility for internal security affairs and party education and discipline as head of the party's political and legal affairs commission/leading group—the leading group for rectification of central departments, the discipline inspection commission, and the central party school.

Qin Benli: Veteran journalist in Shanghai, typical of better-educated reformist wing of the party, labeled a rightist in 1957. Editor of the *World Economic Herald,* Shanghai's semi-independent progressive newspaper, which attracted some of China's best young journalists and a wide readership but was shut down in 1989 as a counterrevolutionary organization.

Rectification commission: Central [Committee] Commission for Guiding Party Consolidation, set up in 1983 to run a three-year campaign to thoroughly inspect, reeducate, and reshuffle the party's membership nationwide and at all levels. Headed by Hu Yaobang, with many elders on its standing committee and representation from every major organization involved with personnel. The campaign was largely a failure, like so many before it, since the patronage system protected many corrupt officials from discipline and leaders used it for personal power building. The executive vice chairman, Bo Yibo, used this platform to attack Hu Yaobang, and the commission was disbanded by Zhao in 1987, after declaring the campaign a victory.

Reform commission: State Council Commission for Restructuring the Economic System. Set up in 1982 to plan and locally experiment with a program for comprehensive reform by Zhao Ziyang, who as its founding director gave it additional prestige and power. Prominent economic officials headed it, and young economists in the reform institute headed by Chen Yizi served as its brains and legs. Gao Shangquan was its leading member and chief spokesman. Zhao turned the commission over to Li Tieying in 1987, but in early 1988, when Premier Li Peng became its head, he downgraded its role and reorganized its membership. Li turned instead for policy advice to a new State Council research office headed by official government spokesman Yuan Mu.

Reform institute: The reform commission's Institute for Research on the Restructuring of the Economic System, headed by Chen Yizi. The young reform activists in the institute carried out data surveys in factories, designed and monitored local experiments with both economic and political reform, and pioneered the use of public opinion surveys as a tool of governance. They had direct access to Zhao through his secretary Bao Tong as well as through normal channels. The group sought to build a position of financial and organizational independence from the bureaucracy, seeking overseas financing for business ventures for this purpose. In 1989, the institute was accused of collaborating with leaders of the democracy movement to use demonstrations to strengthen Zhao's weakening political position.

Regional planning offices: Offices set up under the State Council in the mid-1980s to do regional planning focused on large-scale, long-term development projects. These regions included the northeast economic zone, the Shanxi energy base, the third-front area in the west and southwest, and the Shanghai economic zone, which gradually expanded to cover much of the Yangzi River basin.

Rural development center: Central [Committee] Rural Policy Research Center and State Council Rural Development Research Center. Ostensibly two different organizations, they were basically the same body with the same director, Du Runsheng. Founded in 1982 with high status as policy-making as well as research body(ies). After 1983, a group of young reform scholars and activists under Chen Yizi, who worked under Du's umbrella on the rural reforms, separated with some staying with Du's center(s), some under Chen creating the reform institute, and some going to the social science academy's rural development institute.

Science academy: Chinese Academy of Sciences, the prestigious and elitist body of senior scientists in Beijing. Run according to a Soviet model of centrally funded and party-directed research. A locus of efforts by administrators at the science and technology commission to reform management of research institutions to better serve economic development.

Science and technology commission: The main organ of the State Council aimed at funneling scientific and technological work into the economic development program. Key administrators associated with the commission have been at the forefront of ideological and managerial reform. These included Zhang Jingfu, Wu Mingyu, Yu Guangyuan, Tong Dalin, and Lin Zixin.

Science and technology development center: The commission's policy research center, founded and headed in the 1980s by Wu Mingyu, who headed up the effort to draft the science and technology white paper (on policy strategy), blue books (sectoral policies), and reform decision (adopted by the central committee in 1985).

Science and technology leading group: The party's policy-making and coordinating body for this arena, headed by Premier Zhao Ziyang through the 1980s. Source of policy guidance and personnel appointment for the commission, its development center, and its newspaper, *Keji bao*.

Scientific and technical information institute: Organization under the science and technology commission responsible for collecting, translating, and disseminating foreign sources of information on developments in science and technology. Headed by Lin Zixin in the early 1980s; the main research body for the first China 2000 study.

Secretariat: Chief executive body under the Politburo for party affairs, including propaganda, personnel, rural work, and united front work with noncommunist, youth, and women's organizations. Under Hu Yaobang, the Secretariat and State Council were nearly the same in membership and function, overseeing policy for all arenas, almost replacing the aging Politburo in function. After 1987, Zhao sought to separate the Secretariat and State Council, relegating both to executive functions with the now younger Politburo taking back its policy-making function.

Secretariat policy research center: The nerve center for all policy research under Deng Liqun during the 1980s. Gradually, its influence was weakened as it shared power and influence with research centers set up by Zhao in the State Council that answered to his party leading groups for economics and science. After the 13th Party Congress, the center may have been reorganized or disbanded.

Shekou industrial zone: The China Merchants Steam Navigation Company, with Yuan Geng taking the lead, pioneered China's first "special industrial zone" in January 1979; the intent was to concentrate on industrial exports. In 1980, larger "special economic zones" were set up to allow many different types of economic activity such as tourism and property development, with Shenzhen SEZ in the area around Shekou but administered separately. The zones were allowed to adopt preferential land-use, employment, and taxation mechanisms to attract foreign investment. After 1984, the open coastal cities set up similar "economic development zones" but often aimed at attracting more advanced technology.

***Shijie jingji daobao* [World Economic Herald]:** A semi-independent newspaper developed and housed by the Shanghai Academy of Social Sciences, printed by the party newspaper office. Editor Qin Benli had a large measure of editorial autonomy for his ostensibly nongovernmental newspaper and used it to advance the frontier of journalistic reporting and comment, making the paper a favorite of the progressive elite in China. The paper's bold efforts in 1988–1989 to seek foreign funding, promote a nonparty member to the editorship, advance the cause of Zhao Ziyang and radical reform in the face of conservative opposition, and defy censorship orders from the Shanghai party chief Jiang Zemin led to reorganization and repression of the staff.

Social science academy: Established as an elite research organization in Beijing independent from the science academy for the first time in 1977. Hu Qiaomu was the founding president and retained strong influence there, along with his chief deputy, Deng Liqun. The academy's graduate program and participation in policy research continued to improve through the 1980s under president Ma Hong and executive vice president Zhao Fusan. In 1989, many staff members of the institutes participated in the civil rights movement and demonstrations and the academy as a whole came under a dark cloud of repression.

Song Jian: A member of the select group of military scientists who participated in China's missile program. Song helped pioneer the science of cybernetics and its application to social and economic problems. Song helped create projections of China's population in 1980–1981 and the resulting population control program. Promoted to head of the science and technology commission in 1984 and to state councilor and deputy director of the science and technology leading group in 1986.

Song Ping: An experienced economic administrator and apparently favored by Chen Yun's group, Song followed Yao Yilin as head of the planning commission in 1983; he was appointed director of the party's organization department in June 1987 and a member of the Politburo later that year. In June 1989, he was promoted to the Politburo's standing committee, the pinnacle of power.

Special economic zones: See Shekou industrial zone.

State Council: The executive branch, nominally appointed by and answerable to the National People's Congress, but in fact appointed by the top party leadership, supervised by the party committee for government organs, and directed by the functional party leading groups or commissions. The standing committee is headed by the premier and includes all the senior leadership, vice premiers and councilors (many concurrently ministers), and the secretary general and deputies who run the administrative offices.

Su Shaozhi: Second director of the social science academy's Marxism-Leninism institute. Respected theorist, trained as an economist, who has led the way in revising Chinese orthodoxy to suit the needs of the modern world. Criticized in 1983 and threatened with removal from the party in 1987, Su lost his job directing the institute but successfully argued his appeal to retain party membership to the discipline inspection commission. Su left China just after the Beijing massacre, having accepted an offer to teach at Marquette University for 1989–1990. He was attacked as a counterrevolutionary during the ensuing campaign.

Sun Yefang: China's best-known Marxist political economist, who independently of East European economists in the 1960s created a theoretical basis for market socialism. Returning to his old post as director of the social science academy's economic research institute, Sun helped reconstruct the field of economics in the years just before his death in 1983.

Technical economic center: See development center and economic policy research groups.

Tian Jiyun: An economic official who served with Zhao Ziyang in Sichuan early in the 1980s. Appointed vice premier in 1983, Tian helped supervise the drafting of the 7th FYP, especially its reform strategy. Tian joined the Politburo in 1985 but after 1987 gradually lost overall economic responsibilities, shifting his work focus to foreign economic relations and rural policy. Tian managed to survive the purge of Zhao in 1989.

Tong Dalin: As vice chairman of the science and technology commission and head of the economic policy research group on systemic reforms in 1979, Tong played a major role in launching and supporting the reform drive in the 1980s.

Wan Li: Veteran party leader, and friend and bridge partner of Deng Xiaoping, Wan was vice mayor of Beijing in the 1950s and 1960s. Wan returned to power as party secretary of poverty-stricken Anhui province, where impoverished peasants and desperate rural cadre pioneered rural decollectivization reforms that, with those in Sichuan under Zhao Ziyang, were used as models for the nationwide reforms. As a Politburo member and senior vice premier in the 1980s, Wan played a major role in formulating and implementing rural reforms, promoting science reform, and overseeing general economic and foreign affairs. In 1987–1988, Wan reportedly was Deng's choice for the premiership but was passed over in the factional horse-trading and semiretired as chairman of the National People's Congress. After Zhao's purge in 1989, Wan was a small reform minority of one at the senior levels of leadership.

Wang Ruoshui: Deputy editor-in-chief (responsible for theory) of *Renmin ribao* prior to his removal from office in the 1983 antispiritual pollution campaign. His writings attacking the Cultural Revolution and promoting Marxist humanism made him popular, especially among youth, and the attacks on him, which culminated in his dismissal from the party in 1987 despite his appeal to the discipline inspection commision, made Wang a folk hero. By 1988–1989, however, his continued loyalty to Marxism made even Wang seem antiquated to the avant garde.

Wang Zhen: Veteran revolutionary and leader of the armed forces that entered and occupied Hainan and then Xinjiang, where Wang and his associates maintained influence into the 1980s. Protector of Deng and his family during the Cultural Revolution and mid-1970s. Avid fan of computers but fierce opponent of bourgeois liberal, antiparty thinking and of Hu and Zhao for allegedly promoting it. Wang reportedly was not happy to leave the Politburo in 1987 and as consolation prize became vice president of the PRC.

World Bank: The International Bank for Reconstruction and Development, headquartered in Washington, D.C. China joined the bank in 1980 and by mid-decade was a primary recipient of development assistance and advice.

World Economic Herald: See *Shijie jingji daobao.*

World economics and politics institute: A research institute of the social science academy formed by the merger of the world economics and world politics institute. The institute's founder, Qian Jiazhu (who left China after the Beijing massacre), was a renowned noncommunist economist and bold critic of government policy. Under a subsequent director, the institute carried out the China 2000 study's pioneering survey of long-term global trends.

Xue Muqiao: China's most famous economist after Sun Yefang, his relative. Xue helped reconstitute the statistical system after Mao's death and headed the planning commission's research institute and the 1979 economic policy research group responsible for economic reform as well as its successor organization, the State Council's economic research center. Xue helped draft the first, abortive, economic reform plan in 1980 and reigned as the dean of Chinese reform economists, influencing many younger researchers, before ill health limited his activities in the late 1980s.

Yan Jiaqi: In 1985, Yan became the youngest institute director in the history of the social science academy, when he founded the newly formed political science institute after nearly five years of research, preparation, and controversy. Trained in natural science before the Cultural Revolution, Yan turned first to philosophy until its sterility under leftist dogmatic strictures aroused his interest in comparative political systems. He and his wife, Gao Gao, coauthored a book on the high-level politics of the Cultural Revolution that was banned in China in 1987, when Yan was criticized. His views became increasingly heterodox in the politicized atmosphere of 1980s academic life, and Yan was radicalized by the conflict in 1989 between the party and citizens of Beijing. During the demonstrations, he organized petition drives and negotiations, gave lectures in Tiananmen Square on constitutional democracy, and founded both an independent intellectuals organization and a free university. Fleeing China in early June, Yan joined student leader Wuer Kaixi as the organizers and symbolic leaders of the Front for a Democratic China.

Yang Shangkun: One of the famous returned students from the Soviet Union in the 1920s, veteran of the revolution, and close associate of Deng Xiaoping's from the late 1930s, Yang was responsible before the Cultural Revolution for the elite unit of bodyguards for top leaders and for the general office of the Politburo, which was the nerve center for communication and repository of central committee files. Returned to influence in the late 1970s, Yang helped launch the special economic zones as mayor of Guangzhou, then served on the National People's Congress in Beijing. As Deng's deputy on the military commission after 1982 and President of the PRC after 1988, Yang was a de facto if not de jure member of the Politburo standing committee, playing a pivotal role in the purges of both Hu Yaobang and Zhao Ziyang. By the end of June 1989, after directing the Beijing massacre, Yang was best placed to replace Deng as paramount leader.

Yao Yilin: A senior economic official in China for decades, with expertise in finance and planning, Yao is Chen Yun's closest associate. Yao retained great influence over the economy throughout Zhao's tenure as premier, and he rather than Li Peng was running the economy after late 1988.

Yu Guangyuan: Yu played a key role in drafting the first science reform policies favoring better treatment of intellectuals under Zhou Enlai and Nie Rongzhen in the late 1950s. Thereafter, he was responsible for science in the propaganda department until the Cultural Revolution. As a deputy director of the science and technology commission after 1977, vice president of the social science academy, and head of the 1979 economic policy research group for theory, Yu played a major role in pushing forward the frontier of reform policy. Due to conflict with more conservative theorists Hu Qiaomu and Deng Liqun, Yu was passed over for the post of academy president, forced into semiretirement on the advisory commission in 1982, and severely criticized in 1983, 1987, and 1989.

Zhao Fusan: Executive vice president of the social science academy for much of the 1980s, Zhao greatly expanded its graduate training and foreign exchange programs. A man of erudition and intellect, educated at St. John's University in Shanghai, Zhao's rise to such influence was remarkable given that he is an ordained Anglican priest and a vice president of the state-sponsored Protestant religious organization. In June 1989, Zhao extended his visit to Europe indefinitely.

Zhao Ziyang: A widely experienced provincial leader in south China before the Cultural Revolution, Zhao was sent to Deng's home province of Sichuan to get the economy back on its feet, which he quickly accomplished through rural reforms that then were adapted nationwide. Promoted to the premiership by Deng in 1980, Zhao quickly began to reshape national economic policy and institutions to promote reform and development. He fleshed out Deng's general guidelines with the help of the best minds in the nation, whom Zhao used to staff think tanks and whom he encouraged to boldly explore new ideas. When Hu Yaobang fell in 1987, Zhao quickly and ably limited the political campaign and purge, drafting a mandate for a third wave of bold reforms centered on marketization of the coastal economy, and its interdependence with the Asia-Pacific region's dynamic economies. Zhao helped protect reform intellectuals in 1983, 1987, and 1988 and into early 1989 tacitly sought their support as his political position began to slip. In the wake of the crackdown, Zhao and his associates were removed from office at the fourth plenum in late June 1989 and were placed under arrest and investigation for supporting counterrevolution. If convicted of such serious crimes rather than being accused of mistakes, Zhao and the others would be subject to trial and a death sentence rather than merely party disciplinary measures.

Zhou Yang: Veteran propaganda official from the 1930s on, responsible for persecution of many liberal intellectuals before the Cultural Revolution, when he himself became a victim. In 1979, Zhou publicly apologized for his former leftist ways and by 1983 was a target of criticism by conservatives for his newly found liberal views. Zhou actively supported Wang Ruoshui's explorations in socialist humanism and Hu Jiwei's attempts to free up the press until the conflict of 1983 damaged his health. After years in the hospital, Zhou died in the midst of the June 1989 crisis.

Suggestions for Further Reading

The Cultural Revolution and Late Mao Era

Fox Butterfield, *China: Alive in the Bitter Sea* (New York: Times Books, 1982).

Anita Chan, *Children of Mao: Personality Development and Politial Activism in the Red Guard Generation* (Seattle: University of Washington Press, 1985).

Nien Cheng, *Life and Death in Shanghai* (New York: Harper & Row, 1986).

John Fraser, *The Chinese: Portrait of a People* (New York: Summit Books, 1980).

Roger Garside, *Coming Alive: China After Mao* (New York: Mentor Books, 1981).

Carol Lee Hamrin and Timothy Cheek, eds., *China's Establishment Intellectuals* (Armonk, N.Y.: M. E. Sharpe, 1986).

Liang Heng and Judith Shapiro, *Son of the Revolution* (London: Fontana/Collins, 1983).

Barry Naughton, "The Third Front: Defence Industrialization in the Chinese Interior," *China Quarterly* 115 (September 1988), pp. 351–386.

Anne Thurston, *Enemies of the Peoples: The Ordeal of the Intellectuals in China's Great Cultural Revolution* (Cambridge: Harvard University Press, 1988).

Economic Reform Policy

David Bachman, *Chen Yun and the Chinese Political Systems* (Berkeley: University of California Press, 1985).

Robert F. Dernberger, "Mainland China's Development Strategy: Investment Financing Needs and Sources," *Issues and Studies* 22:12 (December 1986), pp. 74–103.

Joseph Fewsmith, "Special Economic Zones in the PRC," *Problems of Communism*, November-December 1986, pp. 78–85.

Joseph Fewsmith, "Agricultural Crisis in the PRC," *Problems of Communism*, November-December 1988, pp. 78–93.

Nicholas R. Lardy and Kenneth Lieberthal, eds., *Chen Yun's Strategy for Development: A Non-Maoist Alternative,* trans. Mao Tong and Du Anxia (Armonk, N.Y.: M. E. Sharpe, 1983).

William Parish, ed. *Chinese Rural Development: The Great Transformation* (Armonk, N.Y.: M. E. Sharpe, 1985).

Elizabeth Perry and Christine Wong, eds., *The Political Economy of Reform in Post-Mao China* (Cambridge: Harvard University Press, 1985).

Denis Fred Simon and Merle Goldman, eds., *Science and Technology in Post-Mao China* (Cambridge: Harvard University Press, 1989).

Lawrence Sullivan, "Assault on the Reforms," *China Quarterly* 114 (June 1988), pp. 198–222.

George Wang, ed., "China's Special Economic Zones," *Chinese Economic Studies,* Winter 1985–1986.

The World Bank, *China: Long-Term Development Issues and Options* (Washington, D.C.: World Bank, 1985).

Foreign Policy and the Military

Forum, "The Chinese People's Liberation Army 60 Years on: Transition Towards a New Era," *China Quarterly* 112 (December 1987), pp. 541–630.

Forum, "Peking's Foreign Policy After the 13th Party Congress," *Issues and Studies* 24:10 (October 1988), pp. 13–93.

Harry Harding, ed., *China's Foreign Relations in the 1980s* (New Haven: Yale University Press, 1984).

Harold K. Jacobson and Michel Oksenberg, *Toward a Global Economic Order: China's Participation in the IMF, the World Bank, and GATT* (Boulder, Colo.: Westview Press, 1989).

Samuel S. Kim, ed., *China and the World: New Directions in Chinese Foreign Relations,* 2d ed. (Boulder, Colo.: Westview Press, 1989).

Eugene K. Lawson, ed., *U.S.-China Trade: Problems and Prospects* (New York: Praeger, 1988).

Jonathan Pollack, "China's Changing Perceptions of East Asian Security and Development," *Orbis,* Winter 1986, pp. 771–794.

Lucian Pye, *Chinese Commercial Negotiating Style* (Santa Monica, Calif.: Rand Corporation R-2837-AF, January 1982).

Richard Solomon, *Chinese Political Negotiating Behavior* (Santa Monica, Calif.: Rand Corporation R-3295, December 1985).

Michael Yahuda, *China's Foreign Policy After Mao: Towards the End of Isolationism* (London: Macmillan, 1983).

Methodology

Paul A. Cohen, *Discovering History in China: American Historical Writing on the Recent Chinese Past* (New York: Columbia University Press, 1984).

Harry Harding, "Competing Models of the Chinese Communist Policy Process: Toward a Sorting and Evaluation," *Issues and Studies* 20:2 (February 1984), pp. 13–36.

T. C. Kuo and Ramon H. Myers, *Understanding Communist China: Communist China Studies in the United States and the Republic of China 1949–1978* (Stanford, Calif.: Hoover Institution, 1986).

Michel Oksenberg, "Politics Takes Command: An Essay on the Study of Post-1949 China," *Cambridge History of China*, vol. 14 (New York: Cambridge University Press, 1977), pp. 543–590.

Amy Wilson, Sidney Greenblatt, Richard Wilson, *Methodological Issues in Chinese Studies* (New York: Praeger, 1983).

Political Culture, Dissent, and Democracy

Geremie Barme and John Minford, eds., *Seeds of Fire: Chinese Voices of Conscience* (Hong Kong: Far Eastern Economic Review, 1988).

R. Randle Edwards, L. Henkin, and Andrew Nathan, *Human Rights in Contemporary China* (New York: Columbia University Press, 1986).

Helen F. Siu and Zelda Stern, eds., *Mao's Harvest: Voices from China's New Generation* (Oxford: Oxford University Press, 1983).

Lucian and Mary Pye, *Asian Power and Politics* (Cambridge: Harvard University Press, 1985).

Andrew Nathan, *Chinese Democracy* (New York: Knopf, 1985).

Wang Ruoshui, "Writings on Humanism, Alienation and Philosophy," David Kelly, ed. and trans., *Chinese Studies in Philosophy*, Spring 1985.

James H. Williams, ed. and trans., "The Expanding Universe of Fang Lizhi: Astrophysics and Ideology in People's China," *Chinese Studies in Philosophy*, Summer 1988.

Judith Shapiro and Liang Heng, *Cold Winds, Warm Winds: Intellectual Life in China Today* (Middletown, Conn.: Wesleyan University Press, 1986).

James Tong, ed., "Between Party and Principle: The Exit and Voice of Fang Lizhi, Liu Binyan, and Wang Ruowang," *Chinese Law and Government*, Summer 1988.

Perry Link, ed., *Roses and Thorns: The Second Blooming of the Hundred Flowers in Chinese Fiction* (Berkeley: University of California Press, 1984).

Political Reform and Leadership Succession

John Burns, "Reform of Contemporary China's Civil Service System: Proposals of the 13th Party Congress," paper presented to the annual association of the Asian Studies Association, Washington, D.C., March 1988.

Benedict Stavis, "Reform of China's Political System," *Chinese Law and Government*, Spring 1987.

Su Shaozhi, *Democratization and Reform* (London: Spokesman, 1988).

Frederick C. Teiwes, *Leadership, Legitimacy, and Conflict in China: From a Charismatic Mao to the Politics of Succession* (Armonk, N.Y.: M. E. Sharpe, 1984).

Political Structure and Policy Process

A. Doak Barnett, *The Making of Foreign Policy in China: Structure and Process* (Boulder, Colo.: Westview Press, 1985).

John P. Burns, ed., *The Chinese Communist Party's Nomenklatura System* (Armonk, N.Y.: M. E. Sharpe, 1989).

Deng Xiaoping, *Selected Works of Deng Xiaoping* (1984); *Build Socialism with Chinese Characteristics* (1984); and *Fundamental Issues in Present-Day China* (1987) (Beijing: Foreign Languages Press).

David M. Lampton, ed., *Policy Implementation in Post-Mao China* (Berkeley: University of California Press, 1987).

David M. Lampton and Kenneth Lieberthal, eds., *The Structure of Authority and Bureaucratic Behavior in China* (forthcoming).

John Wilson Lewis, *Political Networks and the Chinese Policy Process* (Stanford, Calif.: Stanford University Press, March 1987).

Kenneth G. Lieberthal and Bruce J. Dixon, *A Research Guide to Central Party and Government Meetings in China: 1949–1986* (Armonk, N.Y.: M. E. Sharpe, 1989).

Kenneth Lieberthal and Michel Oksenberg, *Policy Making in China: Leaders, Structures and Processes* (Princeton, N.J.: Princeton University Press, 1988).

Melanie Manion, "Cadre Recruitment and Management in the People's Republic of China," *Chinese Law and Government,* Fall 1984.

Jonathan Unger, "The Struggle to Dictate China's Administration: The Conflict of Branches vs. Areas vs. Reform," *Australian Journal of Chinese Affairs* 18 (July 1987), pp. 15–46.

Post-Mao China

A. Doak Barnett and Ralph N. Clough, eds., *Modernizing China: Post-Mao Reform and Development* (Boulder, Colo.: Westview Press, 1986).

John P. Burns and Stanley Rosen, eds., *Policy Conflicts in Post-Mao China: A Documentary Survey, with Analysis* (Armonk, N.Y.: M. E. Sharpe, 1986).

Jonathan Chao and Richard Van Houten, eds., *Wise as Serpents, Harmless as Doves: Christians in China Tell Their Story* (Hong Kong: Chinese Church Research Centre, 1988).

Harry Harding, *China's Second Revolution: Reform After Mao* (Washington, D.C.: Brookings Institution, 1987).

John P. Hardt, ed., *China's Economy Looks Toward the Year 2000* (Washington, D.C.: GPO, 21 May 1986).

Liang Heng and Judith Shapiro, *After the Nightmare: Inside China Today* (New York: Macmillan, 1982).

Orville Schell, *To Get Rich Is Glorious: China in the 80's* (New York: Pantheon Books, 1984).

Social Change

Judith Banister, "The Aging of China's Population," *Problems of Communism,* November-December 1988, pp. 62–77.

Anita Chan, Richard Madsen, and Jonathan Unger, *Chen Village: The Recent History of a Peasant Community in Mao's China* (Berkeley: University of California Press, 1984.

Timothy Cheek, "Habits of the Heart: Intellectual Assumptions Reflected by Mainland Chinese Reformers from Teng T'o to Fang Li-chih," *Issues and Studies* 24:3 (March 1988), pp. 31–52.

Ann-ping Chin, *Children of China* (New York: Knopf, 1988).

Deborah Davis, "Unequal Chances, Unequal Outcomes: Pension Reform and Urban Inequality," *China Quarterly* 114 (June 1988), pp. 223–242.

Thomas B. Gold, "After Comradeship: Personal Relations in China Since the Cultural Revolution," *China Quarterly* 104 (December 1985), pp. 657–675.

Merle Goldman, Timothy Cheek, and Carol Lee Hamrin, eds., *Chinese Intellectuals and the State: Search for a New Relationship* (Cambridge: Harvard University Press, 1987).

Huang Shu-min, *The Spiral Road: Change in a Chinese Village Through the Eyes of a Communist Party Leader* (Boulder, Colo.: Westview Press, 1989).

Harald Jacobson, *Television in the PRC* (Washington, D.C.: U.S.I.A., 1988).

Stacey Peck, *Halls of Jade, Walls of Stone: Women in China Today* (New York: Franklin Watts, 1985).

Stanley Rosen, ed., "The Impact of Modernization on the Socialization of Chinese Youth," *Chinese Education,* Spring 1985.

Stanley Rosen, "Youth Socialization and Political Recruitment in Post-Mao China," *Chinese Law and Government,* Summer 1987.

Stanley Rosen and David Chu, *Survey Research in the PRC* (Washington, D.C.: U.S.I.A., December 1987).

Vera Schwarcz, *The Chinese Enlightenment: Intellectuals and the Legacy of the May Fourth Movement of 1919* (Berkeley: University of California Press, 1986).

Margery Wolf, *Revolution Postponed: Women in Contemporary China* (Stanford, Calif.: Stanford University Press, 1985).

Michael Yahuda, "Political Generations in China," *China Quarterly* 80 (December 1979), pp. 793–805.

Zhang Xinxin and Sang Ye, *Chinese Lives: An Oral History of Contemporary China* (New York: Pantheon Books, 1987).

Theory: Communist Party Rule and Modernization

David Apter, *Rethinking Development* (New York: Sage, 1987).

Milovan Djilas, *The New Class: An Analysis of the Communist System* (New York: Harcourt, 1957).

Kenneth Jowitt, "An Organizational Approach to the Study of Political Culture in Marxist-Leninist Systems," *American Political Science Review* 68 (September 1974), pp. 1171–1191.

Kenneth Jowitt, *The Leninist Response to National Dependency* (Berkeley: University of California Institute of International Studies, 1978).

Kenneth Jowitt, "Soviet Neotraditionalism: The Political Corruption of a Leninist Regime," *Soviet Studies* 35:3 (July 1983), pp. 275–297.

Janos Kornai, *Contradictions and Dilemmas* (Cambridge, Mass.: M.I.T. Press, 1986).

Suzanne Ogden, *China's Unresolved Issues: Politics, Development, and Culture* (Englewood Cliffs, N. J.: Prentice Hall, 1989).

Judith Stacey, *Patriarchy and Socialist Revolution in China* (Berkeley: University of California Press, 1983).

Michael Voslensky, *Nomenklatura* (New York: Doubleday, 1984).

Andrew Walder, *Communist Neo-Traditionalism: Work and Authority in Chinese Industry* (Berkeley: University of California Press, 1986).

Index